Grace Towns Hamilton

AND THE POLITICS OF
SOUTHERN CHANGE

. . .

Grace Towns Hamilton

AND THE POLITICS OF SOUTHERN CHANGE

Lorraine Nelson Spritzer

and Jean B. Bergmark

. . .

The University of Georgia Press

ATHENS AND LONDON

© 1997 by the University of Georgia Press
Athens, Georgia 30602

Designed by Omega Clay
Set in Adobe Minion by G & S Typesetters, Inc.
Printed and bound by Maple-Vail Book Manufacturing Group, Inc.

The paper in this book meets the guidelines for permanence
and durability of the Committee on Production Guidelines
for Book Longevity of the Council on Library Resources.

Printed in the United States of America

01   00   99   98   97   C   5   4   3   2   1

Library of Congress Cataloging in Publication Data
Spritzer, Lorraine Nelson.
    Grace Towns Hamilton and the politics of southern change /
Lorraine Nelson Spritzer and Jean B. Bergmark.
        p.   cm.
Includes bibliographical references and index.
ISBN 0-8203-1889-2 (alk. paper)
1. Hamilton, Grace Towns, 1907–   . 2. Afro-American women
legislators—Georgia—Biography.   3. Legislators—Georgia—
Biography.   4. Georgia.   General Assembly.   House of
Representatives—Biography.   5. Georgia—Politics and
government—1951–   . 6. Afro-Americans—Civil rights—
Georgia—History—20th century.   I. Bergmark, Jean B.   II. Title.
F291.3.H36S67   1997
328.758'092—dc21
    [B]   96-48849
British Library Cataloging in Publication Data available

For my family, Ralph, Ron, Sherri, Kathleen, Pam and Rob

LNS

For my children, Jan Robitscher, Christine and Christopher Ladd,
John and Linda Robitscher, all engaged in good causes

JBB

Contents

. . .

Acknowledgments

· · ·

T HIS BOOK began as the project of one author and became a collaboration between longtime friends. In November 1982, when the University of Georgia Press published Lorraine Nelson Spritzer's *Belle of
Ashby Street*, a biography of Helen Douglas Mankin, Georgia's first elected
congresswoman, Grace Towns Hamilton called her to commend the work.
Hamilton, the first black woman state legislator in Georgia, therefore came
easily to mind when Lorraine was ready to choose the subject for her next
biography, and on January 29, 1984, she wrote Hamilton: "You have led a
life of unusual achievement, the story of which, I'm convinced, would have
a wide audience . . . I'm writing to ask if you'd consider letting me do it."
In one of her rare personal letters, Grace Hamilton replied on March 13,
1984, "I'm very flattered that you are considering me as a possible subject . . .
and would welcome an opportunity to be in such good company." On
March 20, Lorraine, then living in Philadelphia, wrote her friend of forty
years, Jean Begeman Robitscher (later Bergmark) in Atlanta, telling her,
"I'd love to have your help on the project. Do you want to collaborate?"
Jean, who knew Hamilton well, accepted with enthusiasm. And so the
book began.

· · ·

Much of the time we were two thousand miles apart. Lorraine moved to
Tempe, Arizona, but regularly returned to Atlanta to join Jean in interviewing Grace Hamilton and her friends and colleagues. Together we taped

thirty-nine interviews in addition to the many with Hamilton, and we wish to thank all who gave so willingly of their time and memory:

Betty Barnes, Vivian Beavers, Lorenzo Benn, Sanford D. Bishop Jr., Julian Bond, Warren Cochran, Betty J. Clark, Grace Holmes DeLorme, Austin Ford, Rebecca Gershon, John W. Greer, Philip G. Hammer, Annie Ruth Simmons Hill, Robert Holmes, Alton Hornsby Jr., Harriet Towns Jenkins, Patricia Johnson, Ward Lamb, Wenonah Bond Logan, James Mackay, Tom Malone, Laughlin McDonald, J. E. Billy McKinney, Eleanor Hamilton Payne, Lisa Payne Jones, Linda Meggers, Yoriko Nakajima, Georganna T. Sinkfield, Richard Sinkfield, George T. Smith, Katherine Stoney, Franklin Thomas, Mable Thomas, Robert A. Thompson, Horace T. Ward, Osgood Williams Sr., Osgood Williams Jr., Penny Williams, and Asa G. Yancey.

Others helped us along. The Atlanta Historical Society (later the Atlanta History Center) assisted our research and transcribed a number of our interviews, and we were bouyed by the enthusiasm of Anne Salter and John Ott, when he was AHS director. Carol Merritt, director of Herndon House, the historic residence of Alonzo F. Herndon, gave us time and space to meet with Grace Hamilton's friends and shared her own research with us. The doctoral dissertation Sharon Mitchell Mullis (later Sharon Sellers) wrote for Emory University, entitled "The Public Career of Grace Towns Hamilton, a Citizen Too Busy to Hate," literally became our "road map" for this book. Also earning our special appreciation were Minnie H. Clayton, at Atlanta University Center's Division of Special Collections and Archives; Herman "Skip" Mason, who traced for us the Towns family in the U.S. census reports; Kathryn L. Nasstrom, who provided material from the oral history collection at the University of North Carolina, Chapel Hill, when she was a doctoral student there; and Deanna L. Colbert, who produced for us a summary of Grace Hamilton's legislative history. Mary Lynn Morgan McGill and John Griffin read the manuscript in its early stages and gave us helpful suggestions. We are indebted to Jane Maguire Abram for the use of her files on the disposition of Hamilton's papers and to Harriet Towns Jenkins, Grace's sister, for her advice and encouragement. Special thanks to Eleanor Hamilton Payne, who loaned us the family pictures that bring her mother's story to life.

In gratitude we salute Nicole and Michael Dowling and Pamela Fichtner, who kept us computer knowledgeable. If finally our work is worthwhile, it will be largely owing to the patience and skill of Trudie Calvert, our editor at the University of Georgia Press.

Throughout the work, Jean's husband, David, was a positive and useful force for us both, reading more than once every chapter of the book, while Lorraine's husband, Ralph, was unfailingly helpful and understanding, seeing her through yet another biography of an important political woman.

Introduction

. . .

NOT LONG into her first term as a state representative in the Georgia General Assembly, Grace Towns Hamilton posed for a special picture. She had been photographed extensively in the previous months because she was the first African American woman elected to public office of such high consequence anywhere in the Deep South, but this was a picture she wanted for her own reasons.

Some black schoolchildren from her legislative district were visiting the state capitol and, finding her in a corridor chatting with a news reporter, had asked to be photographed with her. Assenting, she said, "Well, let's go downstairs and have the picture taken with one of my ancestors." And so they did.

The ancestor was George Washington Towns, Georgia's governor from 1847 to 1851, whose portrait was among those displayed on the capitol's main floor. He was Hamilton's great-grand-uncle, a blood connection she had discovered only after the death a few years before of her father, George Alexander Towns, a professor for much of his life at Atlanta University (AU). Among papers Professor Towns willed to the university archives was a Young Women's Christian Association (YWCA) pamphlet (chosen apparently as a random scrap of paper), on which he had written two significant paragraphs, one stating that his grandfather, Luke Towns Sr., was "half brother of Governor George W. Towns whose father was John Towns,

Scotch-Irish," and the other briefly sketching the enslavement history of his father, Luke Towns Jr., giving names of the men who owned him.

Mulatto offspring of slave masters had no more recognition than the master was willing to provide, and proof of parentage was limited to those few whose fathers acknowledged them. Because such recognition was never accorded his forebears, Professor Towns doubtless relied on word-of-mouth in the black community, a grapevine nevertheless known for the quality of its fruit. Yet during his lifetime, he never so much as whispered the story within his family nor, as far as Grace Hamilton knew, had he ever shown anyone his jottings on the YWCA pamphlet. His reticence surely had its roots in the intense hatred among mulattoes after the Civil War for further miscegenation across the color bar, associating it, as they did, with the pernicious exploitation of Negro women by slave owners, a taboo that within a generation brought a virtual end to new issue mulattoes and created between mulattoes and blacks a racial affinity culminating in their permanent fusion as one people. Studying the Atlanta mulatto elite between 1918 and 1932, Caroline Bond Day—like Towns, a member of that elite—found most of them reluctant to discuss their white ancestry; it was part of a past they wanted to forget.

Times had changed, and the civil rights revolution of the 1960s that made possible Grace Towns Hamilton's election to the Georgia legislature had also begun to lift the veil separating whites from blacks. Her curiosity piqued by her father's jottings, Hamilton obtained a copy of George Washington Towns's will from the Georgia Department of Archives. In this testament, dated 1854, the governor gave to his son, George Washington Towns Jr., a "Negro boy named Robert, a son of my Negro woman, Helen." This woman was not among the twelve Negroes willed by name to the governor's wife, nor was she otherwise mentioned or disposed of in the will. Knowing the history of antebellum miscegenation, Grace Hamilton reasoned that the slave child "Robert" was the governor's son, for whom he was providing in a manner common at the time by deeding him over to a legitimate family member. The governor, she reasoned, had sired his own mulatto son, just as his father before him had sired her great-grandfather, Luke Towns Sr. Like his own father, the governor was unwilling (more than indirectly) to acknowledge paternity. In Grace Hamilton's mind, the proof of her ancestral link with the white Townses was no longer missing.[1]

With this family genealogy in mind, Hamilton had taken a close look at Towns's portrait when she assumed her duties in the capitol, finding that her slave-owning ancestor had a "kind and sensitive face." Now before the

portrait again with her young constituents by her side and a camera record-ing the event, she was at last publicly laying claim to kinship with the man.

Hamilton later related the story to anthropologist Margaret Mead when the two met in Atlanta at Emmaus House, a community center for under-privileged youth, whose director, Father Austin Ford, was their mutual friend. Mead noted the act with respect in the book *A Rap on Race*, a record of her lengthy conversations with James Baldwin, and she recommended that other blacks likewise "claim their white ancestors." She saluted Hamil-ton as a myth slayer. For years southerners to whom people listened, such as Margaret Mitchell in *Gone With the Wind* and, before her, Edgar Gardner Murphy in *Problems of the Present South*, had contended that the mulatto population was a postbellum phenomenon that could be laid to the lust of Yankee soldiers and southern scalawags. Grace Hamilton's simple act dra-matically illustrated a fact respected historians in her day were more and more bringing to light, that the blood of southern slave masters ran stronger than any other strain in the veins of the American Negro, her own in-cluded. And she wanted her world to know.[2]

Revealing the blood link with her white political ancestor at the outset of her own political career foreshadowed the original approach that would characterize her subsequent years in the Georgia legislature, where she would come to wield more effective power than any African American be-fore her. In a milieu previously inhospitable to her gender and kind, she would reach a pinnacle never before achieved by any woman, but her con-cerns were people concerns, unbound by race or sex. Indeed, she never mounted the battlements in the civil rights struggle—confrontation was not her style—but she cheered from the sidelines, and ultimately the rise of black power in Atlanta owed much to her influence as a legislator. Widely known for ceaseless promotion of interracial harmony and cooper-ation, she believed passionately that character, not race, should be the mea-sure of a person's worth, and she scrupulously refrained all her life from identifying anyone by color. Those unsympathetic to her approach accused her of bias in favor of whites, but one ardent supporter called her Atlanta's only real integrationist. Another called her a healer, a bridge builder. But in the legislature, where she made her most lasting contribution to her city and state, all agreed she was that rare person who gave politics a good name.

Grace Towns Hamilton

AND THE POLITICS OF
SOUTHERN CHANGE

• • •

1

Genesis

. . .

WHEN Grace Towns was born on February 10, 1907, no one could dream that this girl child would have a notable political future, for conditions and prospects for the American Negro had never been more dismal. Even as she grew in her mother's womb, Atlanta, where she arrived in the world, was the scene in September 1906 of a ferocious racial massacre. For whites, the decades bracketing the turn of the century were the Progressive Era. Even if progress was more cosmetic than real, it was a time of government reform, trust-busting, moral uplift, and, not least, at its close, voting rights for women. But as historian Rayford W. Logan said, it was "the nadir of the Negro's status in America," and even the female franchise had a lesser reach for black women than for white. Racism rode high in the saddle everywhere, and blacks, though they were no mere passive victims, struggled most often in vain. Racism had helped bring down Reconstruction, and in the wake of that aborted struggle for a new kind of democracy in the United States, the Negro emerged as a despised and disfranchised class made up primarily of dependent laborers, possessing little land and virtually no political rights.

As this color caste system became the nationally accepted substitute for slavery, it facilitated racism's further spread so that by the time Grace Towns was born, prejudice against the Negro, as Eric Foner put it, was "more deeply embedded in the nation's culture and politics than at any time . . . perhaps in our entire history." Though an estimated three-quarters of the

American Negro population by then was of "mixed" ancestry—the Towns family among them—deepening racism reinforced the white world's old commitment to the "one drop rule" that lumped all blacks together, forcibly confining them in a caste all whites considered inferior. Caught in this wide net, all people even remotely Negro were condemned (with rare exceptions) to a life in the shadow of violence, exclusion and oppression, injustices that existed everywhere but most inescapably in the old Confederacy. Harvard-educated W. E. B. Du Bois, the sociologist and historian then teaching at Atlanta University, wrote in *The Souls of Black Folk*, published in 1903, that Atlanta and the South "seemed an armed camp for intimidating Negroes." [1]

Amid the rampant racial turmoil, the campus of Atlanta University on the city's western reaches was an island of tranquillity, and for Grace Towns it was a lucky birthplace. Her father was on the faculty there, a colleague and close personal friend of the celebrated Du Bois and a resident with his wife, the former Nellie McNair—along with the Du Bois family—of AU's South Hall. Racial fraternity and equality were a way of life at AU, and at no time in her formative years was Grace Towns forced to feel inferior. Neither white supremacists nor the concept of white supremacy ever penetrated its confines. The institution's attitude toward prejudice and discrimination against Negroes was as strong, unbending, and steadfast as it had been in 1887, when it refused to repudiate its principles as the price of an annual, much-needed state appropriation. Both faculty and student body were integrated, though the faculty would remain heavily white until well into the twentieth century and its white students were few, all of them children of teachers and professors. Grace Towns had little reason to venture beyond its protective embrace when she was growing up, and this sheltered existence was the seminal influence in her life. Many blacks left Atlanta in the wake of the 1906 massacre, many for temporary refuge, some permanently, and the state was tense as agitation mounted for a constitutional amendment (approved by public vote in 1908) that put a final cap on the Reconstruction era of Negro voting. But George Towns and his wife had roots firmly planted in Georgia soil and the young couple never really thought of leaving. [2]

Of the Towns's four children who survived to adulthood, Grace was the eldest. Their firstborn, Helen Dorothy, died in July 1905 at the age of seven months. The three who followed Grace were George Alexander Jr. in March 1909, Myron Bumstead in October 1910, and Harriet in 1920. Grace remained close to her parents all her life, the closest of all her siblings, and was much influenced by them. She entrusted her own daughter to their care for an extended period of her childhood; she and her husband, Henry Cooke Hamilton, lived with them in the family home for nearly a decade of their married life; but above all she shared with them a profound attachment to Atlanta University and, like them, lived most of her life within earshot of the campus chimes.

Grace Towns inherited her mother's fair skin and fine hair, her strong will, and her imperial bent (for it was said of Nellie Towns that she was a housewife and mother in the classic sense "but always a queen, never a drudge," and the adult Grace, Margaret Mead thought, had "a sort of upper-class Englishwoman's style"). But it was her father who most influenced her, professionally and politically. He was her mentor and idol.[3]

· · ·

George Alexander Towns lived for ninety years, a span that encompassed some of the best and worst of the American Negro experience, and the times that bore on his life resounded profoundly in the lives of his children, not least in that of his eldest daughter.

He was born March 5, 1870, in Albany, Dougherty County, Georgia, in the heart of the southern Black Belt, where slavery and cotton had flourished as scarcely anywhere else in modern history. His parents, Luke Towns Jr., a freed slave, and Mary Colt Towns, of Indian blood, married in 1867 and had six children, four sons and two daughters, before Mrs. Towns died of tuberculosis sometime around 1880. George Alexander, their second son, with his sisters, Ella and Mary, became the surviving family unit. A first son died in infancy in 1868, the third son, Mack, disappeared from the family orbit soon after reaching adulthood, leaving no trace of his whereabouts, and a fourth son, Walter, drowned in adolescence.

Luke Towns Sr., like most mulattoes in the lower South before the Civil War, was a slave, but little else is known of him. He had a wife named Maria, believed by the family to have been Cherokee Indian, and he was the unrecognized son of John Towns, a white Virginian who fought in the Revolutionary War, migrated to Georgia, acquired land and slaves, and settled finally in Morgan County, later becoming known as the father of George Washington Towns, a congressman during the 1830s and 1840s and governor of Georgia from 1847 to 1851. So far as is known, neither the governor nor his father ever established any personal relationship with Luke Towns Sr., and, indeed, their blood tie has been disputed. An indignant Anna Walker Terrell, of Hiawassee, Towns County, Georgia, a great-granddaughter of Governor Towns, wrote the *Atlanta Constitution* on December 10, 1979, hotly denying kinship between her family and the Negro Townses. No proof existed of the tie nor would any ever be found, she insisted, probably correctly. Dean Rowley, who wrote a master's thesis at Atlanta University in 1975 on the life of George Alexander Towns, acknowledged that the blood tie was unrecorded and confined himself in scholarly skepticism to saying only that it was a relationship the "family claimed." Perhaps it was a sign of decline in the old southern reluctance to acknowledge the principal origin of American mulattoes when the *Dictionary of Georgia Biography* in 1983 ran a profile of Towns, stating without equivocation that his grandfather "was the half brother of a Georgia governor, George W. Towns." Where Luke Towns Sr. was held in bondage is not known, though it probably was Albany, or its vicinity, for in that town his son, Luke Towns Jr., is believed to have been born around 1840, soon after the town was founded. Little attention was paid to black family records during slavery, and Towns's descendants have no certain knowledge of his birthdate or birthplace. They know only that the 1870 census gave his age as thirty, that he lived more than one hundred years, and that he passed most of his life in Albany.[4]

Lying astride the Flint River where it bends westward in its southward flow toward the Chattahoochee and the open sea, Albany was founded in 1836 as the seat of Dougherty County, which was then carving its own niche in history. Its rich black soil watered by swamp and river, Dougherty County had become on the eve of the Civil War the cornerstone of the Cotton Kingdom. Men called it the Egypt of the Confederacy, and Albany was its thriving capital.

For decades, especially in the boom years of the 1850s, the clank of chained feet resounded over the great fertile lands, as more and more slaves were marched from Virginia and the Carolinas, where slavery was no longer profitable, to the flourishing cotton plantations of Georgia. By 1860, west Dougherty County was perhaps the richest slave kingdom the modern world has ever known, a monarchy where 150 masters, commanding the labor of 6,000 slaves on plantations sprawled over 90,000 acres, reaped profits from human and material property valued at $5.5 million.

W. E. B. Du Bois made an intensive study of Dougherty County at the turn of the century, when he and George Towns taught together at Atlanta University, and he later published his findings as two chapters of his literary classic, *The Souls of Black Folk*. Of antebellum Dougherty, Du Bois reported: "Twenty thousand bales of ginned cotton went yearly to England, New and Old; and men that came there bankrupt made money and grew rich. In a single decade the cotton output increased fourfold and the value of lands was tripled. It was the heyday of the nouveau riche, and a life of careless extravagance among the masters." For whites, Du Bois wrote, it was a land of show and tinsel, of hedonism and quick fortune; for blacks it was "a little hell." As slaves, they toiled by day on the plantations in gangs driven by the whip of overseers; by night they rested in one-room, windowless hovels within sight of the master's mansion. A former slave told Du Bois, "I've seen niggers drop dead in the furrow, but they were kicked aside and the plough never stopped. Down in the guard-house, that's where the blood ran."[5]

When the Civil War broke out, slaves outnumbered whites five to one in Dougherty County, one of the densest concentrations of blacks in all the South. Most were bound to the plantations, but a few, artisans for the most part, lived in the town of Albany. Luke Towns Jr., a cotton sampler, probably was one of them, for skilled slaves typically lived in towns. The facts of his life as his son George knew them were few but stark. His owner was Benjamin Franklin Gullett, son of an Albany doctor, who may have acquired Towns as an investment because that practice was common among slave owners. How Towns learned cotton sampling is unknown, but masters often trained their slaves in trades, for they could hire them out at good earnings and if the slave were ever offered for sale, he brought more money than a field hand of similar age. A few skilled slaves were even allowed by lenient owners to hire their own time, but Towns appears not to have been so fortunate. Other than town living, the artisan's life was little distinguished from the field hand's, for both were human chattels classed with the owner's horses, mules, or oxen, and having this skill made the artisan more liable than the field hand to be used as security for loans, which had its own peculiar hazards.

In the prime of his young manhood, Towns was mortgaged by his owner, who defaulted on the loan. Required to forfeit his security, Gullett in 1858 put Towns on the auction block at the Dougherty County courthouse in Albany. At the public outcry, Towns was bought by John S. Moman, who resold him—or possibly lent him, as masters were often generous with the labor of their slaves—to his brother-in-law James Gardner. Towns later went to war with Gardner as a body servant, remaining a loyal retainer even after his emancipation until Gardner was killed in battle in 1864. When he returned to Albany, having the right at last to claim his own wages, Luke Towns may have found no work as a cotton sampler, for the 1870 census listed him as "black," aged thirty, and a "laborer," but by

1880, when the census taker changed his description to "mulatto," he was shown as once again following his trade.[6]

. . .

The decade after Appomattox was a critical one for all Americans; it determined the Negroes' fate for another century. The revolution of war and emancipation destroyed both slavery and the Confederacy, where money was worthless, one-third of the male population killed or wounded, and the survivors divided, stricken, and embittered. Civil authority no longer existed, and many despondent southerners abandoned their farms or left the region. Others did not know how to start over. Everywhere there was suffering from disease and starvation. Amid the wasted landscape wandered rootless, illiterate Negroes, homeless and jobless, many in weary search of husbands, wives, or children from whom they had been separated sometimes years before by a plantation sale or some other transaction, many simply experimenting with their freedom. The vagabondage bred fear and loathing among whites. Violence against freedpeople was rampant everywhere.[7]

Coping with the disorder and destitution became the task of the Freedmen's Bureau. Created by Congress in March 1865 as the Bureau of Refugees, Freedmen, and Abandoned Lands, this agency set to work before the smoke of battle was cleared, delivering rations, medicine, and clothing to the needy of both races, but its impartiality earned it little credit among former Confederates, and its work was handicapped from the start and ultimately checked entirely by white hostility.

Before expiring in 1870, the Freedmen's Bureau had delivered a whole panoply of services to the South, and though whites were not excluded, blacks were the main beneficiaries. It tried to ease the freedmen's transition to voluntary labor, helping them find jobs and putting many back to work under labor contracts that specified fair wages and sometimes succeeded in mitigating the harshness of their working conditions. The bureau also acted as the Negro's friend in court and set up courts of its own where Negro interests demanded it and resettled thousands of refugees away from congested areas. And when the reality dawned in Washington that the South would never willingly acquiesce in political and civil equality for the black race and Congress enacted the Reconstruction Act of 1867, imposing martial law on the South, enfranchising the Negro, and requiring recognition of the newly enacted Fourteenth Amendment to the U.S. Constitution guaranteeing "due process of law" to all, the Freedmen's Bureau soon added more than seven hundred thousand Negroes to the voting rolls as well as some six hundred thousand whites. Thirty-seven Negroes were elected to the Georgia Constitutional Convention of October 1867, and in elections between 1868 and 1872, roughly the life span of Reconstruction in Georgia, thirty-two blacks won seats in the state legislature and another, Jefferson Franklin Long, of Macon, was elected to Congress, the first of his race ever seated there. Even after Reconstruction's end, one or more blacks remained in the Georgia legislature until 1907, when Negro disfranchisement was written into the state constitution.[8]

The bureau's educational work was its greatest achievement and its most enduring legacy. It went forward in cooperation with the American Missionary Association (AMA) and other northern evangelical philanthropic societies that had flocked south to aid the freedpeople and with blacks who begged for learning "as a thirsty man would beg for water," giving generously "of their poverty" to attain it. Enforced illiteracy, like enforced illegitimacy, had been among slavery's most hated and humiliating oppressions. A small town like Albany, for example, with a black population of no more than seven hundred, raised up to $350 a month—a princely sum among impoverished freedmen—for construction of school buildings, and in all of Georgia in 1867, the Freedmen's Bureau recorded a Negro contribution to school building and teachers' salaries fully half the combined sums given by the bureau itself and the northern societies. In the span of its brief life, the bureau built or helped create close to four thousand schools (by 1867, one or more schools existed in the most remote counties of each Confederate state) and employed some nine thousand teachers, mostly New Englanders brought south by the private societies, who gave rudimentary education to 250,000 formerly illiterate blacks, old and young alike. Spurred by the bureau's achievements, southern legislatures in which blacks sat as members soon established free common schools for all.[9]

• • •

In 1867, as the curtain was rising on the drama of Radical Reconstruction in Georgia, Luke Towns Jr., aged about twenty-seven, married seventeen-year-old Mary Colt, of Indian blood, settling on Albany's south side among the seven hundred freedpeople living there. Though segregated housing was not yet required in Georgia, the races in Albany had always been rigidly divided. No longer the hub of a prosperous plantation society, the town had turned mean, and whites' resentment at the loss of their old pleasures and privileges fed their rage against the Negro and his ambitions for land, education, and the ballot. One observer described Albany in 1867 as a town where whites "would as soon shoot a man as a dog." By 1870, for reasons unknown—perhaps for greater safety—Luke and Mary Towns were living with their three-month-old son, George Alexander, among Albany whites in the large household of J. L. Ingraham, a teacher from Massachussetts, who, according to local legend, arrived in Albany before the Civil War.

Regaining control of the Negro was every southern white man's preoccupation; vigilante terror usually perpetrated by the Ku Klux Klan was the chosen weapon, and the combined forces of the Freedmen's Bureau, federal troops, and the courage and determination of many freedmen themselves were insufficient to thwart him. Violence was worst in Black Belt areas such as Dougherty County, where freedmen, like slaves before them, outnumbered whites five to one. Assassinations, whippings, and torture were common, and Negroes were fleeing Georgia by the thousands in search of safety and work in the West. Some from Albany may have joined the migration. In the wake of a bloody incident at nearby Camilla in 1868, where whites attacked a biracial Republican political rally, killing and wounding scores, Albany freedmen petitioned Congress, protesting their lack of protection and asking to be "removed to some other land." The Freedmen's Bureau helped those it could in their flight, but its capabilities were limited and former slaves lacked both the means and often the desire to uproot themselves. Most remained in the South, where they were born, as did Luke and Mary Towns, who clung to Albany even in the shadow of terror.

Many blacks were then moving into Dougherty County from elsewhere in what Du Bois later called "primarily a huddling for self protection," a search for refuge, emotional support, and collective self-help in the sheltering company of their own kind and culture. The South's "peculiar institution" had undermined and destabilized—but could not destroy—either the strong family tradition or the impulse to communal, cooperative action that was part of the Negro's African heritage, and in their new life, surrounded by an old world of prejudice and injustice, freed people simply strengthened what had served them well in days of slavery. In their numbers, they often found strength to protest their bleak condition. Negro political rallies were frequent in Albany during the peak years of Reconstruction, and a black man, Philip Joiner, represented Dougherty County at the Georgia Constitutional Convention in 1867, later serving in the Georgia legislature. Black laborers on a plantation near Albany in 1868 struck for higher wages and with encouragement from Joiner and other black politicians maintained the holdout for a year. When Black Belt solidarity yielded them little economic or political advance, Negroes moved in a growing stream toward the great cities, but most, like Luke Towns, never left their native locale.[10]

Luke Towns Jr. was doubtless among the 10 percent of Dougherty County's black population whom Du Bois, in his turn-of-the-century study, classed as the area's "well-to-do, the best of the laborers." As an artisan and body servant to his master before emancipation, Towns had occupied a place in the successful class of Georgia blacks that produced the Reconstruction politicians. Common slaves during the centuries of bondage lived a brutish existence, lost in a cultural void between their African heritage, nearly forgotten, and the best of the southern white culture, expressly forbidden to them. In contrast, house servants and sometimes artisans enjoyed bonds of intimacy, affection, and even blood relationships with the masters, proximity to whom often gave them advantages of food, clothing, and occasionally education and experience. From such exposure came a sense of self-worth and awareness of human possibilities denied the slave who toiled in the field gang.

Yet being "well-to-do" in the harsh circumstances prevailing in Dougherty County could hardly have denoted more than minimal economic security. Probably illiterate at emancipation, Towns nevertheless fully shared the freedmen's passion for learning, and he passed along his attachment, as well as his own good humor and self-confidence, to his children.

By 1880, Towns had lost his wife, for the census that year listed Towns alone with his five surviving children, all of whom were shown as living again on Albany's black side in a household headed by Wiley Semore, a warehouse hand. In caring for his motherless brood, Towns relied on the extensive network of emotional support and kin relationships that united the Negro community. Family legend has it that his mother and a female cousin helped raise the children and when his mother died, other family friends took in the youngest children, leaving George and the next brother, Mack, with the father. The female cousin may have been the mulatto nurse, nineteen-year-old Matilda Crawford, who was listed in the 1880 census as a resident of the Semore household. Even if details are obscure, Towns somehow provided his children with a stable family life, and, as George would say in later life, with many "happy memories of birthday parties and other pleasures." Nurtured in the communal warmth of his environment, shielded from the pervasive violence of the time by the protective embrace of a loving family, young Towns left Albany at the age of fifteen to matriculate at Atlanta University. He had received an elementary education, all he could get at the time in Albany, and though some public schooling had become available to Georgia blacks, family recollection is that he attended a private school, probably one of the several established in the town by the American Missionary Association. His teacher had been trained at the AMA's Atlanta University, and family legend holds it was she who so inspired him with admiration for the institution that he determined to make his way to the big city and enroll there. Once he entered the university, it would remain his home—professionally, physically, and spiritually—and later a towering inspiration for his daughter Grace as well, until the end of both their lives.[11]

· · ·

A prime mover among Christian abolitionists in the antebellum North, the American Missionary Association, whose evangelical inspiration and basic funding derived from the Congregational Church, became the most influential of all the benevolent societies working in the South in behalf of the formerly bonded after the Civil War. It arrived in Georgia hard on the heels of General William T. Sherman's army, bringing "the book, the Bible and the New England way."

Under shrewd and dedicated leadership and helped by massive contributions from the Freedmen's Bureau, the AMA quickly established a dominant position in the education of freedpeople throughout the lower South. Almost every AMA college and normal and secondary school was partially built with bureau funds and, upon the federal agency's demise, the AMA inherited additional school property and real estate. This contribution to Negro education, the effects of which echoed and expanded down through the decades, gave the AMA a permanent place in the history of the American Negro.

Common schools, a dire necessity in the early postbellum period, were the AMA's initial focus, but it never intended to stop at rudiments. Between 1866 and 1869, it chartered seven Negro colleges, including Fisk in Tennessee, which became the best-known black university in the world, and Atlanta University, its crowning achievement in Georgia.[12]

Atlanta had barely emerged from ashes when an AMA representative reached the city in November 1865 and found two former slaves conducting a school for fellow freedmen in the remains of an old church building. Possessed of more zeal than competence, these pioneer teachers were glad to turn their task over to the better-trained New England "schoolmarms" brought in by the AMA, and the society soon supplemented the church facility with a second school, housed in a renovated old railroad boxcar. Out of the church and the "car box"—as it was called—arose a new and larger facility, Storrs School, named for the pastor of the Congregational Church in Cincinnati that contributed most of the money to build it. Though it had not a single pupil yet ready for advanced education, AMA leaders pressed on and in 1867 chartered an institution they called Atlanta University. As Jacqueline Jones later wrote, "Although idealistic northern teachers often dubbed an intermediate school a 'university' in hope it would become one someday, Atlanta University just about lived up to the name." [13]

Ironically, the site chosen for the university, the best land available to the founders, was on the high hills of western Atlanta, the very heights from which the Union army had recently laid siege to the city. From here the Confederacy had waged its fiercest defense against the Yankee onslaught, and battle ramparts had to be leveled before landscaping could begin on the new university's grounds. On bare slopes stripped of trees by the shelling rose North Hall, the first of the red brick buildings of Victorian architecture that eventually formed the AU complex. Grounds were terraced, grass and trees planted, and AU's first students, none of them at college level, were marched from Storrs School to begin preparatory classes in October 1869. In 1876, when Atlanta University graduated its first college class, all but one of the seven males in the group had received some pre-college training on the AU campus. To fill its corridors with students qualified for the advanced training they were ready to provide, all missionary colleges had to "raise" their own. The great literacy drive, despite the massive energies poured into it by the Freedmen's Bureau and the northern benevolent societies, had reached no more than 5 percent of the freedpeople and public education was still little more than a dream for blacks. During the first quarter-century of its existence, Atlanta University had more students in its grammar and high schools than in its college classes. Long afterward, the heaviest enrollment would be in the normal department, where students were learning how to teach others. Until AU was near its sixty-fifth year, a student there could begin in the primary class and leave a college graduate. [14]

Other evangelical societies were also establishing colleges in the South alongside those of the AMA. The American Baptist Home Mission Society founded Atlanta Baptist College for Men in 1867, renaming it Morehouse College in 1913 for Henry Lyman Morehouse, and with financial aid from the John D. Rockefeller family established Spelman Seminary (later College) for women in 1881. The Freedmen's Aid Society of the Methodist Episcopal Church in 1870 launched Clark College and Gammon Theological Seminary, and the African Methodist Episcopal Church, wishing to give blacks an institution they alone controlled, established Morris Brown College. Once scattered about Atlanta, all these institutions would eventually relocate near AU, forming the Atlanta University Center.

Yet no other benevolent society matched the zeal of the AMA for freedmen's education. Uncompromisingly radical on race, the AMA dreamed of a casteless society and, practicing what it preached, allowed nothing less than full equality in all its institutions. It aimed to demonstrate to a skeptical nation — only marginally less racist in the North than the South — that blacks, though degraded by centuries of slavery, were equal to whites when given the same advantages. AMA colleges gave blacks access to all levels of training, from classical studies to teacher training and industrial and technical education, and at Fisk and Atlanta Universities it sought to build first-rate institutions where blacks might acquire advanced education equal to any the country had to offer.

Egalitarian though its impulses were, the AMA, as Joe Richardson noted in a study of the organization, sometimes "failed to live up to its lofty ideals." Both its leaders and the New England teachers it brought south assumed their own cultural superiority, and some were themselves racist. They were often paternalistic and arrogant in their assumption that the quicker blacks conformed to northern white standards, the sooner artificial barriers would be dismantled. But evangelical piety, self-control, and hard, steady work, the values that most informed the AMA educational system, had an individualistic thrust that clashed with the black culture's own rich and vital traditions of self-help and solidarity, and the dichotomy did not fail to stir controversy through the years within the African American community. The AMA also never seemed to comprehend blacks' insistence on sharing control of institutions devoted to their education and uplift. The association was so reluctant to promote black teachers, administrators, and trustees at its schools that Atlanta University, for instance, was headed by white northerners for more than sixty years after its founding.[15]

Misguided though some of their educational approaches may have been, the university's Yankee missionary teachers' willingness to put their ideals into practice in a land bitterly hostile to the notion of black uplift won them enormous goodwill and many adherents among freedpeople. The president of AU in the last years of the nineteenth century, when racism reached a new crescendo in the South, was Horace Bumstead, who had been educated at Yale University and in Germany, yet only a single white home in Atlanta, that of a German family, was open to this cultured gentleman, and no AU teacher could safely venture off campus, so great was the risk of assault. White society most abhorred AU's communal dining hall, where students, nearly all black, ate together with their teachers, most of whom were white, and the integrated classrooms where white children from faculty families were educated with blacks.

Adherence to its principles was not without cost to the AMA and its institutions. When two black state legislators, Philip Joiner of Albany and James Porter of Savannah, failed in an attempt to establish an all-Negro university under state aegis, the Georgia legislature in 1870 instead gave $8,000 to help meet AU's operating expenses and in 1874 earmarked the sum as an annual donation. But in 1887, amid rising racism, the appropriation was rescinded when AU, with AMA backing, refused to abandon its commitment to integrated education. The loss threw the university into a financial crisis that was only partially alleviated by the sympathy and contributions its principled action inspired in the North. But such a strong demonstration of its commitment to equality profoundly affected the Negroes' faith in the institution, and George Alexander Towns and his family were among those deeply and permanently moved.[16]

• • •

Arriving at Atlanta University in October 1885, Towns entered the eighth grade of the grammar school. He went on to the university's preparatory department, then its high school equivalent, entering college in 1890 and graduating in 1894, in an all-male class of seven. One of his classmates, his roommate in his senior college year, was James Weldon Johnson, who would later achieve fame as author, lyricist, newspaper editor, diplomat, and race leader.

Tuition and board at AU cost students in this early era between $80 and $100 a year. The modest charge was a matter of principle with AU's founders, but it was a practical possibility, in part because they had had the good sense to establish a farm adjacent to the university where food was grown to supply the college tables and student boarders were required to contribute an hour's work every day. The low costs notwithstanding, Towns and Johnson were compelled to eke out their financial resources by working summer months as country schoolteachers. Highly motivated young blacks of their day typically paid for their education by passing on their own learning to others as quickly as they acquired it.

Johnson taught only one summer, an experience "in the backwoods of Georgia" he lovingly evoked in his autobiography, *Along This Way*, but Towns, impelled by greater financial necessity, served various stints as a teacher between 1885 and 1895, at about $30 a month, in Worth, Mitchell,

Houston, and Douglas Counties. Once he took a year off from AU and taught in Albany to build up his savings. In Pleasant Hill in Talbot County one summer he had so many pupils he earned $241.66, a princely sum for the ambitious but impoverished young man. These early black schools provided from 60 to 120 days of instruction a year and paid student teachers by the pupil, with public funds covering a portion of their salary and parents footing the rest of the bill. The plan had only one thing to recommend it— the economic incentive it gave student teachers to get and keep in school as many pupils as possible.[17]

In their early years at AU, the campus was, as Johnson described it in his autobiography, "a little world in itself . . . a green island in [the] dull red sea" of surrounding Atlanta. There, said Johnson, ideas of social conduct and the approach to life "differed from those of the city in which it was located as greatly as a Boston drawing room differs from the wilds of Borneo." Nevertheless, race pervaded all student life at AU. Service to the race was an idea impressed upon all who studied there. Students talked race; essays, debates, and oratory touched on little else. Though the shortcomings of American democracy in relation to the Negro was not a part of the classroom instruction, practically everything imparted was designed to fit an AU student into a particular system of which race was the center. At AU, Johnson wrote, "the atmosphere was charged with it."[18]

For all its positive focus on race, the institution promoted white values and white religion at the expense of the Negro's African heritage, believing black customs and culture were part of the baggage of slavery that was best forgotten. AU students lived under a puritanical code of conduct that was as high-minded as it was narrow. Protestant religious observance was required, and religious students were preferred; the high spirits and emotionalism that were typical of the Negro church were discouraged. Fighting, loud talk, and tardiness were punishable offenses; students had to sign a pledge promising to refrain from smoking, alcohol, and profanity, and the penalty for the slightest infraction, even beyond the campus, was suspension. Once a student barely escaped the penalty when he was seen smoking in Pittsburgh, Pennsylvania. Johnson, a self-acknowledged agnostic as a student, was luckily occupied elsewhere one day when four of his closest friends spent a few of their free hours at a place outside the city limits of Atlanta drinking wine and smoking tobacco. Professor Cyrus Francis, the university's pastor, tracked down the culprits, all promising students, and forced them out of school. None of them ever returned. Johnson, years later in his autobiography, still remembered with disdain the "fanaticism" of Professor Francis. Towns, however, never chafed under the school's strict discipline, and he believed Francis was one of the "principal sources of the traditions of Atlanta University." Nor did Johnson's agnosticism ever rub off on Towns, who would later say, "Within the walls of Atlanta University I became a Christian . . . [and] was set in the way to become a scholar." [19]

Indeed, there were many differences between the two young men. Towns had grown up in rural, racist Albany; Johnson was raised in Jacksonville, Florida, a town known long after Reconstruction as a good place for Negroes. And in the complicated hierarchy of color and class that overlaid the postbellum solidarity of the Negro people, Johnson, the son of freeborn parents of West Indian origin, had status a cut above Towns, the son of former slaves. Yet their commonalities easily transcended their differences. Both were fortunate in having no undue fear of, or esteem for, the white race, so the effects of racial prejudice scarcely penetrated beneath their conscious selves. Both were talented athletes—Johnson was the star baseball pitcher in his college years at AU, while Towns, good at both baseball and track, was voted the college "all round athlete." As preparatory students, they reveled in the compulsory courses in mechanical arts. Towns, who aimed to be an architect, showed such skill in woodworking that he was soon made shop assistant, and Johnson, likewise gifted, recorded in his autobiography the joy he experienced at the lathe while turning a piece of wood "into a thing of geometric beauty." [20]

When they graduated from AU in 1894, Towns and Johnson had received a classical education based on the curriculum of the best New England colleges, primarily that of Yale, alma mater of AU's founders and its first presidents. They had mastered Greek and Latin, mathematics, and ancient history and studied the best texts on English literature, philosophy, astronomy, chemistry, geology, political economy, the United States Constitution, and international law. The college had a reputation for thorough work and scholarship that was unsurpassed by any similar institution in the South. The strict Ivy League–trained New England teachers demanded no less of the AU students than had been exacted of them. The study of Greek so fascinated Towns that he read Greek classics in the original for the rest of his life.

At graduation, the class of 1894 was photographed wearing the bowler hats and high collars of the period, all staring earnestly and confidently at the camera, except for George Towns, who, sitting in a lateral position in front of the others, was gazing just as earnestly and confidently to his right. These were handsome, high-minded young men, embodying, it seems, all the qualities AU felt the American Negro could and should aspire to. The class photo was one of the most widely reproduced of any ever taken at AU and is still being reproduced today.[21]

Times were not promising for young blacks, no matter how handsome or ambitious, and the challenge in 1894 that most engaged AU students like Towns and Johnson was how to make use of their education. At the dawn of the twentieth century, white America seemed in broad agreement that no political order could survive in the South unless founded on the principle of racial inequality. Reconstruction, which had introduced blacks to politics, was dead, and the North, having acquiesced in its interment, stood by as the South proceeded to nullify the Fourteenth and Fifteenth Amendments to the U.S. Constitution (the former providing "due process," the latter underwriting male Negro suffrage), which Congress had insisted upon as the Negro's due. But white supremacists seemed insatiable, clamoring for ever more racial subjugation. Even as Towns and Johnson set forth on their careers, the U.S. Supreme Court sanctioned disfranchisement of the Negro by state constitutional amendment in Mississippi, and other southern states, Georgia among them, soon succumbed to the same temptation. Having little use for the Negro's plight, the Supreme Court had already struck down the Civil Rights Act of 1875 and in 1896 came up with the "separate but equal" doctrine enunciated in *Plessy* v. *Ferguson,* a decision that opened the door to wholesale segregation of the Negro, and not just in the South. "The Negro is an outlawed inhabitant in [his own] country," cried Henry McNeal Turner, who had been Georgia's most powerful black politician during Reconstruction. That "massive experiment in interracial democracy," as Eric Foner called it, was undergoing hostile review at Columbia University, where respectable northern intellectuals soon joined southern white supremacists in proclaiming the Negro an inferior being and Reconstruction "a monstrous thing." And in the South, where violence had been the final undoing of Reconstruction, lynching had become a growing outrage against the black race. In the 1890s, when such atrocities reached a peak, more than 1,600 blacks were killed by mobs, a record 241 losing their lives in Georgia alone between 1882 and 1903. Savage torture and mutilation of the victims were common; many were burned alive. No Negro was safe from such a fate; maintaining self-respect in the face of pervasive threat was the unceasing dilemma, especially of the Negro male. After his marriage, Towns was arrested while driving with his fair wife, who was taken for white, and Johnson barely escaped with his life when he was accosted by a mob while in the presence of a woman who was legally a

Negro though wholly Caucasian in appearance. Years later, the horror of the experience lived in Johnson's memory, and he recounted the story in vivid detail in his autobiography.[22]

AU impressed upon its students that its rigorous classical course would make them better and nobler and of higher value to the race they would have to serve. It was a naive notion belied by the facts, for by the end of the nineteenth century, the only professions freely open to educated Negroes like Towns and Johnson were teaching, preaching, and undertaking. Recognizing that architecture was effectively foreclosed to him, Towns went home to Albany, where he taught for a year in a Negro public school. His talent for woodworking and carpentry had impressed AU, however, and in 1895 he was employed at the university as an assistant in the mechanical and science department. University trustees had long been leery of adding Negroes to the faculty, though a few had served briefly, but in 1895 the institution not only employed Towns but also added Adrienne McNeil Herndon to the faculty as a teacher of elocution. Two years later, W. E. B. Du Bois, who had studied at the University of Berlin and held the first doctoral degree ever awarded an African American at Harvard University, was hired to direct AU's conferences on problems of the urban Negro. Towns and Johnson served the earliest of these events as researchers and recording secretaries. Johnson had returned to teach in his hometown of Jacksonville, but in his spare time he studied law and became one of the first Negroes admitted to the Florida bar. He also founded there the first Negro daily in America, calling it the *Daily American*; George Towns was among his financial backers, contributing $100 to the venture. When the paper failed, Johnson abandoned his Florida pursuits for New York, where he won recognition with his songs, poems, and books and later became a diplomat, editor of the *New York Age* and, later still, first field secretary of the National Association for the Advancement of Colored People (NAACP). Though Johnson's achievements eclipsed those of Towns, the two remained close friends, visiting and corresponding for the remainder of their lives.

Perhaps inspired by Du Bois, Towns wanted a Harvard degree, and in 1898 he took a leave of absence from AU to get it. Harvard granted two and one-half years' credit for his AU degree and graduated him as the only African American in its class of 1900. Towns later was fond of recalling that at Harvard he had "lived like a gentleman on $600 a year." Upon his return to Atlanta University, he was made a professor of English and pedagogy, a position he held until he retired from the institution nearly three decades later.[23]

In his marriage, too, Towns followed a pattern already traced by Du Bois, for both married women they met in their classrooms. Nina Gomer Du Bois had been her husband's student at Wilberforce University in Ohio, and their marriage in 1896 roughly coincided with the meeting in an Atlanta University classroom of Towns and Harriet Eleanor McNair, a pretty and strong-minded young woman who sat in the front row of his course on geology and mineralogy. She was known to all as Nellie. Upon encountering George Towns, or so a family friend tells it, she determined that "this man will be my husband." Happily, the young professor reciprocated Nellie's sentiments, but neither was in a hurry, both cared deeply about their education, and their courtship was a long one. She completed AU's normal course in 1897 and taught school in Covington, Columbus, and Albany while George, meantime, earned a new degree at Harvard. They were married in September 1902.[24]

Born in 1879, Nellie McNair was the second of the three children of Felix and Hattie Cherry McNair. She had an older brother, Ernest, born in 1876, and a younger, Arthur, born in 1882. The family was listed as "mulatto" in the 1880 census, but both McNairs were as reticent about their white ancestry as others of Atlanta's "mixed" population of this era, preferring never to discuss it. Their Negro blood, nevertheless, must have amounted to little more than the proverbial "one drop," for both they and their children were all "fair" enough to pass for white. Ernest was the only one who chose to do so. He joined the U.S. Cavalry and entered white society, his family believed, for they never heard from him again. "Passing" was common enough and understandable, given the bitter and growing hatred of Negroes, but it was perilous for anyone who was found out, and separation from family and friends was the first requirement for its success. Arthur McNair had freckles, red hair, and blue eyes, and as a young man he went to work for the railroad, married a "distinctly" brown woman, and moved to Chicago, where he spent the remainder of his life. Nellie, deeply attached to her mother, remained at home in Atlanta.[25]

Felix and Hattie McNair separated sometime before 1900, and Felix McNair played no further part in his family's life. Bitterness between the couple must have been intense for afterward, as one family member related, "we never heard anything about grandfather." With her skill as a "baby nurse," caring for newborns usually within the infant's home, Hattie McNair became the family's sole provider. Because her referrals were handled by a prominent Atlanta Jewish physician, she worked in the homes of many Jewish families living in the Washington Street and Capitol

Avenue area of Atlanta, near the McNairs' Summerhill home, and her services were elsewhere also in great demand. The family had long been members of the First Congregational Church, which had grown out of Storrs School and was closely connected with Atlanta University. Fully sharing the Negro's abiding faith in the value of education, Mrs. McNair arranged for her daughter, at age fourteen, to enter AU's normal department. It was said at that time in the Negro community that families sent their daughters to Atlanta and Fisk Universities—alma mater of the era's black male elite—as much to find husbands as to get an education. If such was her family's wish, Nellie McNair pleased them well.[26]

After their wedding, George and Nellie McNair Towns honeymooned in Boston and Niagara Falls, then moved into rooms at South Hall, the boys' dormitory on the AU campus. Until well into the twentieth century, black faculty and staff as well as most white professors either lived in South Hall or in nearby areas, clustering together for both companionship and safety. Their three oldest surviving children were born in South Hall before the Townses moved to a new home of their own. This home, too, would be within the campus confines of Atlanta University.[27]

• • •

Amid a triumphant white supremacy, with racial repression at its peak, Atlanta University remained a protective oasis. It was the scene at the turn of the century of a black intellectual flowering which, in the judgment of John Dittmer, who looked back on it in his *Black Georgia in the Progressive Era*, was "unmatched anywhere." Du Bois, with *The Souls of Black Folk* and his ongoing AU studies, figured prominently in the movement, as did John Hope, classics professor at Atlanta Baptist (later Morehouse College), who in 1906 would be named that college's first Negro president; Bishop Henry M. Turner, chancellor of Morris Brown College, who had moved from politics to the African Methodist Episcopal Church in 1876; Henry Hugh Proctor of the First Congregational Church; J. W. E. Bowen at Gammon Theological Seminary; and Max Barber, who was then editing a courageous black periodical, the *Voice of the Negro*.[28]

George Towns was a colleague of all these men, and by any criterion he was a member of Georgia's Negro leadership in this era. Yet he lacked the charisma and intellectual originality of those who stood out. His values stemmed from the educational heritage of Puritan New England, as did those, for example, of Du Bois, Hope, and Johnson, but Towns's aspirations were more defined by the limits of such values than were those of his more celebrated colleagues. Faithfully reflecting his missionary teaching, Towns did not esteem the white race more than his own, but his cultural ideal was patterned on white standards, with little heed to his African roots, leading one critic later to say, "He has more of the Yankee brogue in his speech than a down right Easterner." Still, he was a gifted teacher, strict but enthusiastic and energetic, imposing scholastic demands on his students that mirrored the New England way of his own teachers. He earned his place as a race leader with courageous acts in the political struggles of his day.[29]

Towns was among the group of progressives and radicals who rallied around Du Bois in his clash with Booker T. Washington, then the dominant Negro in America. Washington's prescription for Negro betterment called for an emphasis on industrial instead of higher education and a surrender of civil and political rights in exchange for larger chances for economic development. His standing among black masses and in the centers of white power was so high that he had escaped challenge until Du Bois included in *The Souls of Black Folk* a telling attack on his dubious remedies. Du Bois believed that imposed inferiority sapped the Negro's manhood, that his economic betterment was a mirage in the absence of suffrage, and that industrial education depended on teachers trained in Negro colleges. In his daring challenge to the great man, he eloquently defended this thesis and soon issued a call for a conference at which "organized . . . and aggressive action" would be taken against Washington's accommodationist approach. Towns was one of four Georgians signing Du Bois's call. The others were Hope, Dr. Loring B. Palmer, and Monroe Work, later a distinguished scholar at Tuskegee Institute. Out of this conference, held at Niagara Falls in July 1905, came the Niagara Movement, forerunner of the National Association for the Advancement of Colored People, which was founded in 1909, and the ultimate decline of Washington's power as a Negro leader. Du Bois, who is considered the father of the NAACP, resigned from Atlanta University in 1910 to edit the *Crisis*, the NAACP's magazine published in New York. His militant ideas marred relations with AU administrators in his last years, for the institution's financial health depended on money from northern white philanthropists, nearly all of them Washington admirers, and, indeed, Du Bois's persistence in his conflict with Washington may have sped his departure from Atlanta.[30]

If Du Bois could escape AU pressure, his young protégé, George Towns, who also insisted on boldly speaking out, could not. In 1903, when Towns and his new wife were expecting a child, he wrote a letter of support to William Monroe Trotter, an outspoken Washington foe, after Trotter, editor of the *Guardian*, a Boston Negro newspaper, was arrested and imprisoned for his part in a public fracas with Washington supporters. Trotter published the Towns letter in the *Guardian*, to the chagrin of Horace Bumstead, then AU president, who demanded a retraction from Towns. Fearing for his job at such a critical time in his life, Towns had to yield. At first he said he regretted the publication of the letter though not its contents. When Bumstead was unmollified, demanding a specific disavowal of the letter's "peculiarly offensive" remarks about Washington, Towns struggled to comply without doing damage to his convictions. By hand he composed three statements before finally coming up with a fourth that satisfied the adamant AU head. The three rejected statements, each heavily edited, were preserved among his papers, but the final, accepted version was not. Perhaps he was ashamed of it so did not preserve it. However much soul-searching the letter cost him, it served its purpose, winning Towns a reprieve from the university's Board of Trustees, who issued a statement expressing their "great astonishment and profound regret" and cautioned him against future "irresponsible" use of his academic freedom. There the matter was laid to rest. Bumstead was not personally a Washington supporter and became active in the NAACP after his retirement from AU, while Towns, the chastened heretic, and his wife gave their second son, born just after the NAACP's founding, the middle name of Bumstead.[31]

But after the Trotter affair, Towns's approach to the racial struggle was practical and never again confrontational. When in the face of mounting proscriptions blacks continued to make modest educational and economic gains, southern whites—determined upon ever more subjugation—set out to disfranchise the entire race. Hoke Smith, whom blacks had considered a fair man when he was President Grover Cleveland's secretary of the interior, successfully ran for Georgia governor on a platform whose main plank was a state constitutional ban on the Negro's right to vote. Disfranchisement had already taken hold in other southern states without hindrance from the U.S. Supreme Court, the Fourteenth and Fifteenth Amendments notwithstanding, and Smith enjoyed a free hand. He stumped the state in 1905 and 1906 in a gubernatorial campaign so inflammatory in its anti-Negro rhetoric that historians cite Smith as the single most important instigator of the September 1906 Atlanta riot, which occurred a month after his election, resulting in pillage and destruction that killed at least 25 blacks, seriously wounded 150 others, and caused many to flee the city in search of refuge elsewhere. Stunned by the absence of support for their safety in city, state, and nation, for even President Theodore Roosevelt would not publicly condemn the riot, Negroes had only themselves to turn to as the move to strip them of the franchise gathered force in Georgia, and despite the odds against them they did not surrender the ballot without a struggle. Inspired by Du Bois's Niagara Movement, Negroes formed the Georgia Equal Rights League in February 1906 at the height of Hoke Smith's anti-Negro incitement. Though the League was hampered by dissension within the race, its members and supporters, including George Towns, registered protests at mass meetings and sent memorials to the Georgia legislature in the summer of 1907, when it was debating the disfranchisement scheme. One such memorial, with Towns among the twenty-one signers, was considered important enough to rate a mention in the *Atlanta Constitution*. Once approved by the Georgia legislature in August 1907, disfranchisement had to win majority support in a public referendum, and Negroes with help from a few whites organized the Georgia Suffrage League to promote black voter registration in the hope of defeating the measure at the polls. In pursuit of its goal, the Suffrage League sponsored mass meetings, public exhortations, and individual solicitations throughout the state, with Towns again among the supporters. But the best efforts of all concerned could bring to the polls only a minor fraction of those Negroes eligible to vote, and in October 1908 the disfranchisement amendment won approval by a two-to-one margin, apparently on a straight racial divide. Though the vote's color composition was never officially established, analysts at the *Atlanta Journal* concluded that less than 10 percent and probably no more than 5 percent of the forty thousand votes garnered in opposition (against seventy-nine thousand in favor) were cast by white men. Blacks would not vote again in Georgia in such numbers for another forty years, but even such complete disfranchisement as was provided in the 1908 law gave much discretion to registrars, and in cities such as Atlanta several thousands remained on the registration books throughout the ensuing decades. In rural areas blacks after 1908 virtually disappeared from voting rolls.[32]

With the Negro suffering constantly thwarted hopes for improvement in his lot, Towns joined with Du Bois, John Hope, the Reverend H. H. Proctor, and Dr. William Penn, a physician, in planning a black colony on the Georgia coast near Brunswick. They were intrigued by the possibility that a seacoast settlement, where they and their families might escape white dominance, would be the starting point of a black belt stretching through the West Indies clear to the bottom of Brazil. The project remained a dream, but the political struggle for racial justice continued, and when an Atlanta chapter of the NAACP was finally formed in 1917, Towns and Hope were on its first executive committee.[33]

Though denied an unfettered franchise during much of his life, Towns never lost his belief that "the ballot is the right preservative of all rights." In 1944, when two world wars and cataclysmic social change had again brought the ballot within the Negro's grasp, Towns sat down at the Fulton County courthouse in Atlanta and, on his own, began a drive to register Negro voters. He persuaded a thousand blacks to sign up. It was a novel idea that would have earned him reprisal in rural Georgia, but in urban Atlanta the racial climate was improving and he was grudgingly tolerated. The Associated Press thought it worth a lengthy story, but newspapers, blind as ever to the black experience, ignored it. Two decades later, voter registration drives became the central focus of the great civil rights movement all over the South. Towns, though deceased by the time the movement reached its peak, may have looked on in satisfaction from the great beyond he so deeply believed in, knowing he had had an idea whose time had come. Here are excerpts from the news dispatch that never got printed:

Atlanta, May 9, 1944 (AP)—A mild-mannered, retired Negro educator, Harvard-graduate George A. Towns, concluded tonight a one-man "citizenship" campaign which by his count has influenced at least 1,000 Atlanta Negroes to seek voting franchise in Georgia's July 4 Democratic primary.

Registrations closed throughout the state tonight and . . . harassed clerks estimated . . . totals (for Fulton County) were 63,157 registrations, of which 4,643 were Negroes. . . . Of the Negroes, about one-fifth, apparently, were shepherded to the registration windows by George Towns.

Spare and 70ish, with heavy glasses, the former Atlanta University professor stood in the lobby of the courthouse daily from 9 a.m. to 5 p.m., beginning March 24.

"The idea occurred to me," he explained, "when I came to the court house to make my tax returns. Every property owner and car owner is compelled by law to make a tax return. When he makes a tax return, he automatically is assessed for poll tax. Hence there is nothing to keep any taxpayer from being a qualified elector except registration.

"The first day I helped about 50 Negro men and women to register as voters. The next day was Saturday and I got about 20. I decided to come back the next week. I averaged 40 to 50 a day. I've been at it every day, ever since. Some people thought I must have an ulterior motive. A city detective came and questioned me to find out my source of income. He thought I was soliciting. I told him I didn't need much to live on, and what I needed, I had.

"Then the sheriff came and got me and questioned me. I told him I was just a retired professor, trying to help some of my people exercise their obligations as citizens. I told him if they didn't want the Negro to participate in this government, they ought not to take his taxes. The sheriff got up and left me and never came back. A police lieutenant came down and threatened to arrest me. I told him I would be here when he came for me, but he never did." [34]

When Towns died December 20, 1960, Du Bois wrote the family: "I grieve at the loss of a friend of sixty years. George Towns was a good man, honest and sincere, a hard worker and a sympathetic friend. He had a deep sense of humor and a wide hunger for knowledge. He will lie buried in the hearts of thousands who knew him and in my memory he will live forever." [35]

Horace Mann Bond, who had been his student at Atlanta University and later himself became a distinguished educator, called Towns "perhaps the finest flower in the garden planted by the American Missionary Association in Atlanta." At the time of the AU centenary in 1969, a poll was taken to determine its ten most outstanding deceased graduates. George Alexander Towns and James Weldon Johnson were among the chosen ten. [36]

2

Growing Up Negro in the
Progressive Era

. . .

GRACE TOWNS never forgot the day she moved with her family from South Hall to a spacious new home at 594 University Place on the edge of the Atlanta University campus. She was then barely three years old, but she remembered all her life that she had "pitched a tantrum" when her parents refused to let her make the short trip there in the little red wagon containing her childhood rocker. Why this recollection and none other remained of that signal event in her family life—for her parents resided at that address for the remainder of their days—she never tried to explain.

In his choice of a home site, as in all else in the life of George Towns, the influence of AU was paramount. Since its inception, the university had acquired land for future expansion, and by the turn of the century it was playing an active role in promoting development of middle-income neighborhoods on its periphery, selling parcels of property to selected buyers willing to build residences. George Towns easily fit the profile of preferred buyers. AU's housing aims were twofold, to encourage the precepts of family welfare taught within its walls and to upgrade the status of its own locale in west Atlanta, otherwise the site of some of the city's worst Negro ghettoes. In a geographically divided Negro community, those better off at that time lived on or near Auburn Avenue in the east; the poor clustered to the west in and around the AU campus.

For his new home, Towns purchased land in what the university called its "Northeast Lot," an acreage along the ridge of a gentle promontory overlooking nearby downtown Atlanta. AU had special ambitions for this lot. Here it built for President Horace Bumstead in the late 1880s a two-story shingle-style house that was always called "Bumstead Cottage" though his successor, Edward Twichell Ware, also long resided there. Later the university came to envision the Northeast Lot as an enclave where that segment of Negro society Du Bois called the "talented tenth" might establish an upper-class haven, building homes at least equal in quality to Bumstead Cottage that would complement the university's handsome Victorian buildings in a manner not possible for the modest housing it otherwise encouraged on its borders.

At the time Towns bought into the Northeast Lot, so did Alonzo F. Herndon, an untutored former slave who was then the South's most successful barber and a skillful entrepreneur. Herndon's Atlanta Life Insurance Company would soon become the largest privately held black-owned corporation in America. His wife was Adrienne Herndon, a teacher of elocution at Atlanta University. Herndon, like Towns, easily qualified as a home builder AU wanted in the Northeast Lot, and, indeed, so eager was the university to have him build there that it may at first have given him the land as an inducement, for only long after his dwelling was occupied did Herndon actually purchase the property. Like Towns, Herndon identified with Atlanta's mulatto elite, having, like most of them, raised himself by his own bootstraps in triumph over racial injustice. Towns, more educated and cultured than Herndon, did not have the talented barber's earnings, and the difference in the homes they built reflected the inequality of their incomes, though each dwelling had its own architectural significance. Towns built a four-square classic box, with brick exterior, neoclassical porch details, Victorian window treatments, and eight rooms, four on the first floor living area and four bedrooms on the second floor, as well as a full basement. Drawing on his latent ability as an architect and his well-honed skills in carpentry and the mechanical arts, Towns participated directly in every phase of his home's construction. Once, when the house was nearing completion, he fell from a scaffold and broke his arm, but the work proceeded while he recuperated, and in mid-1910 the family moved into the finished home.[1]

Across the street, the Herndon home had slowly risen to completion under the artistic guidance of Adrienne Herndon. Five years in the building, it was fittingly called a mansion, for it contained fifteen rooms on two floors, a full basement with a separate apartment, and a rooftop terrace where Mrs. Herndon planned to stage plays for university audiences. An admirer of both Herndons, Du Bois celebrated the home as "the finest Negro residence in the South," but Adrienne Herndon never lived to enjoy it. She died at the age of forty-one, just a week before it was ready for occupancy.[2]

The Northeast Lot never became the upper-class haven AU had envisioned. No others of Atlanta's educated black elite ever sought to build there. Bumstead Cottage, after being divided into apartments for faculty families, was eventually razed to make way for an undistinguished brick "colonial" residence for the president of Morris Brown College, and when AU built a two-story dormitory for women next door to the Towns home, the lot lost its original cohesive character. The ideal was doomed less by this mix of discordant elements, however, than by the relentless pressure outside its walls of racial animosities and proscriptions that were well beyond its control.

In the end, the Towns and Herndon homes stood very much alone, the families isolated socially and culturally not only from whites but also from their black peers. The caustic comments of editor Benjamin Davis, in a column devoted to Towns in his paper, the *Atlanta Independent*, of September 3, 1910, were doubtless no little inspired by malice, but they probably struck a sympathetic note in the wider black community: "Mr. Towns knows less and sees less of Negroes' conditions than many white men. . . . He is so exclusive in his new environment that he does not know whether he is from Boston or Dougherty County. . . . It is true that he is a professor at the University and does possibly good class work but he has no influence that is felt in any phase of our community life."[3]

· · ·

University Place was indeed exclusive. Signs at either end of the one-block street warned all comers, "PRIVATE PROPERTY, NO TRESPASSING." Like the rest of AU's campus in its early years, the unpaved street was windswept and spare of vegetation because tree growth on the battle-scarred hills of western Atlanta was slow to recover from wartime destruction.

The trespass warnings that apparently inspired the ire of editor Davis were no less a source of scorn for youthful Grace Towns and her brothers. "Nobody would come here if they didn't have to," they said among themselves as they grew up. They appreciated the quality of their home life, though they were inclined as children to think casually of their residence as "just another part of the campus." Yet they knew well enough that they lived better than most others of their race in Atlanta. The evidence lay barely beyond their windows to the east in Beaver Slide, a ghetto where unlit dirt streets were lined with shacks that were less shelters than sources of disease and crime, and below them on the north they could see the poor working-class neighborhood of Vine City, called Black Bottom, where conditions were little better. Living comparatively well, they nevertheless looked directly from their lovely Victorian home onto an unpaved street, though it existed a short block from a main city thoroughfare, and the street's only paved sidewalk, truncated and in poor repair, lay on the side of the Herndon mansion. Years later the road was still unimproved and Grace's daughter, Eleanor, recalled that as a child she knew when the family car approached her grandparents' house because it started bumping over the rutted dirt road.[4]

Atlanta blacks might gain in education and economic status, but the upper classes could no more command the amenities and services commonly available to whites than the poorest of the black poor. Particularly to the young of the Towns family, the dirt at their door symbolized the Jim Crow humiliations that awaited them in the white world beyond.

Political disfranchisement of the Negro was completed in Georgia and the last black representative had resigned from the state legislature by the time the Towns family settled into their new home. Outside the grounds of the integrated college where they lived, white supremacists were turning with growing zeal toward perfecting the color line. Whether de jure or de facto, by the second decade of the twentieth century, when Grace Towns entered early childhood, blacks found themselves Jim Crowed at every turn. The wall of segregation was so formidable, so impenetrable, so varied and complex that the entire strength of the American constitutional system would be required to make even the slightest crack in it. Yet it had not always been so.

Two distinct societies, one black and the other white, had existed since slavery, and Jim Crow laws had appeared as early as 1875 in Tennessee, spreading afterward throughout the region. Still in the 1870s and 1880s, when George Towns was growing up in Albany, blacks had more freedom of movement in Georgia than they would enjoy again for most of his lifetime. When he went to Atlanta in 1884, public transportation was integrated, both races used the same recreational facilities and shopped in the same business districts, and residential patterns there as in many other Georgia localities—his hometown of Albany being an exception—were defined by few sharp lines between the races. Courts were in the hands of white men, but as late as the turn of the century, blacks still occasionally served on state juries. Even as Towns arrived in the city, all this was rapidly changing. He and his fellow student James Weldon Johnson traveled from their homes in Albany and Jacksonville, Florida, to Atlanta on integrated trains. Returning home the next summer, Johnson (as he related in his autobiography) was forced by threat of mob violence to ride in a passenger car marked "for colored only." When, in its *Plessy* v. *Ferguson* decision of 1896, the U.S. Supreme Court gave federal sanction to "separate but equal" facilities, Jim Crow's march through the South became a rout. By the end of the 1890s, all facilities related to public transportation were segregated by law. Private hospitals would not admit blacks, and the few beds allotted the race in public hospitals were for the indigent, leaving those able to pay with nowhere to go outside of a few ill-equipped private establishments that grew up to serve their needs. Public schools from their beginning had always been separated by race, where they existed for blacks at all.[5]

By the time Grace Towns was a youngster, theaters, lectures, concerts, athletic events, and public recreational facilities were either barred to blacks or open only on a Jim Crow basis. Atlanta University athletes in 1903 had been driven from football practice in a public park, and George Towns had to raise money in the North for a substitute field on the campus grounds. Barber shops had to designate whether they served black or white patrons. Black businesses were pressured out of "white" downtown Atlanta and then contained along the Auburn Avenue corridor on Atlanta's east side, which afterward became an all-black neighborhood. Black prisoners rode to the stockade in separate vehicles, and black witnesses swore on Jim Crow Bibles. The races rode in separate elevators in public buildings, blacks usually being confined to the freight elevator, and separate passages were reserved for Negroes at the Atlanta zoo. Negroes could not even visit the Carnegie Public Library when it was erected in 1902 and had to wait twenty years for an underequipped branch to serve their needs in the Auburn Avenue locality. Afterward, Negroes needing to use material found only in the main library had to enter the building by the back door and make use of the material downstairs in the janitor's quarters.

Even while the Towns family grew used to integrated University Place, residential segregation was growing. Atlanta in 1913 passed an ordinance assigning Negroes and whites to certain blocks and districts. After the U.S. Supreme Court nullified the city's action, new tactics, ranging from restrictive covenants to terror, coerced blacks into underdeveloped areas or residential sections whites no longer found desirable. It was much the same in all other Georgia cities where black populations were steadily expanding.[6]

. . .

Given the racial intolerance that raged in nearby Atlanta, the isolation of University Place was a blessing, making it safer and more secure for integrated living. "My best friends, my only playmates as a child, were from the families of other members of the faculty," Grace Towns later recalled. They were black and white together. In childhood, she had a racial companion in Yolande Du Bois, only daughter of W. E. B. and Nina Du Bois, and was extremely close to Emma Rush (later Emma Rush Brown), whose mother was a dietitian at AU's dining hall. Across the street in the Herndon mansion lived Norris Bumstead Herndon, but he was a decade older than the Towns children and their friendship with Norris developed only when they all grew older. Nearer their age were the sons of Edward Twichell Ware, AU's president between 1907 and 1920, who lived across the street in Bumstead Cottage, and the children of Alexander S. Huth, superintendent of AU's farm and grounds, and those of George K. Howe, a physics and mathematics instructor and manager of AU's carpentry shop, both of whom lived with their families in nearby campus areas. Grace Towns would develop relationships with a growing number of black peers as she grew older, but she attributed her unbiased outlook in life to the influence of the interracial balance among her earliest playmates.[7]

AU's farm, source of food and dairy produce for the college dining hall, was close to University Place. Faculty members could buy from the farm for their own kitchens, and one of the "stock responsibilities" of the Towns children in their growing years, Grace Towns remembered, was "going to get the milk" every day from the AU dairy. The family also regularly ate such staple items from the farm as sweet potatoes and black-eyed peas. The proximity of the farm, added to its isolation, lent an almost "country" feel to University Place.[8]

Farm produce might have been available elsewhere, but good education was not and, luckily, campus schooling for their children was also available to faculty members. At the turn of the century, education for Atlanta blacks was not only segregated but also meager in quantity and mediocre in quality. In 1903, there were only five public schools in all Atlanta, with forty-nine teachers for the eight thousand Negro children of school age, compared to twenty schools with two hundred teachers for the fourteen thousand eligible whites. Black teachers earned half the salary of their white counterparts and because of severe overcrowding carried nearly double the workload. For white teachers at AU, themselves scorned and shunned in the dominant white society, the educational haven offered their children by the university was as welcome as it was to their black colleagues.

Public neglect of black education was among the reasons why AU maintained primary through high school facilities on its campus until well into the twentieth century and why they were always patronized to capacity. When university building compelled AU to close its own primary and grammar school departments in 1894, it continued for another decade to operate Storrs School, primarily as a practice teaching facility for its own education students, and when it finally handed Storrs over to Georgia in 1904, it then opened Oglethorpe Practice School, where it could continue to control hiring and student numbers and forbid a color bar. Money for the school was raised in the North because (as usual) there were no southern sources of cash for integrated teaching. Oglethorpe's principal benefactor was Mrs. Charles Russell Lowell, whose husband as well as her brother, Colonel Robert Gould Shaw, had been killed in Civil War battles. Colonel Shaw headed the Fifty-fourth Massachusetts Negro regiment, the first of the Civil War's all-black regiments, and died with many of his troops at Fort Wagner, South Carolina. Though it might have honored Mrs. Lowell or her brother, AU chose instead to name the school for General James Edward Oglethorpe, the Englishman who founded the state of Georgia.[9]

Grace Towns and all her siblings attended Oglethorpe Practice School and later received their high school education at AU's preparatory department, long the only secondary school available to blacks in Atlanta. As Grace Towns remembered it, they were long tutored at home before entering Oglethorpe. Just why George and Nellie Towns at first chose private tutoring over Oglethorpe is not known—or no longer remembered in the family. Towns was a professor of pedagogy at the time—in his last years at AU he taught teachers almost exclusively—and perhaps he had his own ideas about teaching and teachers, or perhaps he and his wife thought home education valuable in its own right.

"I can't remember the tutors specifically," Grace Towns reminisced, "but I do remember we had a regular period of study with a teacher who would come to the house. We'd have a school period every day in the morning, in the summertime too. I can remember very well having school work to do every day. The classroom, at least in the summer, was the porch, the front of the porch." Many of the teachers, she remembered, "were my father's students, people who eventually went into the public school system." She did not clearly remember in later life just when she finally entered

Oglethorpe, but she "guessed" she was "in the sixth or seventh grade." She took with her to Oglethorpe a love of reading instilled by her parents. Books were as much a part of her family household as the furniture. "My father," Grace Towns recalled, "was interested in all kinds of reading matter. As children we were read to every day. I can remember a reading period after supper at night, it was just sort of a standard part of the day." Professor Towns clearly implanted in his children the love of literature he had gained at AU as a student of the classics, but it was Mrs. Towns who usually read to the children.[10]

• • •

In the Towns home, life was centered on education, the church, and service to the race. As in most other black families of their standing, George and Nellie Towns sought by precept and example to teach their children the value of community involvement and commitment to the cause of racial justice. The father's active political work served as his example. Having no economic compulsion to work outside her home yet possessed of much spare energy, Nellie Towns set hers as a respected volunteer in important community organizations, most particularly in the many endeavors of the First Congregational Church, to which the family belonged. One of the most socially conscious churches in Atlanta, First Congregational provided a library, gymnasium, kitchen, employment bureau, prison mission, kindergarten, and home for Negro girls, among many other projects, and Nellie Towns was, according to the biographer of her daughter's public career, very active in all of them. Born on the AU campus in 1867 as the nondenominational Storrs Church (so called for Storrs School where it was first located), the church was founded by white Congregational missionaries who that same year chartered Atlanta University, but its communicants in those early years were interracial. By the time the Towns family were members, First Congregational had become an institutional church with its own new building in downtown Atlanta, a Negro pastor named Henry Hugh Proctor—an articulate spokesman for the race, who would later accept a pastorate in New York City—and a heavily black congregation that was mainly connected to AU.

Besides her volunteer activity at First Congregational, Nellie Towns helped found and worked busily with the Gate City Free Kindergarten Association, which sought to relieve the plight of children of the working Negro poor, so poignantly revealed in early Du Bois studies for Atlanta University's conferences on conditions of the urban Negro. At the urging of Du Bois, Gertrude Ware Bunce, sister of AU's then chaplain Edward Twichell

Ware and supervisor of kindergarten work at AU, established the association in 1905, and Nellie Towns was among the "faithful few" who actively assisted her, as were Adrienne Herndon and Lugenia Burns Hope, wife of John Hope. At one time, Nellie Towns was the association's secretary, composing news articles for Ben Davis's *Atlanta Independent* in support of funds for its work. She may have been the anonymous pamphleteer who wrote: "How the money was raised to take care of the work was a mystery even to members of the Association. Many times the promoters wondered themselves how they could carry on, but a way was always provided. . . . Concerts, bake sales, fairs, track-meets, contests and other entertainments of various kinds were used to raise funds. Of course it meant hard work for the 'faithful few.' However, at the end of the twentieth year, the Association had raised and used over thirty thousand dollars in cash to carry on the work." The original association eventually became the Gate City Day Nursery Association, giving full-day care to children in five centers, and its funding after 1924 was provided by the Atlanta Community Chest.[11]

Nellie Towns also found time to work with the Young Women's Christian Association when a branch for Negro women and girls (named for Phillis Wheatley, the Negro poet) was finally established in Atlanta in 1919, and she was the first black woman to serve on the central board of the city's YWCA. Her associates remembered Nellie Towns as "reserved and very unostentatious" in all her organizational activities. One of her colleagues in the Gate City Day Nursery Association enumerated the "eloquent qualities" she admired in Nellie Towns—"integrity in all actions, strong convictions in service to others, firm belief in people, faith in change . . . [and] the pervasive Christian love which penetrated each of [her] endeavors." The colleague added, "She enriches every person who knows her." [12]

In her home life, as a friend remembered her, "Nellie Towns was a housewife and a mother in the old classical sense, but she was always a queen, never a drudge." Said another who knew her well, "She was a mother without being sentimental," a "formidable" woman in rearing her children, and a "very strict" disciplinarian. In a day when discipline was usually corporal, Nellie Towns may have spared her daughter, for Grace had no memories in later life of being disciplined as a child by mother or father. "I don't remember getting a spanking," she said, though for the boys it apparently was otherwise. "My brothers probably got switchings, I can remember hearing about switchings." George and Nellie Towns seemed to complement each other's parental talents, the professor leaving discipline to his wife and acting himself "more as an intellectual guardian for his children," thought the biographer who studied Grace Towns Hamilton's later public career. This writer saw them as "a couple who showered affection and devotion on their children and on each other." [13]

A home that was "filled with so much love," as numerous acquaintances described it, gave the Towns children in their growing years a sense of security and self-confidence. Their maternal grandmother, Hattie McNair, lived with the family until her death in 1920, giving them continuity with the past, a source of self-knowledge and self-esteem. The year her mother died, Nellie Towns had her last child, a daughter called Harriet, the name she herself was given at birth. Never knowing Nana, as Grace and her brothers had always called their grandmother, was a loss for Harriet. All her siblings had "loved to curl up" in Nana's ample lap whenever she allowed it. Though Mrs. McNair shared her daughter's penchant for strong discipline, the children also experienced her intercession when she thought their mother's demands needed to be tempered. Sometimes Nana took Grace to play with children of the white families where she worked as a baby nurse, and Grace also remembered "going with her to weddings of some of the children of those families." [14]

Reared in a household where religion and discipline were imposed by loving and sensible parents, living and going to school in a sheltered community where racial equality was the overriding principle, Grace Towns experienced an uncommon childhood, suffering virtually none of the humiliations the dominant society inflicted on all Negroes within its reach and consequently never developing the feeling that all whites are evil, which scarred the subconscious of many of her race. In years to come, when asked what childhood experience had most influenced her life, she invariably replied, "I grew up without the burden of hating white people." Grace Towns called that world in which she came of age "a closed yet open society, closed in the fact that we were a little island of academic folks shut off from the snubs which are everyday incidents for Negroes working in a white world, yet open in the sense that there were no categorical distinctions between Negroes and whites." As she later looked back on it, the lesson she learned from her early environment, one that shaped her thinking ever afterward, was that people should be evaluated "in terms of their character, not their color." [15]

Yet in the city beyond Atlanta University as she grew to adolescence, people were more and more evaluated by their color. In health care, for example, the very benefits that came with the economic status conferred by the AU connection carried a savage penalty. Atlanta's private hospitals, following southern custom of the time, excluded all blacks and admitted only the indigent (and no more than forty to fifty of them out of Atlanta's forty thousand Negroes) when Grady Hospital opened as a public facility in 1890. Those like the Towns family who possessed (even if limited) means to pay "had to get independent medical advice, nobody ever suggested hospitalization," Grace Towns recollected. If the illness was serious enough, "you had to seek service elsewhere, you had to go to Mayo [the Mayo Clinic then located only in Rochester, Minnesota], or you had to go somewhere else." When she was eight, Grace Towns had pneumonia, and later she developed a spinal problem—an outcome of the pneumonia, her family surmised— but both illnesses were treated successfully by their friend and physician Dr. Loring B. Palmer, a graduate of the University of Pennsylvania Medical School.[16]

In the early 1920s, the Towns family managed to evade the obstacle posed by their "affluence" and got George Jr. and Myron into Grady's Jim Crow ward for tonsillectomies. Grace Towns remembered it as the work of Ludie Andrews, a family friend who had recently been appointed director of nursing for "Negro" Grady, the first black to hold the job. "She must have convinced my parents and the doctor that Grady would be the best place for them to be," Grace Towns said. She could not recall "the details," but when pressed, she said, "I guess it was like anything else, it can be arranged." Once admitted to Grady for the tonsil procedure, the Towns boys were placed under staff care because no private doctor could treat them there. For blacks of education and some means, especially, this was a humiliating experience and doubtless designed to be so by the white society that inspired the prohibition. After these tonsillectomies, the Towns family happily had no further need of hospitalization in the years when Grace and her siblings were growing up.[17]

In 1919 Grace Towns entered high school at Atlanta University's preparatory department. Because it was the only high school for Negroes in the city, students from all black Atlanta whose families could muster the modest tuition flocked to the facility. Previously somewhat isolated from her peers by home tutoring, Grace Towns now met classmates who would become lifelong friends, and, in contrast to her childhood playmates, most of them would be of her own race. AU then turned out more normal than college graduates, and upon entering the preparatory department, a student had to choose between college and the normal course. Having developed an interest in psychology, Grace chose to prepare for college, as did most of her new friends. Among them were Annie Ruth Simmons (later Hill) and

Grace Holmes (later DeLorme). Actually, she had had some childhood contact with Grace Holmes when their mothers, both active in the Gate City Free Kindergarten Association, brought them together at bake sales and other fund-raising activities for the organization. But the Holmes family lived on Atlanta's east side, and the distance that divided the city's two Negro areas had kept them apart. Grace Holmes was the daughter of T. K. Holmes, a man so white, she said, "he had a hard time proving he was black," and while carrying the mail he'd "read" law, later practicing successfully as one of Atlanta's few Negro lawyers. Annie Ruth Simmons lived in west Atlanta on Greens Ferry Avenue near the AU campus, and her father earned a living as a hauler while also running a grocery store with the help of his wife, who in addition supplemented family income as a seamstress.[18]

Jim Crow circumscribed the lives of these young girls, making them more vulnerable every day and in every way than their white peers, but the two Graces and Annie Ruth were less preoccupied with the potential evil that surrounded them than they were with the common pursuits of all adolescents. The young girls and others of their circle, as Annie Ruth remembered it, would get together in the afternoon for "what we called sock parties" or perhaps it would be a "spend-the-day party." These affairs began at various times in the afternoon, but they always ended well before dark. "We had to be back home before the sun went down," Annie Ruth recollected. It was a rule. Wherever you were, even if the streetcar was not running, "you just got back home." In Negro Atlanta, the Towns family was not alone in imposing strict discipline on their children.[19]

· · ·

Grace Towns entered Atlanta University's Preparatory Department when powerful forces were shaking the stereotyped conceptions that had defined the Negro's "place" in America with increasing fixity since the collapse of Reconstruction. Yet the status of the race remained precariously poised between gain and further loss.

On the positive side, new organizations had risen to champion the Negro. There was now the NAACP, formed in 1909 under leadership of Du Bois and an interracial group of like-minded northerners who were inspired by his Niagara Movement to work for the political and civic equality of blacks. There was also the National Urban League, founded in 1910 by George Edmund Haynes to address the problems of blacks as they moved increasingly to urban centers. Their work was hampered by the pervasiveness of the very racism they sought to counteract, but hitherto powerless Negroes at last found voices publicly raised in their behalf.[20]

Minuses nevertheless prevailed. Long lacking both representation and a sympathetic ear in Washington, the Negro was again bitterly disappointed when Woodrow Wilson took office in 1913, the first Democratic president in sixteen years. He had promised fair treatment for the Negro, but as Du Bois, an erstwhile Wilson backer, later wrote, "A campaign pledge has never been more persistently and thoroughly broken than this splendid word of Mr. Wilson." For Wilson quickly moved to segregate Negro and white workers in federal offices, to dismiss Negro workers outright, even postal employees with civil service status, and to replace nearly all black Republican appointees with white Democrats. Wilson's moves to "nullify what remained of the Negro's national citizenship" (the words of James Weldon Johnson, who was stripped of the consular post he had long held in Latin America) only slowed with the advent of World War I. As American industries tooled up to supply the warring nations across the Atlantic, the labor vacuum created by decreasing migration from Europe put a premium on Negro muscle and brain, and half a million southern blacks, fleeing poverty and repression, went north to fill the gap.[21]

When the United States entered the war in 1917, the exodus became the "great migration," described by historian John Dittmer as "the most important event in black America since emancipation." Skilled and unskilled labor, professionals and tradesmen joined the flight. Georgia's migration was heaviest from its "cotton belt" in the southwest. In the area around Albany, more than forty-five hundred Negroes departed in 1916 alone and more than fifty thousand left the state forever during the entire war period. The congregation of blacks in northern industrial cities facilitated their political resurgence and gave rise to new race militancy. Yet the economic competition Negroes represented for whites in areas where they settled in numbers, coupled with the virulent race prejudice abroad in the land, also touched off violence. In July 1917 one of the worst of many racial massacres occurred in East St. Louis, Illinois, triggered by black employment in a war factory. Thousands of Negroes were forced from their homes, at least forty were killed, including children and infants, and many were burned to death in houses set fire over their heads. Only weeks later, when a riot in Houston, Texas, killed two blacks and seventeen whites, sole responsibility for the murders was laid on Negro soldiers on leave in the town from Fort Sam Houston. Seventy-odd men were court-martialed (despite strenuous efforts by NAACP lawyers to have the men tried in civilian courts), and before dawn the day after their conviction thirteen were summarily hanged. Another sixteen were later condemned to die and over fifty were sentenced to life or long imprisonment. "The Negroes of the country were agony stricken," Johnson, then field secretary of the NAACP, wrote, feeling that mitigating circumstances for the soldiers' actions had been ignored and that their execution without right of appeal savored of "vengeance rather than justice." Even President Wilson's prejudice seemed shaken, for he responded to a powerful plea from the NAACP for clemency for the remaining condemned by commuting ten death sentences to life imprisonment, though he allowed six more to go to the gallows. Wilson also found opportunity to make a strong statement against violence and lynching, and he prohibited further executions behind military lines before sentence review. Nevertheless, violence and lynching continued.[22]

Even as Grace Towns entered high school in the fall of 1919, the country had just endured "Red Summer," months that ushered in what historian John Hope Franklin called "the greatest interracial strife the nation had ever witnessed." Twenty-five cities suffered riots that summer, killing scores of both races, and soon a revived Ku Klux Klan was recruiting members in the highest places throughout the land. In 1920, Thomas M. Hardwick, who sponsored Negro disfranchisement in Georgia at the turn of the century and was then serving in Congress, was elected governor, and Tom Watson's anti-Negro campaigning in the same election won him a Georgia seat in the U.S. Senate. Georgia continued to lead the nation in lynchings. Among the most atrocious was the killing in mid-1919 in two rural southeast counties of eleven blacks, including a pregnant woman whose unborn child was slit from her stomach while she still lived and stomped to death before her eyes. Though the NAACP supplied the Georgia governor with the names of the killers, no one was ever prosecuted.

But the conscience of southern whites was beginning to stir, and in 1919 Hugh M. Dorsey, then governor of Georgia, published a personal manifesto called "A Statement from Governor Hugh M. Dorsey as to the Negro in Georgia," summarizing with hitherto unexpressed candor a series of crimes regularly committed against blacks. Among his suggested remedies was an antilynching law. In Georgia it was an unprecedented appeal. His frankness enraged white supremacists who labeled the governor a traitor to the state, and lynch mobs continued undeterred. Dorsey had been persuaded to publish his statement by the Commission on Interracial Cooperation (CIC), which white ministers, teachers, and professionals had recently formed under the leadership of Will W. Alexander, former Methodist minister and YMCA worker, as a forum where black and white leaders could meet regularly to discuss ways of averting racial conflict. As the CIC addressed the symptoms and sought to ameliorate the consequences of a racially polarized society while leaving the causes untouched and as black leaders whom it invited to its deliberations were—in the words of Du Bois, writing to a CIC leader—"too much the sort of colored men that we call 'white folks' niggers," the CIC never became more than a "gesture organization," a symbol of goodwill. For all its timidity, it nevertheless activated the idea of permanent dialogue, breaching for the first time in years the wall that isolated the races, and it also helped get convictions in several lynching cases—a landmark accomplishment at the time—while its threat of court action in 1924 helped Atlanta Negroes finally obtain a public high school. During World War II, the CIC dissolved, relaying its functions to a more militant organization, the Southern Regional Council (SRC), of which Grace Towns, by then Grace Towns Hamilton, was an organizer.[23]

After graduating from AU's Preparatory Department in 1923, Grace Towns entered the university's freshman college class that fall, beginning the advanced education that would enable her to contribute more fully to the forces then redefining the Negro's place in American society. For the Towns offspring, "it was just always understood that we would go to Atlanta University," she recalled. "I did have a friend who attended Mount Holyoke, but for us there never was any alternative. It was there and it was expected we would go." Affordability doubtless also played a role in the choice.[24]

And go they did. Grace and her brother Myron Bumstead would receive undergraduate degrees at AU just before it closed out its college course. Myron's class of 1930 was the very last of AU's undergraduates. Harriet, who was ready for advanced education only after AU became solely a graduate school, would receive a degree from Spelman College, by then a constituent unit of the Atlanta University Center. Only George Jr. would find AU incompatible with his needs and outlook. After two years as an undergraduate in the mid-1920s, he left Atlanta for New York, earning his living at various jobs and settling finally in California, where he worked as an accountant after studying at Stanford University and the University of California at Berkeley. He and his father may have quarreled, for George Jr., in a letter home shortly before George Sr.'s death in December 1960, was scornful of AU, saying the institution was too concerned with producing

"more black-faced Bill Grahams." Myron, who earned a doctor of philosophy degree in chemistry at the University of Michigan, was frequently mentioned along with Grace and Harriet in the papers Professor Towns willed
to Atlanta University. George Jr.'s name never appeared.[25]

When Grace Towns and her brothers entered Atlanta University, the institution was changing, but it still resembled in many respects the institution that had nurtured their parents. The college environment still evoked
that of Puritan New England, AU teaching still upheld the values of white
culture at the expense of the black heritage, the rules regulating student
conduct were as strict as ever, and the paternalism that tempered their application still gave way at times to heavy-handed authoritarianism. Grace
Towns and her friends were inclined to ridicule the campus code, viewing it
as essentially "Victorian," but the vigorous protest similar codes provoked
in the 1920s at black colleges such as Howard and Fisk never occured at AU,
where, as Grace Towns remembered it, "most students accepted the rules
and regulations as given." Whatever frustration she felt as an AU student,
she shared none of her brother George's determination to kick over the
traces. As with her father and mother, her profound loyalty to the institution was never shaken.[26]

And in fact, the hoary traditions were finally giving way. When she ma-
triculated at AU, the classical education of her father's time, grounded in
Greek and Latin, had been liberalized in line with the trend at Ivy League
schools, as always the model for AU's curriculum. More stress was laid
now on modern languages and the social and physical sciences. Blacks also
were gaining more control of colleges within the Atlanta University orbit,
though at some of them this happened earlier than at AU. Of the five
missionary-founded institutions that eventually surrounded the university
on its hilltop site in western Atlanta, three, Clark College, Gammon Theological Seminary, and Atlanta Baptist (later Morehouse) College, had been
turned over to Negro presidents by the early twentieth century and faculties at each quickly thereafter became predominantly black. Black-run
from its founding, Morris Brown University, of course, had no conversion
problem. Atlanta University, however, remained under white control until
1929, when John Hope, then head of Morehouse College, became AU's first
Negro president, and Spelman, the last to yield, had white leadership until
1953. Faculties at both AU and Spelman long remained heavily white. Grace
Towns attended AU between 1923 and 1927, and in her student years, as her
classmate Annie Ruth Simmons remembered it, "Most of our teachers
were white." Simmons also recalled: "Most of the teachers were black in the

normal college. But in the college department, our teachers were mostly white. I can't think of but maybe one or two who were black." Such racial imbalance on the faculty doubtless influenced Grace Towns in those years, perhaps enough to explain why her colleagues in the future included those who complained that she thought "white is right" and why others would say unsympathetically that she lacked race consciousness.[27]

Achieving interracial understanding through face-to-face encounters became her goal in her student years, and she continued to pursue this goal for the rest of her life. She joined the Young Women's Christian Association, which welcomed even though it segregated its Negro members, and tried to persuade her friends to do the same. Wenonah Bond (later Logan) was one of her converts, but she had no luck with Grace Holmes, who recalled, "It was all a bit too solemn for me." Holmes told Towns, "Grace, you just go right ahead. I'm not interested in the YW," and Grace Towns did just that, focusing her energy on the National Student Division, then the YWCA's "sharpest cutting edge" and increasingly a magnet for the new generation of Negro women—able, articulate, and far more vocal and aggressive than their elders. Reared with few exceptions under the influence of black churches, these women were increasingly critical of a conservative approach to the Negro's dilemma, and in the Student Division they found a white contingent that readily rallied to their cause. Grace Towns and Wenonah Bond were exhilarated by "Y" work, feeling the student movement was a "beacon light for young women in the South and a spearhead for social change." By the time Grace Towns became involved, the Student Division had pressured the YWCA into permitting integrated regional student conferences, even in the South, making it the first national organization to embark upon such a "radical" course. In April 1926 Grace Towns, while serving as a delegate to a YWCA convention in Milwaukee, Wisconsin, was elected vice-president of the National Student Division, the first black woman in the organization to win such a high post.[28]

Back at the AU campus, Grace Towns was also active in the Atlanta Interracial Student Forum, organized in 1923 by her own First Congregational Church. At the forum, students from both black and white Atlanta colleges met monthly to discuss a wide range of topics, including those most racially sensitive. But for Grace Towns, the important point was that the forum brought black and white students together. In her senior year as editor of the *Scroll*, AU's student newspaper, she explained her view: "We are getting used to meeting with each other. Most of us now feel comfortable together, and how can friendship grow without contact? The Forum has given us contact. We have heard each other's music. We have talked as fellow students. . . . Yet how can we estimate the value of anything that has even the possibility of fellowship? For are we not brothers? Must we not love one another? Does not knowing each other help?" Editorially, she admonished her fellow students to stay away from segregated movies, saying: "As long as we pack the lofts of the white theatres, the lofts will be available to us. Every time a Negro goes around the alley to a white theatre, or in any way voluntarily segregates himself, he is inadvertently admitting his inferiority. . . . What do I suggest? Absolutely refusing to voluntarily Jim Crow ourselves. Self-pride and self-respect are far more valuable than the admission of inferiority by going up high to see a 15-cent show." [29]

She wrote there with the voice of her father, but years later she made a confession that wrapped this editorial of her youth in a benign contradiction. "It wasn't a family order," she said near the end of her public career, "but Papa did not approve of any of the children going to segregated galleries of the theater. Now of course we went, my brothers and I, occasionally. Not many times, but I do remember going as a young person." George Towns Sr. was so ardent in his own refusal to bow before Jim Crow that he always rode a bicycle rather than board the segregated streetcars, and he probably never knew his children sneaked up to the peanut gallery of Atlanta's Fox Theatre. Yet had he known, he might have ruefully understood. Protest was possible, contacts across the color bar occurred here and there, but in fact choices were few, limited by the very caste system Negroes were fighting. Most blacks of the period, as Grace Towns herself later explained to John Dittmer, arranged their lives so that they touched as few raw edges as possible, accepted the status quo as a necessary evil, and tried to live within it. It was an adjustment from which she and her family deviated little until the death at last of old Jim Crow himself.[30]

Yet friends remember Grace Towns as a student leader who was "always out front." She was also deeply serious about the study of psychology, and she was popular among her peers. A good pianist—all the Towns children took piano lessons—she played for any campus production that needed an accompanist. Because Jim Crow, combined with AU's "Victorian" restrictions, narrowly circumscribed social outlets for AU students, Grace Towns took the lead in 1926 in persuading the college to relax its ban on social sororities and fraternities and allow on campus a chapter of Alpha Kappa Alpha, a sorority founded at Howard University in 1908. The color bar compelled most AU students to confine their socializing to private homes, and University Place was a frequent gathering point for Grace and her student friends. Her sister, who became Harriet Towns Jenkins, recollected: "Grace was a very popular young woman in her college years. Other students would come over to the house and dance and listen to music and socialize. They'd roll up the rug and dance. We had the old RCA-Victor gramophone and that was in the years of Paul Whiteman. His recording of *Rhapsody in Blue*. It played over and over."[31]

Because AU shared the belief that group living away from home had a maturing influence on the young, Grace Towns was required in her senior year to live on campus. She roomed with Wenonah Bond, who later offered this impression:

Grace was a remarkable young woman, even in her teens, she was a gay, witty creature, always intellectually curious. She was a leader as you would expect her to be. We were active in the YWCA. She and I went to student conferences at Talladega. I remember Grace was one of the people on the platform and I remember thinking then, 1926 or 1927, and I remember Grace with her hands on the arm of a chair and how pulled together she was. I guess I was thinking in contrast to most of us at that age, we were sort of gangly, you know. Grace was there, just as calm as anything, with her hands on the arms of the chair ready to cope. Lots of presence, yes, and always lots of fun. I mean giggly kinds of things, you know.[32]

Graduating in 1927 from Atlanta University with a bachelor of arts degree, Grace Towns made immediate plans to pursue a master's degree in psychology at Ohio State University in Columbus, where the National YWCA had offered her a job as girl's work secretary in its Negro branch. George Williams, one of her favorite psychology professors at AU, had a high regard for Ohio State's psychology department and had encouraged her matriculation there, especially because the "Y" job made it possible to finance her studies.

Major changes were simultaneously under way at Atlanta University that would have an impact on all members of the Towns family. In 1924 Atlanta had opened Booker T. Washington High School for Negroes, and AU immediately began phasing out its high school facilities, one year at a time. By 1928 it was functioning solely as a college for the first time since it was chartered in 1867. Oglethorpe Practice School was continued alongside a new high school, called the Laboratory School; both facilities offered training to AU's education majors. And in 1929 under John Hope, its new Negro president, AU ceased to be a college and became at last a true university, awarding only graduate degrees. Morehouse and Spelman Colleges, physically close to the AU campus, then pooled resources with the university in what was called "the affiliation," becoming exclusively undergraduate institutions. Clark and Morris Brown Colleges did the same when they later located nearer AU and joined the affiliation, completing the five-college Atlanta University Center, which in its day was the largest and most prestigious concentration of black learning in the world.

For Professor Towns, the merger brought retirement. With its student body limited to graduates, AU needed a smaller faculty, and Towns was among those pensioned off. Not yet sixty, Towns was unready—and financially ill prepared because his pension was small—to end his teaching career, and in 1930 he accepted a post as principal at Fort Valley, Georgia, Normal and Industrial School, a state-supported training school for blacks, where he remained until 1938. Mrs. Towns and Harriet continued to live on University Place, commuting to visit him on weekends.

When her father retired in 1929, Grace Towns had already studied for two years in Columbus, Ohio, and this, her first experience north of the Mason-Dixon line, had been a startling revelation to her.[33]

3

A Rude Awakening in Ohio

. . .

G RACE TOWNS said later that she never knew "what the real world was like" until she went north to Columbus, Ohio. Emerging for the first time from the cocoon that had surrounded her on the campus of Atlanta University, she was ill prepared, both emotionally and intellectually, for the shock that awaited her in the Ohio capital city. "I did nothing but cry," she recalled many years later. "Part of my tears were due to homesickness, but most came from the fact that I was experiencing racial prejudice for the first time." Once when she was asked what she had expected to find in Ohio, she replied: "I don't remember having any expectations. It was just that I did not know when I was that age that this was the way of life everywhere. It was no better, no worse, than Atlanta." The rudeness of the revelation remained always in her memory.[1]

By the early twentieth century, the caste system that replaced slavery in the South defined the Negro's status to one degree or another everywhere in America. When Grace Towns arrived in Columbus in the fall of 1927, her color barred her from movies, restaurants, hotels, and lunch counters, even though Ohio had on its books antisegregation laws that guaranteed her equal access to all these places. Even public restrooms were forbidden to her except those on the grounds of the state capitol building, where authorities felt constrained to abide by laws that elsewhere were flouted with impunity. As in the South, Columbus blacks scarcely ever found employment outside of teaching, preaching, undertaking, the postal service, domestic jobs, and factory work or as Pullman porters, and they lived in segregated areas no less defined by white society than those of their race in Atlanta. Finding a home away from home was as delicate a matter for Grace Towns in Columbus as it would have been anywhere south of the Mason-Dixon line, but thanks to the network of family and friends that all blacks carefully cultivated in the days of the rigid color bar for use in just such cases of need, she found hospitality in the home of her father's former student Truman Kella Gibson, a 1905 graduate of Atlanta University and a Harvard alumnus of 1908 who had since established his own insurance business in Columbus.

Only on the campus of Ohio State University, where she was enrolled in the graduate program in psychology, did Grace Towns feel accepted among whites without regard to her race. Psychology was a relatively new discipline in those days, a time when gestalt psychologists clashed with American behavioralists. The faculty adviser who helped her thread her way through the conflicting notions about the way the mind works was "a wonderful woman" named Louella Pressey, whom Towns always remembered with admiration and respect. No southern state university would have admitted her, but at Ohio State at least the North gave what the South withheld. Nevertheless, she felt like a "token" black. She recalled: "When I went to Ohio State, I don't remember any other black people in the Department [of Psychology]. However, I don't remember any particular limitations at the University."[2]

Discovering prejudice in the Young Women's Christian Association in Columbus, in her job as girl's work secretary for the Negro branch, was the biggest shock of all, probably because it was so unexpected. "I guess I idolized the YWCA," she later said. Long afterward she could view the discrimination calmly, even wryly: "I had to learn after I was grown the barriers and limitations even in groups working for racial harmony." The discovery was a bitter one, as she later related: "The Student movement was the 'cutting edge' of the YWCA in those days, in terms of opening up its membership to everybody who was in college anywhere. So as a student I had been interested in creating openings, in making opportunities for people to associate on the basis of individual interests. And boy, I didn't really know what to do about it in Columbus! The racial situation there was very hard to understand and difficult."[3]

At Atlanta University she had had "positive experiences" as an activist with the YWCA's student movement. Her election as the vice-president of that organization's National Student Council had marked a signal first for blacks, and she went to Columbus inspired by the notion that students were a "spearhead of social action" who could spur the "Y" into making good on its interracial aspirations. In Columbus she found a different reality.[4]

· · ·

Grace Towns raised eyebrows when she confessed that she reached adulthood before becoming aware of the pervasive grasp of racism everywhere in America. Even given her sheltered life on the Atlanta University campus, such a slow grasp of reality seemed close to willful blindness, if indeed it were literally true. She had arrived in Columbus, after all, near the end of a decade that blacks called "the terrible twenties," a decade that began with the Red Summer of 1919 (so named by James Weldon Johnson), a time when whites (in the words of John Hope Franklin) "poured out a wrath upon the Negro population . . . that could hardly be viewed as fit punishment even for traitors." Increasingly urbanized, possessed of new self-respect and racial cohesiveness, "blacks bristled into action and showed a willingness to defend themselves that they had not shown before," a resistance that culminated in what Franklin called "war in the full sense of the word," though it was a "one-sided struggle" blacks had no hope of winning. Violence was "not confined to any section of the country," occurring, as Franklin said, "wherever whites and blacks undertook the task of living together."[5]

How had she grown up in these years of raging racial turmoil unaware of its effects? Asked that question for this book, Grace Towns Hamilton replied:

> I was aware of the limitations segregation imposed on all Negro people. It's not true that I was not aware of them. I was aware of them. . . . These were conditions we wished to get changed, that you did not subject yourself to willingly, where you had any alternative. . . . You know how it is when you're growing up . . . it wasn't anything that was at the top of your agenda each day of the year. It was just basic to what we were and what the family values were, my mother and father, all of us. . . . We were aware of the situation but we weren't preoccupied with it. . . . It was only after I was away from home, which happened to be in Ohio, that it affected me more directly . . . the extent of the limitations, the pervasion through all institutions. . . . I think I probably thought things would be different because it was North. And it was not. In some ways it wasn't even as good.[6]

As a service-oriented organization, the "Y" was dedicated to the recreational, educational, and residential needs of all young women, especially

those who worked for a living. But the era's generalized prejudice and violence against the Negro put its goals, not to mention its religious and moral
precepts, to a challenge it often failed to meet. The "Y" described itself as "a
pioneer in race relations between American Negro women and other
women in America," but according to one of its "first principles," it went
only "as far as both the Negroes and whites are agreed to go together." Although this sounded reasonable, in fact it placed determination of the organization's racial stance in the hands of those who had power, and for
practical purposes these were white, well-to-do Protestant women whose
mothers founded the "Y" and who themselves afterward guided it to
maturity. Negro input was limited indeed. Although it had the best of intentions in racial matters, the "Y"'s achievements had long fallen short of
its aims.[7]

From its beginning in Boston in 1866, the "Y" had Negroes among its
members, and as the organization grew across the northern half of America
in the early years after the Civil War, Negro women were always on its ros-
ter, joining the associations "normally and naturally, not as representatives
of a race, but as individual working women among many others who were
dependent on their own exertions for support."[8]

Contributing to this "apparently easy acceptance of Negroes" was their
relative scarcity in the North and West, where the early associations flourished. In the South, where most Negroes lived, the "Y" hardly existed at all
before the turn of the century, in no small part the outcome of southern
unwillingness to tackle the delicate matter of Negro membership. When associations first appeared in the region in the early 1900s, the "Y"'s northern
white leadership quietly agreed that "no work with Negroes was expected
of them." Bowing before the mounting force of Negro prejudice throughout the nation, the national organization itself had already acquiesced in
the segregation of its Negro members in associations of their own, the first
of which was formed by Negro women in Dayton, Ohio, in 1893. After that,
Negro YWCAs proliferated, becoming known as "branches." Nowhere was
it specifically stated that the "central" YWCA should be the white association and the Negro the "branch" association, but this soon was taken for
granted. This "practical working solution," enabling the "Y" to square its
religious principles with America's racial reality of that era, opened the
door to Negro branches in the South, their further expansion in the North,
and a great increase in associations everywhere.

To assuage the feelings of Negroes who were offended by the segregation
manifest in the "branch" idea, the YWCA National Board in New York

took charge of supervising the Negro associations, leaving them free of any direct control, or sometimes even any relationship, with the central association in their respective communities. Blacks, having no choice or voice in the matter, accepted branches as the only "practical opportunity for working together in this period of history" and used their isolation to train a generation of their own leaders. Thus Negroes in the "Y," once accepted as a part of the general membership, became in the Progressive Era a separate (and far from equal) group within the association, their affairs dealt with at national headquarters in faraway New York. The "Y"'s goal remained interracial development, to act as an organization "in which all kinds of girls and women contribute to each other, rather than one in which women of privilege and outstanding gifts did things for others," and there was some small forward motion even amid the retrogression. Thanks to the massive social forces unleashed by World War I, "Negro work" greatly increased in the "Y" during the conflict, becoming a "major rather than a fringe interest." Yet the YWCA remained far into the first half of the twentieth century an organization whose progress in matters of race was determined by its white leadership. And this was a mounting source of trial and frustration for the increasingly educated and militant leadership of the "Y"'s Negro women.[9]

Meanwhile, the YWCA's burgeoning student movement, from its inception on the campus of Illinois State Normal College in 1873, had taken a divergent approach on race, one far less cautious than that of the parent organization. Always more evangelical than their parent, the student YWCAs began and remained interracial in the North, while in the South the movement took hold among white and Negro colleges alike long before adult chapters were formed in the region. One of the oldest was the chapter formed in 1884 at Spelman College in Atlanta.

Atlanta University's own chapter, of which Grace Towns was a member, dated from 1910, though it was preceded by a Christian Endeavor Society for girls, founded in 1890 by Julia A. Ellis, a Wellesley graduate who taught English and Bible at Spelman College. The National Student Council, the movement's governing body, adopted an interracial composition in 1920, well before a Negro was admitted to the YWCA's National Board. Conferences, the main "motor" of the YWCA, were interracial among students from 1923 even in the South, but the southern Negro branches were not accepted in the conference life of their region until the 1940s and until this late date also northern Negro branches were not tolerated in the annual meetings of the central associations where general policy was made and

officers for the whole organization were elected. Indeed, the student associations in the Progressive Era, it was said, "best represented the frontier of
YWCA thinking," or as Grace Towns put it, they were its "cutting edge." [10]

. . .

Her disillusionment with the "real-world" YWCA of Columbus, Ohio,
in 1927 was as intense as that experienced by Anna Arnold Hedgeman a few
years before in Springfield, fifty miles from Columbus, though their re-
sponses differed. Hedgeman was young and idealistic like Towns, had also
worked in the YWCA student movement during her college years at Ham-
line College in Minnesota, had taught for a while in Mississippi, and then
accepted a paying job with the YWCA in Springfield. She later wrote of
her experiences in a book called *The Trumpet Sounds: A Memoir of Negro
Leadership*:

> In Springfield, I met the sugar-coated segregated pattern of social work
> and housing in the north. I would, if hired, service a "neighborhood" and of
> course it was important that the facilities of the YWCA be close to the people
> it serviced. In the North, we didn't call this separate branch the "Negro"
> branch publicly. We named the branch for the street on which it was located.
> The branch did not have a gymnasium, swimming pool, or cafeteria, nor an
> adequate staff. . . .
>
> The first week of my employment in such a Negro branch in the fall of
> 1924 was one of appalled discovery of Northern segregation. I found, for ex-
> ample, that even as a professional worker, I could not eat in the cafeteria of
> the Central Association. The young people I supervised could not use the
> swimming pool or the gymnasium in the Central building. . . . As executive
> of the YWCA Negro branch in Springfield, I was much in demand for lec-
> tures on race relations, but I found such lectures difficult, for there were no
> relations. . . .
>
> It was in this community that I recognized fully that "separate" meant in-
> ferior, despised and unequal. . . . Our Negro committee went to the Central
> board of directors and put the issues squarely: "As a part of the fellowship of
> the Young Women's Christian Association, we request that all facilities be
> open to all members of the fellowship. We believe that it is not sound spiri-
> tually for the fellowship to be separated on the basis of color. . . ."
>
> The Board reviewed our request and reported: "The Community Chest
> will not give us funds for capital investment. The community itself is not
> ready yet to open up the facilities of the Central Association. We are, how-
> ever, making progress in understanding and we ask for the patience of the
> branch leadership as they interpret this to the Negro community."

Describing herself as "furious but helpless," Anna Hedgeman contacted the National YWCA and requested an opportunity to work in the East, a request that was granted.[11]

Grace Towns's experience in Columbus was nearly identical to Hedgeman's in Springfield. The Columbus branch, like the Springfield one, was "close to the people it served"—that is, it was located in a segregated area where middle-income blacks lived. Like the Springfield branch, it occupied an old house in the neighborhood and was inadequately equipped and staffed while downtown the central YWCA was located in a "beautiful new building with gymnasium, swimming pool, cafeteria, auditorium and residences," from which all blacks were excluded except those employed as maids, elevator operators, and cafeteria workers, and, of course, the branch professionals who were permitted to attend certain meetings. It was as appalling to Grace Towns as it had been to Anna Hedgeman on those occasions to be allowed in the building but to be refused access to any of its amenities, even a glass of water in the cafeteria. It was perhaps fortunate that the Negro branch was limited to a peripheral role in the affairs of the central "Y," for it meant Grace Towns seldom had to suffer the humiliations she inevitably encountered at the downtown building. She went there only for the infrequent meetings of the white organization's girl's work staff and for the monthly meetings of the Inter-Club Council of the Girl Reserve Clubs. She was hurt by all this but not "furious," as Hedgeman had been, and she entertained no thoughts of leaving, remaining in her YWCA post for the full year required to earn her psychology degree.[12]

· · ·

As girl's work secretary, she was in charge of programs for teenagers, a relatively new activity inaugurated by the association less than a decade earlier. The "Y" called its teenage members girl reserves, and from the time they were first organized in high school clubs in 1919, they were segregated by race, even in unsegregated schools. Shut out of their school clubs in Columbus, black girls formed their own separate group, but "separateness" humbled the young girls and the "reserve" idea had only limited appeal among them. A single club was enough to accommodate all interested black girls in the city, and Grace Towns was their adviser. She was responsible for shepherding the beleaguered group to the central "Y" for the Inter-Club gathering, which was usually a "covered dish" affair. Lillian Hervey Jackson, a sixteen-year-old member of the Negro Girl Reserve Club of 1927, held a clear recollection of her own part in these meetings: "By the time one reaches high school in this racist atmosphere, certain conditioning has taken place and no one from our club would go to these meetings. I fortunately had had a few very good experiences with white girls in elementary and junior high school. I didn't want to go but I had promised to 'help Grace out.' I remembered some of these experiences and I would go, not to represent our club, but to hold up the professional reputation of Grace. I felt she would be blamed if we didn't show." [13]

The Columbus "Y" in 1927 paid nothing more than "lip service to the idea of ultimate interracial cooperation," but her disappointment in realizing this did not cause Grace Towns then or afterward to dispute the sincerity of the organization's "ultimate goal." In the context of the "terrible twenties," as she looked back on it, she saw even this much concession on the "Y's" part as "quite radical." She wanted to believe in the "Y," and she did, and she would continue to work for it, off and on, for the rest of her life. Anna Hedgeman too had interrupted her bitter memoir with the parenthetical observation: "In fairness to the history of the YWCA, it must be said that the organization was in the forefront by even hiring Negro executives." [14]

Professionally frustrated, Grace Towns was nevertheless personally gratified by her work with YWCA teenagers in Columbus, and in young Lillian Jackson she made a lifelong friend and a recruit for the ranks of YWCA workers. Jackson always remembered how one day she "wandered into the YWCA, found this beautiful young woman . . . and asked her what she wanted me to do." She added: "From that day at 16 years old until I retired at 65, I was in the YWCA—and all because of Grace." After meeting Towns, Jackson said, "the YWCA became my hangout." She became active in the Girl Reserve Club, participating in the group's elocution lessons, dramatics, and summer camps. "Grace always seemed to be around," Jackson remembered, "providing me an adult image which was important." She "became more than my Girl Reserve Secretary, she was my friend," Jackson said. "I remember once having a problem with my dentist who was also our next-door neighbor. He had gotten a little 'fresh' with me once in his office. When I had to go for my appointment, I couldn't share my fear of him with my family. I couldn't trust my father's temper to handle the situation reasonably. I went to Grace, asked her to go with me and sit in his operating room while I was in the chair. She asked no questions about my fears, letting me maintain my privacy, but she said yes and she did. I never forgot that." Jackson looked upon Grace Towns as a mentor, and when she was "faced with making a decision about my life work" she chose the YWCA, beginning as a Girl Reserve secretary and progressing finally to the national staff in New York, before her retirement thirty-nine years later. Even with the hurts and humiliations it meted out to its young black workers, the "Y" to them remained a "beacon light" in a bleak landscape that was otherwise void of professional opportunity.[15]

. . .

Grace Towns was not sorry to leave Columbus in the summer of 1928—she never saw the city again—but she sadly bade good-bye to the Gibson family. Their hospitality had been a boon during her Columbus stay, and in return, she later said, "I maintained contact with them the rest of my life."[16]

Back in Atlanta, she returned with relief to the warmth and security of her family's home on University Place. Having completed the coursework for her master's degree in psychology, she now tackled Ohio State's written requirements (she was awarded the degree in 1929), and to support herself in the interim she searched for a job. She soon found not one but two teaching positions, both using her new competence. The Atlanta School of Social Work hired her to teach a course in human behavior for the 1928–29 academic year, and Clark College invited her to join the faculty as psychology instructor, a job she held until 1930. Teaching was not her real ambition; it was more a "matter of availability and circumstance," she later remarked. As it long had been, teaching remained for educated Negroes, no matter what their ambition, the best—indeed often the only—option. She accepted both jobs gladly, though each required a daily journey far from her campus home. Clark College was then still located in the Brownsville section of south Atlanta (it would move to the AU campus in 1942), and the Atlanta School of Social Work, a fledgling institution, conducted all its classes in a single room of the Herndon Building on Auburn Avenue in east Atlanta. Of the two posts, the latter would have the most effect on her life and outlook, largely because of the school's dynamic director, Forrester B. Washington, who had had some equally dynamic predecessors. The school was founded in 1920, largely the brainchild of Jesse O. Thomas, a dedicated social worker who had come to Atlanta the year before to establish the southern regional headquarters of the National Urban League (NUL), becoming its field secretary, and he soon was pushing for social work as an independent discipline in the city's black colleges. Once established under the directorship of Garry Moore, a professor of sociology at Morehouse College, the school was first quartered at Morehouse, then removed to the Herndon Building on Auburn Avenue after it was incorporated as a separate self-supporting institution in 1925.[17]

Since 1922, when Moore died unexpectedly, E. Franklin Frazier had been the school's director, doing what one biographer called "yeoman and pioneer work in building up the institution . . . from its foundations, working as administrator, teacher, recruiter and fund-raiser, writing articles and giving speeches to promote the program, and infusing the School with his personal convictions and relentless energy." Among Frazier's convictions was a firm belief in the efficacy of organizing both community and workplace as potentially the best solution to personal and family problems, and he urged his students to become involved in community-based institutions and indigenous self-help organizations. Frazier's outspoken opposition to segregation, articulated outside as well as inside the classroom, earned him a reputation in rigidly segregated Atlanta for "impatience with the niceties of interracial diplomacy," and in late 1926 the school's board of directors asked for his resignation. The firing became a cause célèbre in civil rights circles. Loving his work, Frazier managed to delay his departure until June 1927. From Atlanta he went to the University of Chicago, where he later obtained a doctorate, going on to become one of the country's best-known sociologists and the first Negro president of the American Sociological Association.[18]

As Frazier's successor at the Atlanta School of Social Work, Washington lacked his abrasiveness but otherwise carried on much in his tradition. Under Washington's leadership, the institution grew rapidly. By 1938 it was an affiliated member of the Atlanta University postgraduate system, now housed on the campus and renamed the Atlanta University School of Social Work. Like Frazier, Washington promoted civic action as a way to overcome racial discrimination, poverty, and other social handicaps. He likewise fostered participation in community life among his students and teachers, setting a personal example by serving several terms as president of the Atlanta Chapter of the NAACP. Grace Towns's own commitment to combating discrimination through civic education and community cooperation surely had its genesis in the example set by her parents, but she thought it stemmed just as much from her experience with Washington— and, through him, the influence of Frazier—at the Atlanta School of Social Work.[19]

4

The Depression Years:
To Memphis and Back

. . .

N
O UNION was more natural than that of Grace Towns and her longtime beau, Henry Cooke Hamilton. Both came from Atlanta's old-line mulatto elite families, the proud, tight-knit group of Negroes whose success in business and the professions placed them in the upper stratum among the city's black population, a status that naturally made them also its political leaders. Though the elite group expanded as Atlanta Negroes, even in the face of mounting white hostility, moved upward economically, much importance remained attached to the "old families" centered around the institutions most associated with the race's northern white benefactors, the First Congregational Church and Atlanta University. The Hamiltons were as closely tied to these institutions as was the Towns family.

Towns and Hamilton were married June 7, 1930, in Atlanta University's Ware Memorial Chapel, a tribute to their mutual attachment to the institution. Hamilton, always known to his friends as "Cookie," was a tall, light-skinned, good-humored man whose hobbies, at which he excelled, were tennis, bridge, and billiards. He was thirty-one years old at the time of the wedding; his bride was twenty-three. Like Grace, Cookie was born and raised in Atlanta and, like her, received all his early education at Atlanta University, from which he graduated with a bachelor's degree in 1921. While teaching afterward in high schools in Alabama, North Carolina, and Virginia, he worked toward a master's degree in education from the University of Pittsburgh, winning it finally in 1928. Thereupon he went to work for LeMoyne Junior College in Memphis (later renamed LeMoyne-Owen College) in the triple capacity of dean, registrar, and professor of education. After their marriage, Grace joined her husband on the LeMoyne faculty as instructor in psychology, a job she held until 1934, and for the remainder of the decade, though her career often took her elsewhere, her life was based in Memphis.

Cookie Hamilton's father was Alexander Hamilton Jr., who, with his father, Alexander Sr., ran a successful construction and contracting business that the elder Hamilton had established after arriving in Atlanta in 1877 from Eufaula, Alabama. At that time the city's black entrepreneurs still mingled rather freely with their white counterparts, sometimes serving a clientele of both races. Before the turn of the century, the Hamiltons had built beautiful homes along "white" Peachtree and Washington Streets, as well as warehouses, mills, schools, and the first home in downtown Atlanta of all-black Morris Brown University (later Morris Brown College). In 1901, the Hamilton company did $35,000 worth of work, a considerable sum at that time, though later, like most black entrepreneurs, they were compelled to depend on their fellow Negroes to survive in business. A valuable asset in the Hamiltons' success in this later period was the considerable real property they had acquired through the years.

Alexander Sr. had been politically prominent in Eufaula during Reconstruction, winning election to the City Council and serving a term in the state legislature from Barbour County. Possibly he served in the Union army during the Civil War—E. R. Carter, early Atlanta black historian, claimed he did—but records to substantiate this do not exist. When Reconstruction collapsed, he moved to Atlanta, establishing the building business which he and his son maintained for the rest of their lives. Among the homes Alexander Jr. later built was one for his own family at 102 Howell Street in Atlanta's then fashionable Auburn Avenue area, which remained the home of Hamiltons for many years afterward. It was sold only after the death of Cookie's youngest sister, Nell, who never married.

Atlanta University was central to the education of the Hamiltons just as it was for the Towns family. Alexander Jr. had also received his education there, concentrating on the mechanical courses then offered by the institution. W. E. B. Du Bois thought highly of the younger Alexander Hamilton's ability and in 1902 solicited a paper from him for the published proceedings of the Seventh Atlanta University Conference, concerned that year with the Negro artisan. "It is a matter of pride to me," Hamilton wrote, "and I think sometimes I am a little over boastful of the fact that I learned the use of tools at Atlanta University; and to this intelligent beginning I attribute my success as a carpenter and contractor." Ruefully he also confessed that his real ambition was to be an architect, to which he appended a sad qualification: "This desire there seems small hope of gratifying." So too it was with the elder George A. Towns. The desire and talent they shared for architecture might have enabled either of them to succeed in the profession, had not racism and later family obligations compelled them to settle for different—if no less valuable—ambitions.

In the Hamilton veins, just as in those of the Townses, flowed considerable white blood. Alexander Hamilton, the first U.S. secretary of the treasury, and Alexander Hampton, white governor of South Carolina, were said to be antecedents. (Cookie called them "the black sheep of the family.") Alexander Jr.'s wife, the former Nellie Cooke, was part Indian. They had seven children, two daughters and five sons. Cookie was their fourth child and third son.

Growing up in the early 1900s was an anomalous experience for young Negroes of Atlanta's upper stratum. The race was Jim-Crowed, lynched, confined to ghettoes, and for the most part consigned to poverty, yet the fortunate elite lived relatively secure lives, surrounded by doting parents, grandparents, and family friends and essentially free from financial woes. They may have been poor, as Grace Towns Hamilton later said of her own family, "but we didn't know we were poor." Yet comfort gave no security; danger lurked around every corner for all of them, especially the males; at any moment tragedy could strike. On one such occasion in the mid-1920s, Bertram Hamilton, one of Cookie's older brothers, was lucky to escape with his life when he was falsely accused of raping a white woman while spending a weekend in a black summer resort in Kennesaw, Georgia, as a guest in the home of Cornelius King, the real estate entrepreneur who owned the resort. Under cover of darkness, Bertram was smuggled out of Kennesaw in the trunk of a car, and because of the incident the resort was soon closed down forever.[1]

Though the benefits of their status were circumscribed, the "haves" among Atlanta Negroes were envied and resented by many among the masses of "have nots," as one of the latter, a preacher named Benjamin Bickers, made clear in an interview for this book:

I have known the Hamiltons since I was a boy in the seventh grade. I worked in their home, also worked for other families of the Atlanta elite. Helped me stay in school. My father was illiterate, worked for the Fulton Bag and Paper Company, my mother was a domestic servant in a white home. She was a proud woman, fiercely protective of her children. We rented a house that belonged to the Hamilton family, it was on Houston Street, right around the corner from the Hamiltons.

I saw Grace Hamilton in that house, she never spoke to me. She was always arrogant and aloof. Her husband, Henry Cooke Hamilton, never said more than hello to me until the day his daddy died. Then they asked me to ride in the family car to the cemetery and I did. Henry Cooke talked to me that day, said I sure had grown, that kind of thing you know. I never had a word from Grace Hamilton, she looked down on me, on anybody who was poor, not as light as she was. She acted just like all the old Atlanta mulatto elite.[2]

For Grace marriage soon brought motherhood. By the time she joined the faculty at LeMoyne in the fall of 1930 and Cookie resumed his various teaching responsibilities there, Grace was pregnant. A leisurely time out to await the birth of their first child was something she neither wanted nor could afford, and she taught the entire first semester of the 1930–31 term, creating something of a sensation among her students—as she learned from one of them many years later—because pregnant teachers seldom if ever appeared in the college classroom of that time. At semester's end, she took leave for the remainder of the academic year and gave birth at home on March 5, 1931, to a daughter, named Eleanor after her grandmother. She would be their only child.

Black colleges paid poorly, but because of the rampant racism everywhere in the nation they were virtually the sole employer of blacks with advanced degrees—irrespective of gender—and both Cookie and Grace considered themselves lucky to have their positions. Staying on the job, indeed, seemed highly advisable at the time. They had bought a new home at 707 Edith Street near the campus, and Cookie was contemplating further advanced study, so with a child on the way, they needed her earnings as much as his. The new house, into which they moved after a summer of communal living in a faculty boardinghouse, would remain their address for the more than a decade they lived in Memphis.

Grace had always expected to be a working wife; she preferred to work. A white woman of the time might work for a few years, but once married she usually stayed at home until her children were grown, returning to the job market only afterward, if at all. Large numbers of black married women had no such option, no matter their class. They always worked in proportionately greater numbers than white wives, and not until late in the twentieth

century would percentages of married working women of the two races begin to converge. Grace Towns Hamilton, like most Negro women, worked
because it was economically necessary. It was mere chance that it was also
what she herself wished.

LeMoyne Junior College was not a boarding institution, but otherwise it
had much in common with Atlanta University, and for Grace Hamilton it
came close to replicating the life she had known on the AU campus. Like
AU, LeMoyne was founded by the American Missionary Association to educate freedpeople. Its establishment in 1870 was aided by a $25,000 gift
from Julius LeMoyne, a Pennsylvania abolitionist for whom the institution
was named. Just as at AU, LeMoyne in its earliest years "raised" its own students, initially providing the only primary and secondary schooling available to blacks in Memphis, then gradually expanding its curriculum upward toward the higher levels of learning. As at AU, its initial concentration
was on training teachers, and it prepared the majority of those eventually
employed in the Bluff City's Negro public schools. After the mid-1870s,
public primary education for Negroes appeared in Tennessee, as in Georgia, but until the 1920s, both LeMoyne and Atlanta University provided
Negroes the only four-year high school course available in their respective
cities. LeMoyne's faculty, like AU's, was interracial, and Grace Hamilton
was happy to find white faculty members, just as at AU, making themselves
"very much a part of the Negro community." Actually, integration was a
must for LeMoyne's white faculty because they were no more accepted in
Memphis white society than AU's white teachers were accepted in Atlanta.
LeMoyne's growth led to changes, much as they had at Atlanta University.
The very year the newlywed Hamiltons joined the institution's faculty,
LeMoyne dropped all primary and secondary courses, converting itself for
the first time into a college only.[3]

· · ·

"I always felt my mother would have been miserable as a homemaker
only. I can never remember a time when she was not working," Eleanor
Hamilton Payne said in 1984. Her mother, Grace Towns Hamilton, said essentially the same thing but in other words: "I always took for granted that
we would need the money that both of us earned, it was always my intention to work. . . . I always assumed I would work professionally, hopefully
teaching in the same institution where Cookie was. Teaching is what I had
done up to that point."[4]

Holding a job while caring for a child and a new home was not the
problem it might have been for Grace Towns Hamilton, thanks to Annie

Alexander. Miss Annie, as she was known by all, was an Atlanta woman, the granddaughter of a charter member of Friendship Baptist Church, whose bond with Atlanta University rivaled in closeness that of the First Congregational Church. (In 1865, AU's founders had no space to locate their renovated railroad car, called the "car box," in which they proposed holding classes for freed blacks. The newly formed Friendship Baptist Church, a breakaway from integrated First Baptist, which required blacks to sit in the balcony, had land on which to build a structure but no money. Their needs neatly dovetailed so the school and church combined their resources, sharing the "car box" for a year. For Atlanta blacks, the connection long remained a vivid memory.)

At the turn of the century, Annie Alexander, who lived to be 103, was already known to faculty children on the AU campus. She had cared for Yolande, daughter of W. E. B. Du Bois, during the latter's first stint at the college (1897–1910), and she had summered in Maine with the family of AU president Edward Twichell Ware (1910–19), as the nanny to his two sons, Henry and Alexander, early playmates of the Towns children. She later worked at AU's Oglethorpe Practice School as a child care helper. So when Grace Hamilton looked for live-in help, at about the time Eleanor was eighteen months old, she was relieved to find Miss Annie free and willing to move to Memphis. "She came and lived with us from that time until we came back to Atlanta," Grace Hamilton recalled, adding, "She was a rare person. She made possible my being able to work in the way I did at the time."[5]

In the meantime, Grace's husband had been accepted for advanced study at the University of Cincinnati. It was rare for a Negro of Cookie and Grace's generation to go to college but much rarer to get a higher degree. Before World War I, only fourteen American Negroes had received the doctor of philosophy degree and by 1929, when Cookie was ready for such advanced study, the number had increased to only fifty-one.

His sights were set on a doctorate in education, and he had planned it all with Grace before their marriage. "We had a family agreement," Grace remembered. "He would finish his work on his doctorate after we went to Memphis. It was just taken for granted that I would continue to work and we'd manage. I guess we just planned to cope with the resources we had. . . . I remember when we talked about his going away for this period . . . we laughed and said, when you get through, then I'll take some time off and get my doctorate." But she never did. "I didn't wish to," she said. "After that, life had moved on." (Had she done so, Grace would have joined a very select few. Up to 1921 only three Negro women had received the doctoral degree in the United States.)[6]

After Eleanor's birth, Grace's mother and her sister, Harriet, spent the summer with her in Memphis. In the fall, Cookie went off to the University of Cincinnati to spend a full year in resident study, and Grace, engaging temporary part-time help at home (Miss Annie would not arrive until the following year), returned to the classroom. During Cookie's Cincinnati stay, when he was off salary, Grace was the family's sole financial support. Stretching their reduced income to meet twice as much need, while coping simultaneously with work, child, and home, was no easier for Grace than it was for any other woman in these years of the Great Depression, and Cookie did not enjoy his enforced absence from wife and family. In fact, Cookie was a husband ahead of his time. Black males, long targeted for humiliation by a white world intent upon establishing undisputed supremacy, within their own families were often apt to outdo the other race in masculine chauvinism. Not so with Cookie Hamilton. As a mutual friend commented with admiration at the time: "Here was a man about to get his Ph.D., a man who is an excellent tennis player, who with dignity and joy helps in the work of his home." In Memphis, Cookie began making Sunday brunch for his family, often turning it into the day's main meal, always including waffles, muffins, or sweet rolls prepared by his own hands. It became a tradition in the household that lasted throughout his lifetime.[7]

These ample Sunday breakfasts did not mean the living was luxurious in the little house on Edith Street. There was little luxury living anywhere in America of the 1930s. The Great Depression had settled upon the country, and hardship was the common lot, but blacks, overwhelmingly poor because of racism, were the most hard-pressed of all. In her eloquent book, *Labor of Love, Labor of Sorrow: A History of Black Women, Work and the Family*, Jacqueline Jones wrote: "During the 1930s, eight or nine out of every ten black households lived on the thin edge between subsistence and complete economic disaster. Even in northern cities, no more than ten percent of the black population maintained a relatively comfortable, secure material existence characteristic of the white middle class." Though the Negro middle class was minute, it existed in both North and South thanks to the growing urbanization of the race and the social and economic forces this phenomenon had unleashed, and by any standards Henry Cooke and Grace

Towns Hamilton, with well-established professional careers, were firmly fixed within it.[8]

Yet they were forced to live in a world apart. The Negro community was segregated, barred by the caste system from becoming part of the mainstream of American life, and this long-standing exclusion seemed impervious to change. Its existence "in a nation dedicated to the idea of the essential equality of mankind and in which there is a general commitment to the fusion of the races and cultures," John Hope Franklin wrote, "is one of the truly remarkable social anomalies of the twentieth century." Whites who stepped across the line, for whatever reason, were apt to be as decisively shunned as blacks. At LeMoyne, like Atlanta University, the white faculty, no less than the black, knew better than to come near white society, and the taboo on "mixing" remained as rigid in the 1930s as it ever had been.[9]

Even so, the Negro world was changing. "The migration of Negroes from their ancestral homes on the plantations to urban America that began during World War I," Franklin wrote, "placed the destiny of the Negro in his own hands more than ever before." In 1910, no city in America had as many as one hundred thousand Negroes; by 1940, there were eleven with that number, most in the North and West, but Memphis and Atlanta in the South were also among them. From this mass migration emerged in the 1920s what the philosopher Alain Locke called the New Negro, who in company with his fellows in the city was no longer the timid, docile Negro of the post-Reconstruction past. Now he was more than willing to speak out against the injustices inflicted upon him. Protest and service organizations such as the NAACP and the National Urban League flourished, and in the 1930s new political pressure groups joined them, such as the Joint Committee on National Recovery, the National Negro Congress, and the Southern Negro Youth Congress. Though their accomplishments were small, all these groups developed approaches and techniques that would be of value in the decades ahead.[10]

· · ·

The changing shape of the Negro world was also giving new direction to the philosophy and career of Grace Towns Hamilton. Teaching never had been her first love. It was only "availability and circumstance" that led her into the profession, and at LeMoyne, when circumstance compelled her to undertake "a few courses I didn't feel equipped to teach, relative to educational methods," her frustration grew. Suddenly, in 1934, LeMoyne terminated her employment. It had nothing to do with Grace Hamilton's competence—it was a matter of gender and the Great Depression. Impelled by hard times, LeMoyne had adopted a "share the work" policy, limiting faculty positions to one per family and reserving the job for the family's primary breadwinner. Because the male traditionally occupied this role, it was Grace who got the sack. This gender discrimination accorded with the cultural construct of the time, and it did not bother Grace, who was more than ready to look for other career possibilities. Jobs for black middle-class women were scarce, and while she looked for work she did volunteer fundraising for the NAACP, traveled in the South and Southwest for the YWCA National Student Council, and helped establish in Memphis a Negro branch of the YWCA whose programs for the Bluff City until then had totally bypassed the black community. The "Y" branch was obtained soon after Grace and her co-workers set their minds to it, and until the position was permanently filled Grace was its acting director. Other work, more to her liking, came her way in 1935, but not before she had had an offer she also liked but had to refuse. In October a four-member Negro delegation from the National Student Councils of the YMCA and the YWCA was to embark for India to spend four months visiting colleges and universities at the invitation of the country's government, and Grace was asked to make the trip. At first she apparently agreed, for her picture appeared in a 1934 brochure announcing the tour, but she withdrew from the delegation just days before it sailed. "It was when Eleanor was still a baby and I just decided I couldn't do it," she later remembered. Waiting in the wings was a job supervising a Works Progress Administration (WPA) survey of white-collar and skilled Negro workers in Shelby County, of which Memphis was the seat. The job was a preparation for more than she knew at the time, for it gave her, as she put it, "my first direct involvement with anything to do with the political apparatus." When the Negro's civil and political rights were finally restored in the South, politics would become the center of her life.[11]

The WPA survey, for which Grace Hamilton worked through the next year and a half, was unofficially entitled *The Urban Negro Worker in the United States, 1925–1936*. It was one of a variety of WPA projects dealing with problems of the Negro that the New Deal devised and turned over to black specialists whose work, even though they deplored its racial limitations, became a contribution to the emergence of the Negro's renewed political respectability. Administrator of the survey was Robert C. Weaver, who had left Howard University in 1933 to become the first black adviser to Secretary of the Interior Harold Ickes (and later would be a cabinet officer when the Housing and Home Finance Agency, which he headed under

President Lyndon Johnson, was made an executive department). The survey's director was Ira De Augustine Reid, then an associate of W. E. B. Du Bois in the Department of Sociology at Atlanta University. Charles Spurgeon Johnson, a professor of sociology at Fisk University (later Fisk's president) and a former YWCA worker whom Grace had known in her earlier experiences with the "Y", was employed as supervisor of tabulations.

Grace Hamilton always thought she owed her job to Johnson's recommendation, but she also believed the Memphis Republican Robert R. Church Jr., "until 1932 the most powerful Negro politician in the land," had given her strong support. Grace Hamilton was doubtless one of those Jacqueline Jones had in mind when she wrote in *Labor of Love, Labor of Sorrow*: "Few well-educated black women received job assignments [with the WPA] commensurate with their talents or professional training. . . . A handful served as supervisors of racially segregated projects. . . . They often had to rely on direct intervention from sympathetic. . . . officials in order to get and keep their jobs." The WPA frequently reduced even well-educated blacks of both sexes to menial labor, so Grace Hamilton had reason to be pleased with her new employment. She was mainly responsible for choosing and training the staff who conducted the interviews and, according to her own account, "seeing that the reports got up the line." In her case, "the line" often led to the Shelby County Commission, "lily white," of course, at the time. In describing the WPA experience many years later, she said: "Just like today the local political structure had a lot to do with what was done. . . . I don't remember too much about the details, but I know that whatever committee I had to report to involved the County Commission, so you had to get acquainted with the Commissioners. . . . I remember how I would be the only woman in this group of county politicians. . . . I learned a lot from that experience about how government really worked." At the time the Shelby County commissioners may have been meeting their first educated, articulate, well-dressed, middle-class black woman (not the "poor women of little opportunity and few resources" by whom all black women were judged), yet she remembered it as the unique political experience it was for her, preferring to overlook the singular racial encounter it must have been for the commissioners. She apparently was treated with respect within the commission—doubtless white supremacists to a man—for she remembered no discourtesy.[12]

Her path before the commission may indeed have been smoothed by Robert Church, who remained the "Republican boss in Tennessee" even though his party's fortunes had been eclipsed by the Depression and its consequences. Even with reigning Democrats, he was definitely persona grata. Grace Hamilton said of Church and his influence on her: "He was a remarkable man who helped to educate me in the realities of life. He helped me in the understanding of how you had to deal with these county figures who were really the controls of this WPA operation." She looked upon him as a mentor, and he surely sensed in her an apt pupil. Professor Towns, Grace Hamilton's father, had known Church since 1917, when they both were active in establishing the NAACP in their respective cities, each serving on his chapter's first executive committee. Robert Church's daughter Roberta had studied under Cookie Hamilton at LeMoyne Junior College, and when Grace joined him in Memphis, the newlyweds soon became acquainted with the whole Church family. Church was a unique man whose background was a fertile source for the political education of any young black person. He had inherited wealth from his father, the slave-born son of a Mississippi River boat captain. The elder Church's keen business sense enabled him after the Civil War to amass large real estate and banking interests in Memphis, but young Robert Church was less inclined toward business than politics, a leaning he also acquired from his father. Largely through the commercial influence of Robert Church Sr., Beale Street became famous as the "Main Street of Negro America," but even while he built his businesses, the elder Church was a staunch and active Republican. The son, while looking after the family fortune, made himself so valuable to the Republican cause in Tennessee that he frequently was recruited as roving envoy to other states where the fate of GOP candidates was in electoral doubt, always paying all his own expenses and frequently those of others who traveled with him. His probity was such that he even refused national appointments of honor and trust lest they brand him a self-seeker. Though never accepting office for himself, he was, as one writer pointed out, "until 1932 . . . chief dispenser of Negro patronage . . . not only in Tennessee . . . but also in the country at large." The praise he received for his rectitude was balanced by charges of wire-pulling and patronage peddling. Yet, as the writer noted, "for all the vilification. . . . he was purchasing . . . with his leverage . . . significant recognition for the race's aspirations and claims." [13]

Church was, indeed, as much a "race man" as a Republican stalwart, and he fervently believed that "the hope of the American Negro was in the American ballot." With the franchise well out of the Negro's reach in the South except in scattered urban areas, and that only in general elections, Church in 1916 set out to maximize its possibilities in Memphis. In that year, he founded the Lincoln League, which Roberta Church, in her book *The Robert R. Churches of Memphis*, called "the first large-scale attempt to organize Colored people to register and vote since curtailment of their participation in the electoral process during the Reconstruction period following the Civil War." It sponsored voting schools to educate Negroes about their rights, taught them the mechanics of the ballot, conducted registration drives and encouraged poll-tax payments, and on election day it "got out the vote." Church himself defrayed most of the organization's expenses. As Memphis demonstrated the League's potential, the organization spread into other states and a national convention was held in Chicago in 1920. But the League's Republican allegiance, coupled with the subsequent waning of GOP political fortunes and the party's abandonment of the Negro in the South in favor of a white reorientation—southern Democrats all the while remaining as opposed as ever to the Negro franchise—led to demise of the League before the end of its first decade. Robert Church himself, though he remained a lifelong Republican, was incensed enough in 1928 about the Republican turnabout that he refused a place on the party's national advisory committee.[14]

Church nevertheless remained optimistic about the ballot. His influence on Grace Hamilton was gentle and pervasive, not that of a professional politician but of a friend. "He was a person whose judgment I trusted," she said, "and who was a man, a man a lot older than I was, and he was willing to deal with me as an equal in terms of telling me about how things worked." Church preached the power of the ballot to Grace Hamilton, reinforcing what she had already absorbed from her parents, and henceforward, possibly as an added result of his influence, the importance of registering and voting, along with the struggle for a restored and meaningful franchise for the southern Negro, would be the core of her political philosophy. He taught her that in politics "alliances are essential to get anything accomplished," and he schooled her in techniques of convincing others that her goals were beneficial to them. There were lesser influences too. While working with the NAACP's membership drive—really a fundraising effort—Grace Hamilton talked to Church about the goals she had set. "I remember Mr. Church saying, well, now that's maybe more than you ought to bite off at one time, and maybe think about it, you know, plan realistically in terms of what is possible to move it ahead. Of course that was wise." Out of this NAACP drive came one experience that always stuck in Grace Hamilton's mind. "I remember I went to see this prosperous black dentist to get his help," she said. "He gave me a contribution but before I left he said, 'Now what do you expect to get out of this?' I was so taken aback, I didn't know what he meant. I was naive I guess. 'What do I expect to get out of it?' I answered him, 'nothing except a good branch of the NAACP.'" Grace Hamilton and other black middle-class women, working for pay outside the home in greater numbers than their white counterparts, "often perceived themselves as civil rights activists" on behalf of the whole race, Jacqueline Jones noted, and Grace Hamilton fell squarely within that tradition.[15]

· · ·

By 1936, when the WPA project was completed, changes of consequence had occurred within the Hamilton household. The year before, five-year-old Eleanor, approaching school age, went to live with her grandparents in Atlanta and was soon enrolled in the Oglethorpe Practice School at Atlanta University. She would remain in Oglethorpe and Atlanta public schools until she was fourteen years old. Grace and Cookie Hamilton parted in this way with their daughter, Grace said, "because of the state of the schools in Memphis at the lower level." As they were everywhere in the South, the city's Negro schools were poor, inadequate, and segregated. Oglethorpe was integrated, at least in theory—a few children of white teachers were still enrolled—and Grace wanted her daughter to be exposed to the happy experiences she herself had had there. There was, however, another reason why Eleanor went to live with Professor and Mrs. Towns: Grace Hamilton had gone back to work for the YWCA, this time in a higher position than she had held nearly a decade earlier in Columbus, Ohio. Now she joined the staff of the YWCA's National Student Council, an arm of the organization's National Board, and her responsibility was interracial program development. Induced by the same forces that were bringing change to the Negro's status everywhere—not the least of which was increased pressure from Negro women within its own ranks—the YWCA was slowly moving to realign its actual practices with its long-standing interracial professions. The separate pursuit of "Negro work" was muted beginning in the early 1930s, even the idea of Negro branches was coming under question, and a process was beginning to germinate that would lead the YWCA shortly after World War II to adopt its famous "interracial charter," essentially a promise to make the YWCA "an interracial experience... increasingly democratic and Christian." As usual the forward-looking student movement was ahead of the parent organization, and Grace welcomed the chance to work with the National Student Council that had so inspired her in her youth.[16]

She described her duties: "I would work in student conferences, helping set them up. I would have responsibilities for setting up the inter-collegiate council business and working with the student leadership." She held the job until 1941. Actually it was part-time employment, but all of that "part time" had to be spent at board headquarters in New York, from which she traveled frequently to conferences. From 1936, when she began the work, until 1941, when she and Cookie moved back to Atlanta, she was a resident on Edith Street in Memphis only from November to February. While in New York, she often resided with Frances Williams, a friend long active in the National Student Council, and Miss Annie looked after Cookie in Memphis. Eleanor meantime was fully domiciled in Atlanta with her grandparents in the Victorian home of Grace's childhood. Though often away from her mother between the ages of five and ten years, Eleanor nevertheless was seldom far from maternal influence. When she was still a small child, Eleanor played a game she called "going to conference." Grace Hamilton greatly pleased her young daughter one year by taking her to a conference at Lake Geneva, New York, and Eleanor as an adult remembered a childhood pride in "having a glamorous mother who went to conferences." Later, "when I grew up and went to conferences on my own," Eleanor remembered, "it had the feeling of some special achievement." [17]

Any feeling of abandonment Eleanor may have had as a child was mitigated by the close relationship she had always had with her grandparents. "I had spent considerable time with my grandparents even before I started to school," she remembered in later years. Her parents, she said, always came "to visit with me at very special times, and they always came for long periods during the summer." Eleanor had her own way of adjusting: "When I started first grade in Atlanta I used to tell people that I came to Atlanta to go to school instead of Memphis because I was left-handed and they did not teach left-handed children in Memphis. That seemed to me to be the reason." [18]

Eleanor eventually looked back on the situation with deeper understanding: "My mother used to ask often how I felt about it, if she had done a disservice because she had not been around in the earlier years. My recollection is that she got all the affection from me in those days and my grandparents got all the resentment because they had to discipline me. I would feel 'if my mother were only here' of course it would be all right, that my mother was perfect." In maturity she was generous toward her mother: "Yes, she probably feels guilty, because she does talk about it. I also always felt that my mother would have been miserable as a homemaker only and that's probably why our relationship is so good now, because I was away during my adolescence and she had other things to invest in besides me."[19]

Her assessment of the relationship between her parents was also generous and perceptive: "My parents have always had different interests which they pursued on their own . . . and obliquely going their own way. . . . They came to see me separately after I married. My mother would come off and on during the year and my father would come in August. It was so much easier for me if they came separately, so I could do different things with each of them to make them happy. When they both came, I felt split down the middle. . . . I never used to understand their relationship as a child but later I decided that they had something working for them that has lasted for more than fifty years and that I don't have to understand it. It works!"[20]

· · ·

In 1941, Grace and Cookie Hamilton returned to Atlanta where he had agreed to become principal of Atlanta University's Laboratory High School. Their decision to move "home" coincided closely with the outbreak of World War II, but war was not the motivation for their return. Primarily they were influenced by a desire to reunite the family. Although both they and their young daughter, Eleanor, traveled between Memphis and Atlanta regularly during the five years Eleanor lived alone with her grandparents, their separation had been hard emotionally on everyone. Besides, the elder Townses were in their seventies, as were the senior Hamiltons, and getting the family under one roof again would please them all. The roof would be the Towns home on University Place. Nell Hamilton, Cookie's youngest sister and a schoolteacher, still lived at the family home on Howell Street, but the situation was freer with the Townses. Grace Hamilton remembered: "All my family except my parents were away, so we lived at my parents' home, shared cooking but had our own separate living quarters, and living room, upstairs." It was a comfortable arrangement that would endure for nearly a decade. When the Hamiltons eventually moved in 1950, it would be no further than next door, where they built a modern house of their own on the portion of the original Towns lot where Grace's father had once maintained a vegetable garden. The "shared cooking," begun when they lived in the same house, continued after the Hamiltons moved next door. "Grace Hamilton didn't like to cook, her mother did and was good at it," a friend remembered. Until near the end of her life, Mrs. Towns prepared most meals for both families. Cookie Hamilton meantime continued to prepare the Sunday brunch, complete with baked delicacies.[21]

Two years after their return to Atlanta, death struck sharply in the Hamilton family. Cookie's older brother, Alexander Hamilton III, died at age fifty on November 19, 1943, followed within less than two months, on January 14, 1944, by his father, Alexander Hamilton Jr., then aged seventy-three. For Grace and Cookie Hamilton, the consolation was that they were at home to help the family adjust to the bereavement.

Cookie's position as principal of Laboratory High School did not last long. He was aware when he returned to Atlanta that the school's days were probably numbered. For years the school had been a financial burden to Atlanta University, and in 1940 when Spelman College reclaimed for its own use the building it had long lent to house the facility, AU's president, Rufus E. Clement, called upon educators at George Peabody College for Teachers to make an exhaustive study of both Laboratory High and its companion, Oglethorpe Elementary School. The conclusion, finally made public in April 1942, was positive for Oglethorpe but negative for the high school. Ten-year-old Eleanor Hamilton, who was just finishing Oglethorpe, was among those who, in the absence of the private Laboratory High School, would have to attend an overcrowded and segregated public secondary facility. It was to avoid precisely this fate that she had lived separately from her parents for so many years. But protest was to no avail. When the Laboratory High School closed its doors forever in June 1942 (Oglethorpe would function until 1957, when it was turned over to Atlanta's public school system), longtime faculty received separation pay and some, like Henry Cooke Hamilton, with his doctor of philosophy degree in education (advanced degrees were still a rare possession among blacks), were immediately reemployed. He became professor of education at AU, remaining until 1952, when he became registrar and head of the Department of Education and Psychology at Morehouse College, a post he filled until his retirement in 1970.

Eleanor Hamilton entered D. T. Howard Junior High School, chosen—as Eleanor remembered it—because her aunt, Nell Hamilton, was principal there, "so she could look after me." She went on to complete the ninth grade at Booker T. Washington High School, then the only Negro high school in Atlanta. Built to accommodate twelve hundred students, it then had an enrollment, spurred by Atlanta's wartime population growth, of nearly three thousand. Grace and Cookie Hamilton were frightened for their daughter. Grace remembered: "There was all kinds of physical violence in the halls. You know, just too many children . . . and so I decided that we couldn't stand another year. I couldn't stand another year for her, because of the anxiety." [22]

Encouraged primarily by her mother, Eleanor applied to Putney, a popular and prestigious preparatory school in Vermont, integrated (in principle at least) and challenging intellectually. In fact, Eleanor was Putney's only black student in her first year, but (according to her recollection) "others came, two or three." The scarcity of Negro students probably reflected less a policy of tokenism at Putney than the school's costs. Carmelita Hinton, Putney's founder and director, was a staunch egalitarian, but private schools, including those run on the highest principles, were always expensive. Eleanor indeed always remembered Putney as one of "her most beneficial experiences." She often said: "I loved it. Those were the happiest of times." [23]

Through Eleanor, two of her classmates made their first contact with the South's racial realities. In April 1947, during spring break, fellow students Dorothy Russell Booth of Colorado and Elizabeth Heller of California accompanied Eleanor home to Atlanta for the holidays. One afternoon the young trio made a shopping excursion to downtown Atlanta, using public transportation and returning to the Hamilton home on the edge of the AU campus at rush hour. Finding the bus crowded, the girls took seats as they found them, light-skinned Eleanor ignoring the segregation rules as naturally as her white friends. As they proceeded westward into the Atlanta University area, the bus emptied out, leaving predominantly black passengers. Elizabeth and Dorothy, known as "Russ," by then were sitting together with Eleanor. "Russ" later told the family what happened next, a story subsequently retold for this book by Grace Hamilton, who had waited anxiously at home for the girls' return: "The driver stops the bus in the middle of the block and comes up to Russ and says, 'should you be sitting here?' And you [to Eleanor]?' The people on the bus knew Eleanor . . . the neighborhood was not like it is now. And she said the bus just broke out . . . in this chuckle. The girls didn't move. Russ said, 'we just said yes, and then got off where we were supposed to.' She said, 'I hope that teaches him he can't be the motorman, conductor, and census taker too.'" Elizabeth Heller's mother wrote Grace, sending a contribution to the Atlanta Urban League, which Grace then headed, and saying the visit had been a unique experience for her daughter. [24]

Nor were episodes of the kind familiar to all her race lacking in Hamilton's life. Once she took Eleanor to buy shoes at Rich's, one of Atlanta's

biggest department stores. "It was one time when Cookie and I were in Atlanta with Eleanor," Grace Hamilton remembered.

> Now Rich's shoe department had always been, just come and you were
> served. I remember this time the department had been changed to a different
> location in the store. It was on the second floor. And I went with Eleanor and
> sat down and nobody did anything for a while. And then this clerk came and
> said, "if you want to be served you'll have to sit over here." And I said, "in-
> deed not, I'm perfectly comfortable." And Eleanor said, "Oh Mother, don't
> make a thing, don't make a thing." The clerk said, "if you're going to be
> served, you'll have to move." And I said, "we won't." And we just left the de-
> partment and went upstairs to the top people. We didn't stay and we didn't
> go back to buy shoes. I don't think the store continued that policy.

Grace Towns Hamilton's fortitude and strong self-esteem helped her better
than most to deal with such incidents.[25]

Later Eleanor returned home from Vermont to attend Spelman College
for a year. This was not what Eleanor herself wanted, as she explained:

> My father had not been big on Putney. . . . He thought I should stay and ac-
> celerate and go into Spelman. Spelman was much less expensive and he was
> not into big name schools and that sort of thing. When I left Putney, I did not
> want to go back south. My plan was that I would go to Oberlin. I'd been ac-
> cepted there and I had some friends who were going to Oberlin. That's what I
> wanted to do. It was my family who insisted that I come back south. . . . It was
> more my father than my mother who felt it was important for me to come
> back south and attend a black college. . . . I think it was my mother's feeling as
> well [but] my father felt very strongly that I should have the experience of go-
> ing to a black college as well as coming home to the South . . . to experience
> my people.
>
> But I think they were right, and I should have come home for that year, it
> was an important one for me and I enjoyed it. I was glad to leave but I wasn't
> unhappy while I was there.[26]

Eleanor had agreed with her parents to return south for two years but, as
she put it, "I got busy and wrote off and got a full scholarship to Smith College." Grace and Cookie Hamilton could hardly withhold their approval,
especially since a niece on Cookie's side was already attending this prestigious women's college. Though she found that her experience there failed
to measure up to Putney and she eventually lost the scholarship, Eleanor
Hamilton received a bachelor of arts degree from Smith College in 1952.
Ironically, the state of Georgia paid much of her Smith tuition. "It was all

my mother's doing," Eleanor recalled. Georgia then was, in effect, financing out-of-state studies for black students as part of its vain effort to stall legal challenge to its all-white institutions of higher learning. Grace Hamilton by that time had learned much about "how government really worked" and was not shy about using her knowledge to pry from the vulnerable state a large part of her daughter's bill at Smith.[27]

5

The Emerging Leader

. . .

G RACE HAMILTON did not set out to be a race leader, but it is clear
in retrospect that in the years leading up to her return to Atlanta
she had been groomed for just such a role.

She was now thirty-four years old, her formal education included an advanced degree, she had worked steadily at professional jobs for more than a
decade, and under the tutelage of skilled and respected mentors she had
learned the value of community action and the importance of the political
process in the fight for racial justice. She believed the struggle should be
waged through conciliation and negotiation, not confrontation, and her
moderation qualified her as a "realist" of her time. Only blacks so anointed
had a chance of being heard in the South of 1941. Her aims for the ballot
were unambiguous—she wanted an unfettered franchise for all persons,
including Negroes. Otherwise, she clothed her objectives in guarded language and seldom committed anything to writing, habits that were to per-
sist throughout her life. Once, while on the staff of the YWCA's National
Student Council, she wrote a letter advocating "a social order which pro-
vides every individual, regardless of race, an opportunity to participate and
share alike in all the relationships of life . . . and the ultimate elimination of
all segregation and discrimination." It was the nearest she ever came to
putting on record the philosophy that guided her work, said the author of
a dissertation on her public career, and no written evidence exists to the
contrary.

commissioners, and on boards of education and city councils. By the 1930s, as John Hope Franklin wrote, "blacks [were] once more in the thick of American politics . . . [exercising] the kind of strength they had not exercised since Reconstruction." Only now the Negro's political affiliation was in flux. Once unfailingly loyal to the GOP, the party of Lincoln and emancipation, Negroes began to break this historic tie in the 1920s when Republicans, eager for southern influence, ousted old-time loyalists in favor of southern "lily whites." By the 1930s the race increasingly gave its allegiance to the Democratic Party of Franklin Delano Roosevelt and the New Deal, though Roosevelt seemed no more inclined to tackle racial injustice than his predecessors. Largely out of deference to southern Democrats, for instance, he refused repeated NAACP entreaties to support a civil rights plank in the Democratic Party's campaign platform. Yet as president he dismantled some of the segregation in federal offices established by his last Democratic predecessor, Woodrow Wilson, and he appointed Negroes to the federal bench for the first time; his administration employed numerous black specialists and advisers, and his wife, Eleanor, showed an empathy for the black cause that rubbed off on others in the Washington of her day. Negroes in growing numbers went to work for the federal government; Forrester B. Washington, for one, left the Atlanta School of Social Work to direct Negro work for the Federal Emergency Relief Administration, predecessor of the Works Progress Administration, and some even were employed by federal agencies in the South. Roosevelt's personal appeal to Negroes was so profound that by 1936 when he ran for a second term, he captured a resounding 75 percent of the Negro vote. Already the party switch was reflected in Congress, where Chicago's Arthur W. Mitchell, former Republican turned Democrat, occupied the seat once held by Oscar DePriest. Mitchell was the first Negro Democrat in Congress, the herald of a growing contingent.[4]

· · ·

Poverty knew neither locale nor color in the cataclysmic decade of the Great Depression, but Negroes were disproportionately hard hit. Historians Guichard Parris and Lester Brooks gave this graphic accounting: "Two out of every five black families in the nation's cities were on relief. They were the fortunate ones; many in the cities and most in the rural areas received no regular aid." And Jacqueline Jones wrote that up to 90 percent of all Negro households during the 1930s "lived on the thin edge between subsistence and complete economic disaster."[5]

Black unemployment reached epidemic proportions, and even the total number of Negroes in the labor force declined, cutting a gash across the face of Negro progress in the North, while the southern black's condition verged on universal desperation. Losing jobs, even the most menial, to unemployed whites was a threat everywhere in the country, but in the South the threat was backed by terror. Lynchings once again increased, and in Georgia, a KKK-like outfit called the Black Shirts, claiming forty thousand members, became active in the "displacement" movement. Whole counties in Georgia organized efforts to turn Negro jobs over to whites, and their success was more than minimal. Forrester Washington, speaking for the Atlanta School of Social Work, reported: "White men have taken over such positions as elevator operators, tradesmen, teamsters, expressmen, bill posting, city sanitary wagon drivers . . . stewards, cooks, waiters and bell boys in hotels, hospital attendants, mechanics at filling stations, delivery boys from drug stores and not infrequently such domestic service employment as chauffeurs, maids and all-around domestics."[6]

Nor was Roosevelt able to deliver the "equality and fairness" he promised in the New Deal's relief and recovery program. Wage differentials between blacks and whites were widespread, most flagrantly in the South. And Negroes were left out of the New Deal's biggest reforms, the Social Security Act of 1935, providing old age assistance and unemployment benefits, and the Fair Labor Standards Act of 1938, providing for minimum wages and maximum hours. The deliberate exclusion of agricultural and domestic workers, 70 percent of whom were blacks, was the price New Dealers had to pay for passage of both reforms. Even in old age assistance—again especially in the South—lower sums went to blacks than to whites.[7]

Despite its striking callousness toward blacks during the Depression, the New Deal projected the federal government into Negro affairs for the first time since Reconstruction, and one historian concluded that Roosevelt's reforms accomplished much simply because they "took an isolated farmer far back in Georgia's pine barrens and made him realize that he was part of the nation." Above all, by exposing Negroes, especially those implacably repressed in the South, to a larger world from which to draw their standards, by offering them a graphic example of the government's potential for helping citizens solve their problems, it opened up new avenues of protest and aroused the dormant will to dissent. The consequences were both future and immediate.[8]

Georgia blacks, the poor as well as the better off, showed signs of a new awakening as the Depression wore on. Many among the race participated in rallies, voter registration drives, boycotts, and strikes. Meetings held at the Atlanta Urban League to discuss government relief measures drew up to twenty-five hundred people. There was even interracial activity. As early as March 1930 an integrated demonstration of about one hundred gathered at Atlanta City Hall to protest the lack of jobs, a small crowd that attracted a disproportionate amount of police harassment and arrests. The repressive tactics discouraged further marches until June 1932, when an interracial "hunger march" before the Fulton County Commission in Atlanta brought out one thousand people and ended in the arrest and prosecution of the rally leader, Angelo Herndon. (A celebrated defendant, Herndon eventually was freed by the U.S. Supreme Court.) Integrated rallies continued and by 1934 were occurring periodically before Atlanta's City Hall, protesting the general inadequacy of federal relief funds. At the same time, the New Deal's encouragement of labor organizing helped some southern Negroes find a place in the union movement which had largely excluded blacks everywhere. Blacks were even represented in the South's unsuccessful general textile strike of 1934, though they held few and usually menial jobs in the industry.[9]

The black middle class, meanwhile, pinned their hopes for racial justice on a political rebirth in the South to match the one already unfolding for Negroes in the North, and they diligently chipped away at the legal props supporting the southern Democratic Party's white primary, the ultimate barrier to equal Negro suffrage in the region because it was always tantamount to election. The NAACP had been challenging the hoary device in state and federal courts since the 1920s, with only piecemeal success, but by 1940, as V. O. Key Jr. wrote, "a lot of water had gone over the political dam and the United States Supreme Court had acquired some new members," giving the white primary's prospects a decidedly gloomy outlook. In Atlanta, activists were readying their fellow Negroes to take advantage of its demise.[10]

Their efforts had begun in earnest in 1932, when Lugenia Burns Hope, a leader of the Neighborbhood Union, a women's community action group, and A. T. Walden, then serving as president of the city's NAACP, organized what they called a "citizenship school" to instruct Negroes in voter registration procedures and the structure of national, state, and local governments. Clarence A. Bacote and Rayford W. Logan, professors of history at AU, were directors of the school, and during its eight annual six-week sessions, over a thousand Atlanta blacks passed through the course. Elsewhere in the city, meanwhile, John Wesley Dobbs, retired railway mail clerk and a leading Negro Republican, organized the Atlanta Civic and Political League (ACPL) to stimulate voter registration while engaging the Negro in the use of political means for achieving economic and civic ends. Probably the ACPL's biggest achievement was to help push Negro registration in Atlanta from a meager six hundred in 1934 to three thousand by 1939. Both the citizenship schools and the ACPL aimed at more than they accomplished, but later it would become apparent that they had achieved more than they knew at the time.[11]

Indeed, militancy was crackling beneath the surface of the Negro world when Europe was plunged into war in September 1939, and the war would soon set a match to the race's patience with humiliation and injustice. America at first professed to see the war as a purely European affair, but its neutral stance was untenable in a conflict between fascist racism and democracy, and the United States was soon supplying arms to England and France. By 1941 the nation was engaged in preparations for war, both in the buildup of its armed forces and in the manufacture of materials for modern combat. Suddenly jobs at good wages were available in defense plants everywhere in the nation; the Depression was over, the economy responding to preparations for war as it never had done to New Deal programs for social peace. Negroes wondered what their place would be in the new prosperity, and the answer was not long delayed. Five million unemployed whites, the Depression's residue, held first place in line everywhere ahead of blacks for new jobs. Negroes, mostly unskilled and semiskilled workers, were relegated to filling jobs deserted by whites absorbed into the higher-paying defense economy. An executive from North American Aviation frankly stated that it was "against company policy to employ [Negroes] as aircraft workers or mechanics . . . regardless of their training" and he would hire them, if at all, he said, only as janitors.[12]

Blacks were enraged, filled with an anger uniquely logical and compelling at the time, for how could the country fight fascism and racism abroad while condoning age-old discrimination and injustice at home? In the face of this new humiliation, Negroes declared themselves fed up and prepared for action.

Their response was a plan for a massive march on Washington reminiscent of Jacob Coxey's army of unemployed in 1894 and the bonus expeditionary force of 1932. The idea surfaced in January 1941 at a Chicago meeting of Negro leaders. A. Philip Randolph, head of the Pullman porters' union, got the credit for organizing the march, but the idea originated, one historian insists, with a woman who is reported to have said: "Mr. Chairman, we ought to throw fifty thousand Negroes around the White House—bring them from all over the country, in jalopies, in trains, and any way they can get there until we can get some action from the White House." Randolph liked the idea, seconded it on the spot, and went on to lead the movement. It was to Randolph that President Roosevelt turned in trying to deflect the race from its purpose. Though the president brought in his secretaries of war and the navy to pressure Randolph, the Negro union leader remained adamant, and by late June 1941 Negroes from all over the United States had packed their walking shoes and were heading for the nation's capital. Randolph refused to yield to last-minute persuasion even from Eleanor Roosevelt and Mayor Fiorello LaGuardia of New York, nor would he heed entreaties from Walter White, then head of the NAACP. Only when Roosevelt capitulated on June 25, 1941, issuing his famous Executive Order 8802, did Randolph call off the march. The order, indeed, gave Negroes all they wanted. It flatly forbade "discrimination in the employment of workers in defense industries or Goverment because of race, creed, color or national origin" and enjoined employers and labor organizations "to provide for the full and equitable participation of all workers in defense industries, without discrimination." The Fair Employment Practices Commission (FEPC) was set up to administer the order and ensure compliance.[13]

Negroes were elated. John Hope Franklin wrote: "Negroes hailed the order as the most significant document affecting them since the Emancipation Proclamation." In the end, the fair employment decree no more fulfilled Negro hopes than had the proclamation long before. The South was generally opposed to the order, and discrimination continued, especially in that region, in defiance of the FEPC, but as Franklin succinctly noted: "Its existence had a salutary effect on the employment status of Negroes."[14]

· · ·

It was in this climate of racial triumph that Grace Towns Hamilton and her husband, Henry Cooke Hamilton, returned to Atlanta in mid-1941. It would be their last homecoming. Neither of them would ever again permanently depart their beloved city and state.

Grace Hamilton recalled the Atlanta University seminars with Professors Du Bois and Reid that she undertook immediately upon her return as very rewarding, but her studies were a short-lived interlude. In the winter of 1942, the national YWCA offered her a part-time job with its community division, and soon she was commuting again, this time between Atlanta and New York. Suddenly an opportunity arose for a new and different kind of work. Asked to become director of the Atlanta Urban League (AUL), she accepted at once. It was a career move that would change her life.

Talking about it later, she recalled: "W. Y. Bell, who'd been the director for years, had taken a job with the USO [United Service Organization]. I was glad to have a base of some responsibility in Atlanta. A. T. Walden was the one who suggested me, I'm sure. He was chairman of the League's Board of Directors and he urged me to come. He was a dear friend. He used to say, 'I knew you before you knew yourself.' He was a good friend of my parents so I jumped at the chance to take the job. In 1943, there weren't but, oh, six or seven Urban Leagues in the South and that went as far up as Oklahoma." Among the first problems she had to deal with at the agency was a personal one not unknown among her fellow working women, irrespective of race. She told the story this way:

> There was not an expectation among the League's black leadership, men largely, that women deserved full and equal treatment. For example, and this is where it really hit me, when I agreed to come back and head the League, this man who had been the director, very able, recommended that my salary be $1,200 a year. And his had been, I think, $3,600. I didn't even know that. I didn't raise any question about what the salary would be. I just said, "Yes, I'll take it." Then when I got on the spot, I found out that this was really a decision he had recommended to the chairman, and that was it. I got that corrected too. I got it put up to whatever they were paying the man.

Her predecessor had taken a temporary leave of absence from the League position, which meant Hamilton first held only an acting appointment, but when Bell returned he became head of the National Urban League's Southern Field Office in Atlanta and Hamilton's appointment as AUL executive director became permanent. Again she clashed with the man. "He apparently expected to have some oversight role with the Atlanta League, which of course I could not permit," she recalled.[15]

A forceful personality and a strong will were assets to a woman executive in the black world no less than the white, and besides that, her standing in Negro Atlanta was the very highest. The *Atlanta Daily World* called Hamilton's appointment "a fitting tribute to her intellectual ability and social genius," and the newspaper congratulated the Atlanta Urban League's Board of Directors "upon the wisdom of its choice." The new appointee assumed her duties in February 1943.[16]

· · ·

In Atlanta, Walden soon became Grace Hamilton's mentor in much the way Robert Church had been in Memphis. One prominent Negro Atlantan even called her "Walden's Girl Friday," a not very accurate epithet that at least conveyed the closeness of their relationship. Long the quintessential "race man" in the city, Walden had a widespread reputation in Georgia and beyond; his civic, professional, and political activities were numerous and legendary. Like Church, Walden was of an older generation, nearer her father's age than her own; like Church, he was a family friend, an even closer one than Church had been; and in much the same way that Church was "Mister Republican" in the Deep South, so Walden had become "Mister Democrat" in Georgia. Like Hamilton's father, George Towns, Walden was active in the NAACP, heading the Atlanta chapter for over a decade and serving meanwhile as a vice-president of the national organization and a member of its legal committee. A 1907 graduate of Atlanta University, Walden had earned a degree in 1911 at the University of Michigan Law School. He first practiced in Macon, Georgia, then joined the army in World War I, rising to the rank of captain in the segregated infantry. Discharged, he moved his law practice to Atlanta, "where his scholarly understanding and interpretation of the law made him one of the most respected members of the bar," and he handled numerous civil rights cases, even occasionally prosecuting whites with success. Excluded from Atlanta's organized legal fraternity because of his color, he founded the Gate City Bar Association for Negroes and was its first president.[17]

By the 1930s, Walden was a convinced Democrat, proselytizing vigorously among Negroes on behalf of the Democratic Party, and with other middle-class black leaders working hard to overcome the political apathy that prevailed among his race in those years. When the U.S. Supreme Court in April 1944, in a Texas case known as *Smith* v. *Allwright*, finally outlawed the white primary, Walden founded the Association of Citizens Democratic Clubs of Georgia, which gathered black leaders by county and set them on a quiet but all-out campaign of Negro voter registration that ended in the registration of nearly 120,000 Negroes, or approximately 20 percent of Georgia's adult blacks, and a voter turnout of 70 percent in the 1946 Democratic primary. It was the greatest show of Negro suffrage in the South since Reconstruction, and Georgia politics would never be the same again. Grace Towns Hamilton would play a key role in the drama, largely from her director's chair at the Atlanta Urban League.[18]

• • •

Among popular causes of the Progressive Era, justice for blacks ranked at the bottom of the list, for "progressivism in politics," wrote NUL historian Nancy J. Weiss, "went hand in hand with racism." Yet out of this bleak period came not only the NAACP, in 1909, but also the National Urban

League in 1910, two organizations whose contributions to racial reform remain a lasting legacy of the time. Both were the fruit of black inspiration, the NAACP owing its origins to W. E. B. Du Bois and his Niagara Movement, while the NUL's founding was largely the work of George Edmund Haynes, a pioneer sociologist who was the first Negro to receive a doctoral degree from Columbia University. The leadership of both from their inception, however, was interracial, and their financing was heavily subsidized by well-to-do-whites sympathetic to the Negro cause. All founders came from their respective upper-class elites, and several board members, mostly black, served on the founding boards of both the NUL and the NAACP. Without exception they were a special breed of reformer, fired with the belief shared by few of their time that organized interracial cooperation could achieve economic and social justice for the Negro race.[19]

By mutual agreement, the NAACP occupied itself primarily with political, civil, and social empowerment of all colored people, aiming to achieve their full and immediate equality through protest, agitation, and legal action. The NUL, organized to address the special problems of blacks as they moved in ever-growing numbers to the cities, confined itself to questions of philanthropy, social service, and job procurement, employing the tools of negotiation, persuasion, education, and investigation. Given the nature of their goals and methods, the NAACP was seen as "radical," the NUL as "accommodationist." The Urban League in its early years reportedly called itself the "State Department" of Negro affairs, the NAACP the "War Department." Mary White Ovington, an NAACP founder, later concluded that the functional division between the two organizations was "fortunate." She wrote in *The Walls Came Tumbling Down*: "We could not have raised money for 'philanthropy' as successfully as an organization with a less militant program and securing employment is a business in itself. So the two national organizations divided the field, working together from time to time as action demanded."[20]

• • •

When George Edmund Haynes came away from Columbia University with his advanced degree in sociology, he was convinced that the newly urbanized Negro, mostly unskilled, unschooled, and still saddled with a dark heritage of subservience, constituted a problem not only for Negroes themselves but for the entire community. Because social service efforts of the time seldom included blacks—and often specifically excluded them—he determined to remedy the deficiency. With the aid of wealthy, reform-minded Ruth Standish Baldwin, he arranged the consolidation of the two small groups then focusing on the plight of urban blacks, the National League for the Protection of Colored Women and the Committee for Improving the Industrial Condition of Negroes in New York, incorporating their functions in a new group called, infelicitously, the National League on Urban Conditions among Negroes. Renamed the National Urban League in 1920, the agency under Haynes proceeded on the assumption that "the key to changing racial injustices was to educate whites to their existence." The agency's social and employment services, the core of its work, were based at Haynes's insistence on scholarly research and scientific investigations of black life and needs—an adaptation to new times of the studies Du Bois had pioneered at Atlanta University. In another innovative effort, the early NUL promoted the training of Negro social workers, then practically unheard-of in the field. Having set the NUL on its way, Haynes moved to Fisk University to establish a department of social science and in 1919 permanently severed his connection with the League. His successor, Eugene Kinckle Jones, would lead the organization until 1940, guiding it through the cataclysmic years of the Great Migration and the Great Depression, both of which would greatly change the NUL.[21]

Bringing nearly half a million southern Negroes to large cities of the North between 1915 and 1919, the Great Migration magnified the need for NUL programs and converted it into a national organization with affiliates across the nation. A Department of Research was established within the organization in 1921, giving formal recognition to the "importance of facts" in its work. In 1925, a Department of Industrial Relations was launched, charged simultaneously with widening industrial employment opportunities for Negroes and with pressuring labor unions to lower their bars against the race. Modest success in both goals came to a halt during the hard times of the 1930s, when the League was unable to prevent massive Negro unemployment, much less find new jobs for blacks. Instead of progress, the NUL thought "grimly of bare survival" and turned to vocational training, keeping hope alive by preparing Negroes for better jobs in the future and laying the foundation for what would become its Vocational Opportunity Campaign, a permanent NUL program. The radicalizing influence of the Great Depression was not without effect on the NUL, and in tune with New Deal times, the agency, despite division within its leadership on the issue, took up the cause of labor unions, creating what it called "workers councils" across the country to educate blacks about the value of collective action in solving labor problems. A Workers Bureau under Lester B. Granger, who since 1919 had held various jobs with the League in various parts of the country, coordinated the councils' activities and simultaneously continued the NUL's long-standing effort to break the Negro's lockout in most existing unions. Leadership disagreement and financial shortfall, plus Granger's departure from the bureau, soon ended the NUL's labor organizing, but the main legacy of the effort was Granger himself, who returned to the NUL in 1940 to succeed Jones as executive secretary, a job he held throughout the next two decades.

At the time, Granger was considered a good man with a losing organization. Though by 1940 the NUL had won praise from presidents of the United States and executives of powerful foundations, earned applause for its work in leading white newspapers as well as the black press, and enjoyed the respect of professionals in the fields of education, employment, and social services, it aroused much ambivalence within the black community. To John Hope of Atlanta University the League was "the greatest agency" for the uplift of black people in the cities, whereas to Ralph Bunche its policies were unrealistic, expedient, and conciliatory, and he chided the agency for never coming to grips with "the fundamentals of the American racial conflict." The masses found the League's activities complex, intricate, and time-consuming, affecting few of them; the NAACP was easier to accept because its court fights against lynching and the white primary held promise for all African Americans and its membership numbered in the many thousands. Moreover, in 1940, as Guichard Parris and Lester Brooks wrote in their history of the NUL, the agency was debt-ridden and internally demoralized; not a few thought it was sinking into oblivion. Charged with reversing the decline, Lester B. Granger found his task immeasurably aided by American entry into World War II, the consequent revival of American industry, and the upsurge in militancy among Negroes themselves, to which the NUL made its own unique contribution. When Negroes threatened the massive march on Washington in 1941 that produced the Fair Employment Practices Commission, "the solid guts of the call to march, the background for demands," as Parris and Brooks wrote, "were supplied by the NUL, which prepared the roll-call and documentation for these items." Granger felt the Negro would never have a better argument for increased economic opportunity than the need for total national defense, and he made the most of it, beefing up the NUL's industrial relations work and adding clout to the agency's public relations and financial appeals. By 1943 Granger had successfully reinvigorated the National Urban League; in that year, by chance, Grace Towns Hamilton became executive director of the Atlanta affiliate. Her tenure with the AUL and Granger's remaining years at the national headquarters would closely coincide. They were two talented, charismatic, and strong-willed individuals, whose eventual conflict might have been predicted.[22]

• • •

The National Urban League was already nearly a decade old when the Atlanta Urban League was formed in 1919 under the guidance of Jesse O. Thomas, a Mississippian holding a degree from the New York School of Social Work. Thomas had been hired that year by the League to set up a southern regional field headquarters in Atlanta, from which he was charged with establishing southern affiliates as rapidly as possible. The League in those years actively promoted its own national expansion, but Thomas had only limited success in his southern drive. In the region where the bulk of the black population still lived, he had managed by 1940 to add to Atlanta only six new NUL affiliates in the South. Raising money for interracial work was a difficult assignment in the former Confederacy, and the League, believing whites were concerned and indispensable partners in the work of racial advancement, limited affiliates to cities able and willing to establish interracial boards and a paid staff. Early Georgia affiliates in Augusta, Savannah, and Albany foundered on these requirements. In Atlanta, the affiliate lived up to the challenge, but awkwardly. In its early years the organization had two boards, one black and the other white; each met separately three times a month, then convened for one joint monthly meeting. Just as perplexing as maintaining an interracial board in a segregated society was the problem of League funding. Whereas the NAACP relied for support on the dues of its black membership, the NUL depended on public, mainly white, largesse, and its affiliates from the beginning looked primarily to Community Chests for their support. (The AUL had Chest funding from 1923.) Dominated by whites, Community Chests in the South were inclined to view even the moderate, accommodationist approach of the Urban League as radical, and the Chests' effect on affiliates was often chilling. In the 1930s, when workers councils were organized in Atlanta to promote labor unionizing under the joint aegis of Thomas's southern field office and the Atlanta Urban League, Georgia police raided Thomas's headquarters, leading the city's Community Chest to threaten a complete cutoff of funds for the AUL if the organizing continued, a threat that effectively ended the program. But the city had strong black social and economic institutions, and, with their support, the AUL survived the setback. Nevertheless, it would remain the only branch in Georgia until the 1960s.

The caliber of the AUL's support is indicated by its founders, most prominent among whom were Alonzo F. Herndon, the successful Atlanta barber who also owned the burgeoning Atlanta Life Insurance Company, and Heman Perry, founder of the Standard Life Insurance Company. The AUL would find a home for many years in the Herndon Building on Auburn Avenue. John Hope, then president of Morehouse College and a founding member of the National Urban League, was on the AUL's first board of directors, as were C. B. Wilmer, rector of St. Luke's Episcopal Church and a vice-chairman of Atlanta University's Board of Trustees, Plato Durham, the first dean of Emory University's School of Theology, J. L. Wheeler, a banker, Solomon W. Walker, founder of Pilgrim's Health and Life Insurance Company, Ludie Clay Andrews, the head of Negro nurses at Grady Memorial Hospital, Cora B. Finley, a prominent public school teacher, W. A. Fountain of Morris Brown College, and Mrs. D. R. Green, otherwise unidentified.

• • •

William Y. Bell had long been the AUL's executive director, and in 1943 he was ready for a change. When he took a temporary post with the USO, the agency that provided recreational and social services for American servicemen, A. T. Walden, as the League's board chairman, wanted Grace Hamilton as his replacement, and the Board of Directors forthwith approved his choice.

As Grace Hamilton remembered it in later life, she was the "first woman director anywhere in the National Urban League." Her recollection was faulty, for according to Nancy Weiss, there were at least three women executives in local Leagues during the 1920s alone, and at the highest level Ann Tanneyhill had been the National Urban League's director of vocational guidance since 1928. Nevertheless, Grace Hamilton was the first woman executive in Atlanta, and to the work of the Atlanta Urban League she brought unique strength and a useful feminine perspective.[23]

6

The Atlanta Urban League:
A Housing Success

. . .

A T THE HELM of the Atlanta Urban League, Grace Hamilton was soon forging a path of her own design. As she saw it, Atlanta had problems peculiar to its history and status as hub city of the South, and the fabric of the National Urban League's preset program, with its concentration on philanthropy, social service, and job procurement, did not fit Atlanta's needs. Worthy though the NUL's objectives were, they lacked an Atlanta accent, and she wanted to strike out in new, more locally oriented directions. On January 1, 1946, when Robert A. Thompson returned to the AUL from three years in the army and took over as industrial relations secretary, a post virtually mandated at all local affiliates that put him in charge of job procurement, Hamilton found a willing recruit to her cause. He was as ready as she to revamp the agency's agenda, and both agreed that housing should take precedence over jobs.

Under Hamilton's leadership housing soon became what she called the League's "principal activity," but she also, and sometimes simultaneously, promoted equality of school funding, voter registration, better medical care, and training of physicians. "We managed several community-wide projects you don't think of as League things. I think they made a significant contribution to change in the city," she would later say. The housing drive that began with Thompson's return to the AUL was an innovation in a program that by then was already uniquely at variance with the traditional NUL agenda.[1]

Thompson put it this way: "I returned to civilian life determined to do something about housing. I just didn't see myself trying to persuade businesses to employ blacks and minorities, because the controls were not really in my hands. I decided I could do something a little bit better where I had the initiative." What he had in mind was getting Atlanta blacks out of "nigger town," an aim that dovetailed neatly with Grace Hamilton's own thinking. She later related: "Tommy [as she called him] was a great pillar of strength to me, because his training was in sociology and economics. He had been a student of Ira Reid's, a good statistician and a good analyst and was interested particularly in the limitations on housing, the restrictions on where black people could live. He first came back to the League as industrial relations secretary, but that was sort of a hangover. We did not pick up on employment as a major undertaking." [2]

In 1947 Thompson was made the AUL's housing secretary, and under his and Hamilton's leadership, housing, of all League programs during her tenure at the agency, was undoubtedly its biggest success. Thompson inspired and guided the work; Hamilton remained throughout his loyal supervisor. She was "used to being in charge at the League," as one friend recalled, and taking a backseat on housing underlined the respect she had for Thompson and the importance she attached to the problem. Although housing had remarkable long-term results, downgrading job procurement to the point of its virtual elimination was a bold show of independence. Hamilton was a hard and uncompromising fighter, and once she determined upon a course of action she typically pursued it with single-minded intensity. "In terms of the broad purposes of the organization we conformed fully with the objectives of the National Urban League," she always insisted. "They just wanted it cut more to their format." The NUL, observing and approving the early and well-publicized successes of the housing program, never moved to rein in the Hamilton-Thompson local initiatives. Local autonomy could hardly be challenged when the results were good. Nevertheless, when friction with national executives eventually ended her career with the AUL, in retrospect it seemed clear that the trouble might have been mitigated if in her pursuit of independence at the agency she had shown more sensitivity toward the jobs program and the historic importance it held in the NUL agenda. [3]

• • •

The National Urban League's ties with its affiliates in those years were loose and ambiguous. Local Leagues were virtually autonomous bodies, relatively free to originate their own program activities. The NUL looked upon itself as a parent body, yet it actually functioned more as a "super local," expecting of its affiliates a minimum standard of performance, participation in its various national programs, and adherence to its principles and policies. Yet it was unable to compel compliance with any of these objectives because the purse strings were in the hands of local Community Chests, none of which were reluctant to exercise the restraining power thus conferred upon them when they judged it necessary. Under the circumstances, the NUL generally limited its supervision to instances of intraorganizational dispute.

For the duration of World War II, when Thompson was absent from the League, Hamilton went along with ways of the past, energetically promoting Negro employment in defense and government agencies, aware that the war gave Negroes an unprecedented opportunity to advance their status in the employment market. Shortly before she arrived at the AUL, one of its directors, Jacob Henderson, with aid from the National Urban League and Atlanta's NAACP and clout provided by the new FEPC law, had forced Georgia to set up an aircraft training facility at Washington High School, the first such facility for Negroes in the South. Members of the race were soon moving into skilled jobs at the Bell Aircraft Corporation's bomber plant in Marietta, near Atlanta. Hamilton endorsed and promoted the cooperative working relationship Henderson had arranged between the AUL and the plant; she supported him in his further successful effort to place Negroes on the staff of the Office of Price Administration, a federal agency; and AUL prodding under Hamilton led the Georgia State Employment Agency, funded partially by the federal government, to hire Negroes in the early 1940s. It was the first state office to do so.[4]

· · ·

Thompson grew up in Lynchburg, Virginia, graduated from Morgan State College in Baltimore in 1932, entered Atlanta University in 1934, where he studied under Ira Reid, and received a master's degree in economics in 1936. He stayed in Atlanta, working for two years at the Federal Reemployment Center, then headed by Marion Hamilton, Grace Hamilton's brother-in-law, which serviced black clients exclusively, but when the Center's functions were handed over to the state of Georgia in 1938, Thompson and all other Negro employees were summarily fired. Afterward, Thompson, while working for M. R. Brewster at the Georgia School of Technology on a federally funded inventory of real property in Atlanta, counted the city's substandard housing units by census tracts and blocks, a job that Thompson later said gave him his "first orientation in housing conditions in the city of Atlanta." In 1942 he joined the staff of the AUL but was drafted by the army in mid-1943, soon after Grace Hamilton had taken over as the agency's new executive director. The rapport established between them before he departed for war was easily renewed when he got back.[5]

Like all community-wide projects pursued by the AUL under Hamilton's leadership, the housing effort aimed no arrows at segregation, seeking only those improvements sanctioned by Jim Crow. "It was the law of the land," she always said in justification, "it was the only way you had to work." Even confined to this rigid framework, the Atlanta Negro community, spurred by the AUL and energized by its own capable and resourceful individuals and institutions, produced a housing expansion of remarkable proportions. It was a community effort that harked back to black self-help based on racial solidarity that characterized post-Reconstruction years. Whites aided, but mostly by not impeding the determined Negroes. Atlanta's white leadership, then busily engaged in planning the city's postwar expansion (a planning that excluded Negro participation), was determined to preserve and rationalize the city's system of residential apartheid, and as long as the Negroes' housing demands posed no threat to this goal, it was willing to accommodate the race's needs, readily acknowledging them to be desperate.[6]

War had vastly expanded Atlanta's population, black and white, and Negro militancy combined with American postwar prosperity had provided the race with more jobs and income than ever before. But Negro housing, especially for those of moderate income, remained poor, scarce, and largely confined to Atlanta's center city, its most dilapidated area. In 1946, Atlanta encompassed twenty-five square miles, divided into sixty-six census tracts. As a result of a real property inventory, Thompson found that "blacks lived primarily in 20 or 25 of these 66 census tracts, concentrated right down town," and population density in tracts just east of the town's center was twenty thousand persons per square mile. With 33 percent of the population, Negroes had 16 percent of the living space. Health and safety conditions were deplorable; 71 percent of the housing was substandard. Poor, middle-income, and well-to-do Negroes alike had little to choose from beyond slum and neglected neighborhoods. When those desperate for better accommodations in the early postwar years sought to move into adjacent "white neighborhoods"—buying usually from residents moving to the burgeoning suburbs—mob violence erupted, fanned by a revived Ku Klux Klan and a new hate group in Atlanta called the Columbians. Housing won at the cost of such strife was often in semislum conditions and scarcely worth the struggle. When those with sufficient income to build their own homes sought the mortgage loan guarantees offered since 1934 by the Federal Housing Administration (FHA) that were then fueling the postwar explosion in suburban housing for whites, blacks, viewed by the FHA as poor credit risks, were usually turned down. By 1949 in Atlanta, the FHA had approved six thousand dwelling units for whites but only twenty-four for blacks, a discrepancy that reflected the national situation; between 1946 and 1959, less than 2 percent of all U.S. housing financed with federal mortgage insurance was made available to Negroes.[7]

Instead of challenging Jim Crow, Hamilton and Thompson proposed new Negro housing "in areas which may be occupied peacefully." If this effectively excluded Negroes from seeking "housing in old established neighborhoods" (i.e., white neighborhoods), Thompson and Hamilton considered the limitation a worthwhile trade-off, and, later, when League funding was under challenge from white supremacists, she would permit the Atlanta Community Chest to point to the AUL's acquiescence in segregated housing as a point in its favor. Reasoning that Negro Atlanta could escape its center-city ghetto by moving beyond the city's boundaries, especially in directions opposite the white suburban flow, the Hamilton-Thompson team quickly took the first step toward locating what Thompson called "expansion areas."[8]

In October 1947, with crosses burning and bombs exploding in tense transitional neighborhoods, they organized the Temporary Coordinating Committee on Housing (TCCH), composed of prominent Atlanta Negroes, and gave it the task of pinpointing large outlying areas that could be suitably developed for blacks without great white opposition and finding investors willing to put up funds for major projects. W. H. Aiken, a prosperous builder who headed the Empire Real Estate Board, was made chairman of TCCH; among its members were T. M. Alexander Sr., founder of the Southeast Fidelity Fire Insurance Company, J. P. Whittaker of the Atlanta Mutual Building and Loan Association, and representatives of black Atlanta's other leading financial institutions, the Atlanta Life Insurance Company and the Citizens Trust Company.

Searching for open underdeveloped land on the city's outskirts, far enough from white property to allay racial animosity yet accessible to existing Negro communities and Negro work, the committee located six tracts that met its requirements, generally land lying to the west, southeast, and north of the city. Negroes already owned some of the land, but white property was also involved, and certain white neighborhoods lay athwart the proposed expansion routes, posing the threat of racist reaction. Political support that curbed this possibility came from Atlanta's all-white Metropolitan Planning Commission (MPC) in 1952, when it outlined its own ideas for the city's future in a document tacitly accepting Negro housing goals and also suggesting even more black expansion areas. The concept of "Negro areas," whether conceived by whites or blacks, had no legal standing and was, besides, new endorsement for residential segregation in Atlanta, but it also helped ensure peaceful achievement of what Negroes were already determined to accomplish on their own in any case. Eventually all six areas pinpointed by the TCCH and four of those named by the MPC were nailed down for Negroes.

Once the TCCH identified the desired expansion areas, it "faded out of the picture," Thompson remembered, leaving the remainder of the formidable task to the AUL. In a 1951 "Report of the Housing Activities of the Atlanta Urban League," Thompson wrote: "We made land ownership analysis of practically everywhere we wanted to go. Armed with this information, the Atlanta Urban League persuaded the land owners themselves to build houses or make available their land for development. The acceptance or rejection of these proposals varied according to the landowners knowledge of the building and construction industry." When approached, as Thompson recalled, "some owners said, well, they didn't know how to develop it, so we said, with our limited experience and knowledge, we will try to find somebody to acquire and develop it." The result was that on selected sites the AUL "assumed the role of cooperating with developers" and on certain other tracts development became its "direct responsibility."⁹

Where owners were white, as they were in three large tracts on the western rim of the city, an indirect approach, essentially an interracial triangular arrangement, was employed. At one apex of the triangle were three whites—Adam Cates, a leading real estate firm, Laura Galbraith, a Cates agent, and Morris B. Abram, an Atlanta lawyer with interests in real estate and better Negro housing—while at the other two were the AUL and a collection of black buyers.

Thompson described the collaboration: "We found the land and had Morris buy it, that is, he got Mrs. Laura Galbraith, a Cates agent, to buy the land; it subsequently came to Morris who in turn transferred it to waiting black purchasers." As Thompson recalled, "In each of the three tracts Galbraith contacted the white owners, got them to sell the land, Morris was simply the lawyer in the transaction." In a category of its own was Western Land Incorporated, formed, as Hamilton put it, "to get strategically located land in ownership that was sympathetic." "Western Land," Thompson recalled, "was a bona fide corporation formed to buy land, not to build on, but as a beachhead to establish black ownership in the area. I forget how much we put up, maybe $125, $300, $500 a person. It was headed by Dr. J. B. Harris, a black physician. A. T. Walden, Morris Abram, and Grace Hamilton were investors. Whittaker and R. L. Chennault were others. We had about twenty-three investors in all. Morris was the only white one." Across the road from the Western Land acquisition was a large tract owned by a white who refused to sell to blacks. Western Land's purchase had him checkmated.[10]

Walden, Whittaker, and Grace Hamilton as its executive director were members of AUL's Board of Directors, and Western Land was an indirect creation of the AUL, yet the corporation was never discussed by the board. So far as is known, it was mentioned only once, indirectly, at a board meeting held on November 18, 1952, in a minute that stated: "R. A. Thompson reported on Housing. He said about 18 months ago, the AUL recognized that the land available for Negro occupancy was rapidly disappearing. A Corporation has been formed, land has been purchased and an expansion area for the future is assured." Bought for $30,000, Western Land's eighty-five-acre acquisition was eventually sold for $85,000 to a white developer who used it for commercial purposes. The two other tracts purchased through the triangular dealing with whites became the sites of moderate-priced homes. Would white owners have sold if they had known the ultimate buyers were black? "Might have, we don't know," Thompson replied. "It was just easier for Morris to buy it, since he was white."[11]

The Hamilton-Thompson plan for getting Negro Atlanta out of the ghetto worked peacefully as foreseen. Collier Heights was an example. One of the white neighborhoods lying astride the corridor that defined the new "expansion areas," Collier Heights was largely a postwar development financed by the publicly subsidized loans then generally unavailable to blacks. In 1954, Collier Heights woke up to the fact that "Negroes . . . had them surrounded." Opposed to the notion of a mixed neighborhood, Collier Heights was trapped in the arms of a pincer created by the three tract purchases, as Thompson later proudly recalled: "So all these white people in these beautiful homes were pocketed, because we had jumped over, and over, and over and bought land and they didn't like it. They panicked."[12]

Pragmatic considerations prevailed, however, when Collier Heights residents realized the best way to protect property values was to sell out as an entire neighborhood. "Within three months, it was all over and Negroes were the new owners of Collier Heights," the United Press International reported. Indeed, the Collier Heights drama served as a go-ahead signal for development of much of the new land acquisitions, and by the late 1950s, the UPI wrote, "the sound of hammer and saw is everywhere, as the undeveloped area to the west mushrooms." Collier Heights was not without its poignancy and trauma for both races, but for Hamilton and Thompson at the AUL, determined to move Negro Atlanta into new homes on new land, it seemed both then and afterward an unadulterated success. The National Urban League in New York was also impressed, one high-ranking staffer calling the AUL housing program "a magnificent job." [13]

Of the seventeen subdivisions for which the AUL had some responsibility in these years, it was most intensely involved with Highpoint Apartments and Fairhaven, a development of moderate-income, single-family homes. Highpoint best illustrates the processes and obstacles encountered in the Hamilton-Thompson housing drive and the role Hamilton played in them.

Opened in July 1950 as the largest federally insured private rental project for Negroes in the South and the first development of its kind in metropolitan Atlanta, Highpoint provided 452 apartments and was erected at a cost of $2.5 million. Though the AUL played a key role in its development, Highpoint actually was built and owned by Morris B. Abram and his law partner, Hugh Howell. Abram, who had political ambitions and later ran for Congress, eventually became the sole owner, and as late as 1993 the property still remained in the hands of his family.

The land for Highpoint, one of the TCCH's expansion tracts, was easily acquired because its owner, the African Methodist Episcopal Church, was entirely in accord with the Negro housing goals. Thompson made a cryptic review of the AUL's role in this project in his 1951 report:

> The Atlanta Urban League presented land site to present owners. Arranged for conferences between officials of AME Church. Informed local leaders of proposed project and secured endorsements. Participated in conferences between land owners and officials of local Federal Housing Administration who refused to approve loan application. Visited with and urged officials of Housing and Home Finance Agency and FHA in Washington to approve project which rescinded unfavorable state decision. Compiled information relative to housing conditions and income of Negroes in Metropolitan

Atlanta. Appeared before Fulton County Commissioners to help secure rezoning for apartments and general approval of the project. Assisted project manager in locating office space.[14]

Rezoning was a difficult hurdle because white objectors from as far as two miles away had to be placated. Leverage came from the Negro's revived political participation, as Thompson later noted, but as he also wrote, "probably the most important device in getting approval of the project" was the creation of a twenty-seven-acre industrial zone as a buffer between white and Negro communities. (Such industrial zones had long been used by white Atlanta to maintain residential segregation, wrote Ivan Allen Jr., later Atlanta's mayor, in his 1971 book *Mayor: Notes on the Sixties*.)[15]

In February 1950 Hamilton joined Abram in an appearance before the Fulton County Commission to support the rezoning appeal. One incident at the hearing, in Abram's opinion, illustrated in a nutshell Hamilton's "graciousness and self-denial." Abram had made his presentation to the commission and was ready to introduce Hamilton. He was in a predicament and she knew it. His political ambitions would be at risk if he used the polite title in presenting her, for Georgians of the dominant society still expected its public officials to adhere to norms of white supremacy. Privately whispering to him, she said, "Let me introduce myself." Abram assented, thus sparing himself political liability. (It was to no ultimate avail, as he failed in his 1954 bid for Congress; Abram left Georgia thereafter for a prosperous legal career in New York and service on civil and human rights commissions under Presidents Jimmy Carter and Ronald Reagan.) Against the pleas of more than a hundred white protesters, the commission was assured of Highpoint's worth and voted unanimous approval of the project.[16]

The most difficult task of all was obtaining federal mortgage insurance because of the FHA's aversion to lending for Negro housing. Harold Fleming, in an article on Highpoint published by *Survey* magazine in September 1951, told this story: "FHA, which had previously approved only twenty-four dwelling units for Atlanta Negroes, was doubtful that such a development would ever pay for itself. Few Negroes, the objection ran, would be willing to pay rents as high as $45 and $55 a month, however attractive the apartments and their surroundings. Even Negroes of moderately high incomes have traditionally lived in substandard neighborhoods. Who was to say that they didn't prefer it that way?"[17]

In repeated trips to Washington, Hamilton, Thompson, Abram, and Howell, accompanied on one trip by Dorothy Rogers Tilly of the Southern

Regional Council and onetime member of the AUL board, pointed out that Atlanta's ghettoes were created by white restrictions, not by Negro choice. The FHA finally conceded the point.

Within a year Highpoint was fully occupied, showing that Negro families were not in the least reluctant or unable to pay medium rent for a comfortable place to live. A modern shopping center, a church, and a recreation area for the development's children were later constructed, adding to Highpoint's attractions and its value as a community.

The AUL agreed to become a "sponsor" for Fairhaven, built on land owned by Negroes. Thompson described it in a cryptic overview in his 1951 report: "Made land ownership analysis of large area. Persuaded property owners to subdivide property. Secured bids from engineer on cost of subdividing land. Consulted architects. Contacted Life Insurance companies relative to proposed development and financing of project. Secured commitment from Life Insurance Company of Georgia to finance entire project. Persuaded Insurance Company to use Negro realty company for purpose of processing FHA applications and to collect monthly premiums. Negotiated agreement between property owners and construction corporation for the erection of homes. Property owners appointed the Atlanta Urban League as sponsor." [18]

Fairhaven was an example of the integrated approach so valued by Grace Hamilton—the land was owned by Negroes, the builders were white and Negro, and the money came from white lending institutions. Thompson also personally valued Fairhaven; he bought a home there, which he still occupied when interviewed for this book.

· · ·

Estimates vary and no official count was ever made, but the Atlanta Urban League under Grace Hamilton believed it was responsible for nearly half the 10,550 housing units for Negroes constructed in greater Atlanta between 1945 and 1956. Twenty-nine housing subdivisions went up in that period, and the AUL was involved to some degree in seventeen of them. These subdivisions were by and for Negroes, who contributed as developers, contractors, real estate brokers, and financiers. Black financial institutions provided early loan money, but once they had demonstrated the creditworthiness of the Negro market, white banks quickly joined in to supply new black borrowers.

Of the new contruction, two thousand units were public housing built by the Atlanta Housing Authority with aid from the federal government, but these agencies had long been generous to Atlanta's black poor, favoring them over whites in project construction. Although the AUL urged and facilitated location of the new public projects, its major effort between 1945 and 1956 was devoted to housing those of middle income, for whom little had been built in Atlanta in the previous century. By 1958 the community's efforts were beginning to pay off, as a syndicated journalist wrote from Atlanta: "Gone are the days when the only place a Negro of average means could find to live here was a tumble-down shack, a cracked-plaster walkup apartment or in a kind of squalid settlement that has been labelled since Reconstruction times as 'nigger town'. A Negro can stand at a certain spot in Atlanta and as far as the eye can see there is space for him to live. . . . That's perhaps the most significant victory yet for the Negro in this Deep South metropolis. It was won with very little disturbance and with not a little cooperation from the white citizenry." [19]

By 1960, a housing expert contended that the "quality and quantity of housing in Atlanta for blacks is unsurpassed in the U.S." By 1985, segregated housing was on the wane and the same knowledgeable Negro authority could state with confidence, "There is much more dispersion of minorities in the city of Atlanta, I suspect, than in any other major American city." The catalyst for these changes, it was widely accepted, was the housing program pursued in the 1940s and 1950s by Hamilton's Atlanta Urban League. The *Atlanta Daily World* made the point as early as June 23, 1951, when it wrote in an editorial, "Mrs. Grace Hamilton along with Robert A. Thompson, housing secretary, may be credited with changing the face of residential Atlanta." [20]

· · ·

The AUL's housing successes brought Grace Hamilton accolades from the Atlanta press, praise accorded in terms of unprecedented courtesy and respect. At a time when blacks rarely ever appeared by name in white newspapers and the courtesy title before a Negro's name was a rarity, press coverage of Highpoint was extensive and she was always referred to as "Mrs. Grace Hamilton." Praising her "idealism," reporter Robert McKee, writing in the *Atlanta Journal-Constitution*, called her the "driving force behind the new housing development for Atlanta's growing Negro middle class" and, further, he called her fight for Negro housing "the most important and constructive thing that happened in Atlanta in 1950." McKee's story was reprinted by *This Week* magazine, a national publication. [21]

Hamilton's response was typical of her integrationist approach. "Honest cooperation of white persons and Negroes all along the line has made the new housing possible," she said. "This cooperation has proved its worth. We hope there will be a great deal more of it in the future." [22]

Thompson was overlooked in early public notices, but the Negro community recognized his work at the AUL, giving him the "27" Club's 1954 award "for leadership in securing better housing facilities, more educational opportunities and a wider active voter participation." That Hamilton got the spotlight on housing irked Thompson's wife, as he made clear in interviews for this book, though he himself denied feeling any resentment. Hamilton in later years repeatedly acknowledged the value of his work, as she did in 1976, when historian Jacquelyn Hall asked her to describe her housing work at the AUL. "Oh, that's a big story," she said to Hall. "I can't tell you about it. I have to go and let you talk to Tommy on that." In private at least she never failed to give him a lion's share of the credit. If in public the accolades went to her, there was little she could do to prevent it. After all, at the AUL she was still "very much in charge." [23]

Atlanta University College graduates, Class of 1894: front row,
Nathaniel W. Collier, George A. Towns, Samuel Stripling, John D. Jackson;
back row: James W. Johnson, James T. Hodges, Benjamin F. Allen
(courtesy Atlanta University Archives, Class Photographs,
The Atlanta University Center, Woodruff Library)

Harriet Cherry McNair (Hattie),
1856–1920, Grace Towns Hamilton's
grandmother (courtesy Grace Towns
Hamilton family collection)

The Alexander Hamilton family, circa 1913: Alexander Hamilton Jr. and
his wife Nettie Cooke Hamilton; their children, Alexander III, Eunice,
Theron Bertram, Henry Cooke, Marion, Nelle Marie, and Joe Tom
(courtesy the Herndon Foundation)

Family gathering, circa 1917, on the porch of Towns home: George Towns,
George Jr., Harriet Cherry McNair, Myron, Nellie McNair Towns, and Grace
(courtesy Grace Towns Hamilton family collection)

Professor George A. Towns, circa 1917
(courtesy Grace Towns Hamilton
family collection)

Myron, Grace, and George Towns Jr., children of George A. and
Nellie McNair Towns, on the porch of the family home at 594 University Place,
Atlanta, circa 1917 (courtesy Grace Towns Hamilton family collection)

Grace Towns, circa 1928
(courtesy Grace Towns Hamilton
family collection)

Grace Towns Hamilton
and daughter, Eleanor,
circa 1932 (courtesy Grace
Towns Hamilton family
collection)

Grace Towns Hamilton,
circa 1937 (courtesy Grace Towns
Hamilton family collection)

Grace Towns Hamilton,
circa 1950 (courtesy Grace Towns
Hamilton family collection)

Grace Towns Hamilton and the Atlanta Urban League staff, 1951: C. D. Coleman
(community organization secretary), Mrs. Myrtle Mickens (office secretary),
James D. Martin (office manager), Grace Towns Hamilton (executive director),
R. A. Thompson (housing secretary), Mrs. A. Lamar Robinson (office secretary)
(courtesy Robert A. Thompson)

Grace pins a rose from the garden on
her husband's lapel, election year 1965
(*Atlanta Journal-Constitution*
staff photo)

Dr. Henry Cooke Hamilton chalks
his favorite billiard cue
(*Atlanta Journal-Constitution*
staff photo, courtesy Grace Towns
Hamilton family collection)

Portrait of
George Washington Towns
(courtesy Office of Georgia
Secretary of State)

Grace Towns Hamilton with
school children from her legislative
district in front of the portrait of
George Washington Towns on the
main floor of Georgia's capitol building
(courtesy Grace Towns Hamilton
family collection)

Atlanta Journal-Constitution
columnist Celestine Sibley, Grace
Towns Hamilton, and Dorothy Spence,
executive director of the Georgia
Association American Institute
of Architects, circa 1972 (courtesy
Grace Towns Hamilton family
collection)

Grace Towns Hamilton
in the House Chamber, circa 1975

Grace Towns Hamilton signs letters
at her legislative desk, circa 1981
(courtesy Grace Towns Hamilton
family collection)

Grace Towns Hamilton with legislators Calvin Smyre and J. C. Daugherty,
circa 1979 (House photographer, Georgia House of Representatives)

Grace Towns Hamilton, having served in the House for eighteen years,
gets a hug at the State Capitol from Speaker Thomas B. Murphy when
a resolution was offered in her honor by Representative Lorenzo Benn (left),
March 1985 (*Atlanta Journal-Constitution* staff photo)

Grace Towns Hamilton with
Rev. Austin Ford and Jane Maguire
Abram (right), 1989
(courtesy Atlanta History Center)

Eleanor and a portrait of her mother, 1989
(courtesy Museum Services, Georgia State Capital)

7

At the AUL: Equalizing Funds for
Negro Schools and the Rebirth
of Negro Voting

. . .

ESPITE the distance Grace Hamilton would eventually put between the Atlanta Urban League and its parent body in New York,
she always fully shared the national organization's faith in the
power of facts and its conviction that the key to changing racial injustices
lay in educating whites to their existence. She put the AUL in the business
of what she called "preventive social work"—a term not used before by the
NUL—but her tools were those it favored: research, education, and interracial cooperation.

"All community efforts to make for change," she later said, "had to begin by describing what was. . . . We worked on the theory that you gathered
an objective description of the situation and then put together a citizens
group for public education, to disseminate the information gathered in the
report." Once the (white) public knew the facts, she was profoundly convinced that corrective action would follow.[1]

Hamilton also deeply believed in the founding tenet of the NUL, that
without interracial cooperation the black cause was doomed. Upon arriving at the Atlanta Urban League and finding "it was just a staff operated
thing," she devoted much time to what she called "promoting the interracial character" of the AUL's Board of Directors, to giving the agency a
"board that included all the people you needed to do what you said you
were existing to do." This meant in practice bringing in more influential
whites.[2]

The board she soon put together included Mrs. Harry M. (Rebecca) Gershon, Mrs. M. E. (Dorothy) Tilly, and Mrs. Devereaux (Dorothy) McClatchey, all whites known for their dedication to good causes. Also on her new board were Rufus E. Clement, president of Atlanta University; Mrs. Benjamin E. Mays, wife of the president of Morehouse College; Edward M. Kahn of Atlanta's Jewish Welfare Board; and Robert L. Cousins, a white real estate agent. Others were Mrs. C. W. Powell, who with her husband owned Harris Memorial Hospital, a private Negro facility; Alonzo G. Moron, director of a Negro public housing project; A. V. Jett, a black building contractor; P. E. Shulhafer, a white businessman; and Daniel S. Thorpe, a biology instructor at Washington High School. A. T. Walden remained board chairman, Jesse B. Blayton, a professor of accounting at Atlanta University, was vice-chairman, and holdover members from earlier days included Jacob R. Henderson, Solomon W. Walker, and Forrester B. Washington.

She had accomplished her board objective to her satisfaction by June 1944, when the Atlanta Board of Education announced its plan for a $10 million bond issue to finance postwar improvement and expansion of the city's public school facilities, the catalyst that launched Hamilton's first independent project at the League. Changing times offered a new context for tackling old injustices, and the Board of Education's report left Hamilton with her work cut out for her.

Negro schools, serving one-third of the city's school population, were to be allotted one-tenth of the proposed $10 million. It was not the first time the Board of Education had thumbed its nose at Atlanta's Negro population; now it was about to meet a new response.

Segregated schools from their inception after the Civil War had always delivered the Negro a profoundly inferior education, and the later "separate but equal" requirement never altered that fact. Atlanta's Negro schools in 1944 were as disgracefully inadequate as they had been in 1921, when they were studied by George D. Strayer and N. L. Englehardt, Columbia University professors. Typical of their findings at the time was that Negroes— then, as in 1944, constituting more than a third of the school-age population—were served by fifteen, or barely more than 20 percent, of the city's sixty-three public school buildings, a shortfall that was met, as it had been since public education began in the city in 1872, with half-day schooling for Atlanta's black children. Such buildings as were used by blacks, said Strayer and Engelhardt, were overcrowded, in a "wretched state of disrepair," lacked playgrounds, and had "almost no equipment." The professors' indictment was severe. "No plan for adequate housing of colored children has ever existed in Atlanta," they said.[3]

Negro Atlanta had fought as best it could against the outrageous neglect of its children. Nearly impotent politically because they had no vote in the Democratic white primaries that decided southern elections, blacks nevertheless possessed the franchise in general and special elections in which certain city issues were decided. In both 1921 and 1923, when the Atlanta Board of Education proposed bond issues for school construction that slighted Negro needs (but required a majority of all registered voters to pass), the Negro community registered and voted in sufficient numbers to defeat the proposals. Only when white authorities agreed to take black needs at least partially into account did the race allow the issue to pass at the polls. Out of this unique political mobilization came several additional elementary schools and, in 1924, Booker T. Washington High School, the first Negro high school in Atlanta. Now the city's educational authorities were once again giving blacks a walk-on part in the school drama. The Atlanta Urban League, hardly even a bit player in the earlier confrontations, moved to center stage under Hamilton's direction.[4]

Upon reading the board's bond proposal, Hamilton immediately put the Atlanta Urban League to work; her own role was primarily to find experts to conduct the study—"finding people interested in helping get the job done," as she put it—and then to administer and coordinate the results of their work. The experts she found included Alfonso Elder, director of Atlanta University's School of Education, C. L. Harper, president of the Georgia State Teachers Association, Ira Reid, at that time chairman of Atlanta University's Department of Sociology (having recently succeeded Du Bois), and her own husband, Henry Cooke Hamilton, then professor of education at Atlanta University. The researchers issued their findings report in December 1944, and, unsurprisingly, they revealed a situation scarcely different from that Strayer and Engelhardt had described twenty years before. Buildings were still shockingly scarce, and half-day sessions for Negro pupils were nearly universal, giving blacks little more than half the instruction accorded whites. The situation faithfully reflected the statistical disparities in per pupil expenditure—$37.80 for Negroes as against $108.70 for whites—and investment in school property—$2,156 for whites as against $887 for each Negro child. The Negro-white disparity had indeed worsened. For instance, in 1944 Negroes had only thirteen buildings, instead of the fifteen they occupied in 1921, while white children now had sixty-five.

Every white elementary school had a kindergarten; black schools had none. Even where the racial divide was best bridged, in the area of teacher training and experience, equality was effectively canceled out by Negro teachers' lower pay, combined with the longer hours and greater pupil loads imposed on them by the double sessions. The AUL report summarized the situation in one poignant paragraph: "The educational program offered by (Atlanta) to Negro children who spend about half of a school day in buildings without attractive libraries [where there is one], without sanitary, supervised cafeterias [where there is one], without places for school and community assemblies, and without adequate space and equipment for wholesome supervised play can be at best mediocre. Its debit cost is computed daily in personal maladjustments, social disorganization and crime." The report neglected to mention that not one Negro school had a gymnasium.[5]

Nor did Grace Hamilton in introducing the report dwell on the shameful side of the story. Her foreword made up in simple sincerity for what it lacked in passion, underscoring her own belief in objective fact as a catalyst for community understanding and action. "It is believed," she wrote, "that the lack of facilities existing in the public schools for Negroes in Atlanta is not generally known. All citizens, therefore, do not realize the enormous waste of human resources which is taking place within the community. . . . [This report] is published by the Atlanta Urban League in order that the findings may be available for consideration by all who are concerned with the welfare of the community. It is presented with the hope that there may be increased interest and effort to secure for all children equal educational opportunity." Segregation was nowhere challenged in the report; it sought equality of opportunity for Negro children, no more. Neither then nor at any later time would Grace Towns Hamilton associate the AUL with an attack on segregation. Her justification was unapologetic: "It was the law at that time" and had to be obeyed.[6]

Once the report was published, disseminating the facts was uppermost on Hamilton's agenda, and when she later recalled the time, she used gentle words to describe her line of action:

> We decided to do this very careful analysis of the needs of the Negro schools. Which we did and published it. And then we organized the Citizens Committee for Public Education. And tried to make the information from the study widely disseminated over the community, with the objective to force the Board of Education to make a difference in its bond issue. One of the directors of J. Walter Thompson [a well-known New York advertising agency] offered to help prepare what we called public education material. And then

we got all kinds of groups in Atlanta at least exposed to the material. I guess that's how I learned about the impact you can make on public bodies if enough people really know the facts.[7]

Walter O'Meara was the "man in Atlanta" from the J. Walter Thompson agency; Eugene M. Martin, an officer of the Atlanta Life Insurance Company, was chairman of the Citizens Committee on Public Education, Joseph Pierce was its secretary, and J. H. Calhoun its treasurer. Committee members were drawn from sixty organizations, both white and black, including the NAACP, the Committee for Georgia, parent-teacher associations, church groups, fraternities and sororities, clubs, and labor unions. Charged with the task of "building public opinion," the committee worked quietly and methodically, appearing before the Board of Education with resolutions. It also brought the board petitions obtained in the white community as well as the black, circulated the "public education material" Walter O'Meara was turning out behind the scenes, and lent its name to further reports from the AUL that kept before the public the facts of neglected educational needs in the Negro community. More than 250,000 brochures and pamphlets designed by O'Meara were scattered across Atlanta in 1945. A sophisticated New Yorker, he would later write to Hamilton, "My own small part, insignificant as it was, in the Atlanta school campaign was one of the most satisfying experiences of my life."[8]

The Atlanta Board of Education at first seemed barely moved. It refused to answer the report outright but gave it backhanded recognition in 1945 by opening two kindergartens for Negroes; by 1948 it had opened another two and was finally employing Negro clerks at all black elementary schools. Meantime, pressures on the board were multiplying from a variety of directions. In the Citizens Committee, as a historian for the Atlanta Public School System wrote in 1972, the "Atlanta Urban League had constructed a strong coalition of black groups in support of the [equalization] principle," and the group's recognized force lent weight to the fact that some of its members, more aggressive than Grace Towns Hamilton, wanted to institute legal action against the Board of Education. Even though the committee outwardly adhered to Hamilton's more benign strategy of public education, its legal counsel searched for possible plaintiffs among Negro parents and had many takers, laying the groundwork for a legal challenge to segregation.[9]

Just as important, the report had aroused interest in Atlanta's white press, normally indifferent to concerns of the Negro community. The *Atlanta World*, the Negro newspaper, naturally lauded the report, calling it a "unique service to the Negro people of Atlanta and a distinct challenge to the conscience of whites." The *Atlanta Journal* made clear that the white conscience had been touched. "While the facts are unpleasant," wrote the *Journal* editorialist, "we think they deserve the public's attention as well as that of the Board of Education. If Atlanta is duly to progress, the progress will have to be measured in terms of her entire population, not in terms of two-thirds." [10]

The *Atlanta Constitution* defended segregation but said it "was never meant to mean, as it so often means, discrimination against and exploitation of Negro citizens," and conceded that "a beginning should be made toward solving this, one of our great problems of justice and right, looking toward the improvement of the whole community." Newspapers as far away as Milwaukee, St. Louis, and Pittsburgh praised the AUL and its work. The *Milwaukee Journal* commented that a southern voice such as the *Atlanta Journal*'s, condemning the situation and demanding improvement, "has long been needed, more power to it." It was in fact the beginning of Hamilton's extraordinarily favorable relationship with Atlanta's public media. When she discussed the school report in an address to the Southern Negro Youth Conference in early December 1944, the *Atlanta Constitution* covered the event with a four-paragraph story. So did the *Atlanta Journal*. It was Hamilton's first appearance in the city's white press, but southern custom forbidding courtesy titles for Negroes was carefully observed. Her name was given in full at the outset without the courtesy title; thereafter Hamilton was referred to only as "she." Persistence of the pronoun for another three paragraphs must have seemed awkward both to writer and reader. [11]

But there was another pressure at work on the school situation, one stronger than all the others combined, and that came from the federal government, more specifically from the U.S. Supreme Court, which in 1944 had overturned the Democratic Party's white primary. The Atlanta Urban League, even as it molded public opinion on the issue of neglected Negro schooling, was spearheading a massive, well-organized, and emotionally charged registration drive aiming to bring Negroes back into Georgia politics at all levels. O'Meara's pamphlets and brochures were cast broadside about Atlanta's black and white communities, but those scattered in predominantly Negro areas reminded readers that only registered voters would have a voice when the school bond issue went to the polls. In response to this and other appeals, Negroes were signing up to vote as never before.

Desperate for the bond issue that would finance school improvements long deferred by World War II, the Board of Education did not fail to take notice. *From Ivy Street to Kennedy Center, Centennial History of the Atlanta Public School System*, written in 1972, made it clear that the new Negro voter was the decisive factor in the board's ultimate capitulation to AUL demands; it also offered a succinct description of how it happened:

> In the Spring of 1946, the [Atlanta Urban] League conducted a strong voter registration drive which had immense implications for the forthcoming bond election. Then, at that precise moment—April 1, 1946—the courts declared unconstitutional the white primary in Georgia. (Of course, after the decision of the U.S. Supreme Court in the case of *Smith v. Allwright* in 1944 declaring the white primary in Texas unconstitutional, everyone recognized that it was just a matter of time until all similar laws were struck down.) This turn of events made the black vote even more significant. The Board began to consider the implications of all these factors and the danger of losing everything. It came up with a new bond proposal in April which recognized the demands of the black community for its proportionate share—approximately 30 percent—of the facilities to be constructed after the issuance of the bonds." [12]

Having never in its history spent more than 16 percent of its budget on Negro schools—often it was nearer 10 percent—the Atlanta School Board finally squared its mathematics with the "separate but equal" doctrine and sent to the polls a school bond issue pegged at $9.97 million, $3.1 million of it earmarked for blacks. It was approved by a ten-to-one margin on August 14, 1946.

But the board's habit of slighting Negroes was ingrained. Knowing a watchful eye was essential, Hamilton at the AUL issued a supplemental report in 1948, and it offered little good news; indeed, far from a decrease, it found a steady increase in the differential between average expenditures for white and Negro children. Work on promised new school buildings for blacks and additions to old ones had not begun, leaving all but a handful of Atlanta's black children still on half-day schooling, while whites, little plagued by shortages in the first place, were already enjoying new facilities. "Atlanta Public schools," said the new report, "offer little encouragement to the Negro school child, especially at the elementary level." Two years later, high school plans for Negroes had taken a new slide in comparison with those for whites (a reflection certainly of the spurt in building of facilities for whites occasioned by the new bond issue), a slide so severe it more than offset the slight concurrent decrease in inequality at the elementary level. Analyzing the data in a public statement of August 15, 1950, the AUL pointed out that the overall gap between the races in per-pupil expenditure for school facilities obviously was widening.[13]

It is small wonder then that Atlanta awoke September 19, 1950, to find its Board of Education the defendant in a suit challenging segregation. Equalization had been tried to no avail; now the old separate but equal doctrine, guide to racial accommodation in the South for half a century, had become the target. More than two hundred Negro children were listed as plaintiffs; some of their parents had signed petitions circulated four years before by the AUL's Citizens Committee on Public Education. The Atlanta suit, the first challenging Jim Crow schools in a major city (the only other comparable attack was then pending in Clarendon County, South Carolina), would not be among the five cases jointly decided by the Supreme Court in 1954 when, in *Brown* v. *Topeka Board of Education*, it struck down segregation in public schools. (The Clarendon County case was one of the five.) Attorneys for the Negro plaintiffs in the Atlanta suit were A. T. Walden, E. E. Moore Jr., S. S. Robinson, and R. E. Thomas Jr., all of Atlanta, while Thurgood Marshall and Robert L. Carter of New York, NAACP attorneys, were listed as co-counsel.

. . .

As a "private social welfare agency" that had "long studied and sought improvement in Negro education," the AUL was immediately "flooded with requests for information on the relative status of Negro and white schools in the city," Hamilton reported in a public statement on September 22. Her response to this "public demand" was a simple reiteration of the glaring and growing disparity between Negro and white schools as just disclosed in the AUL's August analysis. Grace Hamilton also felt it wise at the same time to point out that "the Atlanta Urban League is not associated with the present court action in any way," a caution compelled by her agency's dependence on Community Chest funding. The disclaimer was a trifle disingenuous, given the AUL's connection with the very actions from which the suit had sprung. Nevertheless, Hamilton was now a recognized member of Atlanta's Negro leadership, thanks to her role in forcing the city's school board to surrender on the bond issue. The Omega Psi fraternity named her "most useful citizen for 1945" and the *Atlanta Daily World* lauded the award, saying it expressed "a sentiment universal among colored Atlantans" and adding that "her leadership and direction of the celebrated study of public school facilities for Negroes in Atlanta remains a monumental task never before achieved here or elsewhere in the nation." Atlanta's white power structure, which was undergoing an attitudinal change because of the specter of black ballot power, found Hamilton an acceptable leader at the AUL and was comfortable with her methodical, nonconfrontational approach to solving racial problems. She would later say, "I think what I tried to do is look at the community situation in terms of getting everybody that had a stake in the solution, to consider it without regard to whether they are white or black . . . of course that's not always possible to do, but that was my objective." The time was not yet ripe for the militancy that would erupt in the South a decade later, sweeping aside her cautious approach.[14]

• • •

For Grace Hamilton and her family 1950 was a time of personal change. She and Cookie left her family residence where they had lived since returning to Atlanta in 1941, but the move merely took them next door. Her father, now eighty years old and no longer the avid and active gardener he once was, gave the Hamiltons the portion of his property where he had once grown his vegetables, and there the couple built a modern, one-story home that seemed an anomaly next to the Victorian structure where Grace had grown up and the Herndon Beaux Arts mansion across the street. Eleanor Hamilton was by then attending Smith College, and Grace and her husband were mostly alone in the new dwelling.[15]

• • •

The currents that eddied beneath the outward tranquillity of race relations in Georgia when Grace Hamilton returned to Atlanta in 1941 were by 1950 unmistakably visible upon the surface. World War II had created everywhere a new situation both in racial attitudes and black employment, and an aroused moral concern plus diplomatic and political considerations, added to the rising militancy of blacks themselves, had put racial advancement once again on the national agenda. The Fair Employment Practices Commission, itself a product of the new Negro spirit, gave the Urban League an added tool for pushing job placement, while the U.S. Supreme Court and later President Harry S. Truman for the first time since Reconstruction stamped the cause of civil rights, long the province solely of the NAACP, with the imprimatur of the federal government.

In Georgia, Negro leaders believed black empowerment lay in the ballot, and the ink had scarcely dried on *Smith* v. *Allwright*, the Supreme Court's 1944 decision finally felling the Democratic Party's white primary, when A. T. Walden, Grace Towns Hamilton, and like-minded colleagues went into action, producing a registration campaign that was and still remains unique in the state's African American history. Georgia's party rulers at first evaded the verdict, saying that because *Smith* v. *Allwright* was a Texas case, it did not apply to them. But Primus King, a black preacher-barber from Columbus, soon tested this assumption in federal court, and *King* v. *Chapman*, a Supreme Court decision rendered April 1, 1946, officially gave blacks the right to vote in Georgia's Democratic primaries, the only elections that counted in the state. In the intervening two years, while whites scarcely noticed, Walden organized registration committees throughout the state, bringing them together for added clout in what he called the Georgia Association of Citizens Democratic Clubs. The registration drive proceeded slowly at first, but it soon found a powerful and welcome ally in Ellis Arnall, Georgia's young reformist governor, who in 1945 brought the state a new constitution which, among other things, lowered the voting age from twenty-one to eighteen years and abolished the poll tax. Under this spur, registration in the state inched upward, and in Atlanta it stood at about three thousand when, unexpectedly, Atlanta's congressman resigned and Governor Arnall called a special election for February 12, 1946, to fill the unexpired term.

Negroes could vote in special elections, and as the election date was the birthday of Abraham Lincoln, the great emancipator, Atlanta's Negroes were seized with "registration fever" as never before, though the upward curve of the fever chart was aided by the work of the NAACP, the Atlanta Civic and Political League, headed by Republican John Wesley Dobbs, and the *Atlanta Daily World*. By election day, the number of eligible Negro voters in the city had more than doubled to nearly seven thousand, and much the same dramatic climb was occurring elsewhere in the state. Had the leading candidate, the congressman's chosen successor, wished it, Democratic Party leaders in the Atlanta congressional district might have held a white primary (*King* v. *Chapman* was still in the offing) in advance of the special election, but Thomas Camp, who bore the mantle, believed he needed no such aid to victory. Among his many opponents was Helen Douglas Mankin, a popular Georgia legislator long associated with child welfare, social service, and labor legislation. It developed during the short race that she, alone among the significant candidates, was willing to seek Negro support. Now welded together in a substantial voting bloc, Negroes rallied to her cause, and when the votes were counted the night of February 12, she won by a mere 710 votes. The leading candidate held a margin of 146 votes until the all-Negro precinct 3-B on Ashby Street reported nearly 956 votes for Mankin. For the first time since Reconstruction, Negro votes had turned an election—an important election—and the outcome, along with pivotal Negro precinct 3-B, captured national attention. It was a great energizer for the massive registration drive in the Georgia Negro community that followed the fall of the state's white primary on April 1, 1946.[16]

White Atlanta paid scant attention to the Mankin election until it was over. But in the black community, whose leaders had discreetly promoted the Mankin candidacy precisely to keep the white world unaware, the outcome was a cause of celebration. Grace Towns Hamilton would remember vividly all her life the family scene before the radio as they waited tensely for the election results and the rejoicing that followed the announcement of Mankin's (and, by extension, the Negro's) victory. Whites would soon write finis to the political career of Helen Douglas Mankin, but her name would remain for years a special memory among Atlanta Negroes.

The AUL had been only peripherally involved in the registration campaign that preceded the unique race; now Hamilton moved with fellow Negro leaders to bring it directly into action. No one, white or black, doubted that Georgia Negroes were on the verge of regaining a full and unfettered franchise and the Mankin race had fully exposed the possibilities. The challenge was to overcome Negro apathy and get the race to the polls. The course Hamilton charted for her agency "was a little unusual for the League," but it was "preventive social work" at its best, in her view. As yet, Walden's statewide registration campaign had scarcely touched the masses; Hamilton felt the time had come to harness their energies, that the momentum of the Mankin-Negro victory had put the "masses in the mood." An intensive registration drive, directed by a community organization operating under the wing of the NAACP, was quickly set in motion. The League had to be discreet about its involvement because the Community Chest, its funding source, frowned on political as opposed to educational activities. "The League did not do that as the League, we provided the Secretariat and most of the analysis," she pointed out years later. Hamilton's recollections so long afterward apparently still reflected Chest restrictions. It was little more than a fiction, even in 1946, of course, because the aim of Hamilton and all her colleagues was political indeed.[17]

In the immediate offing was a Democratic Party primary in July 1946 where the black vote, if exercised in sufficient numbers, could profoundly influence racial politics. Eugene Talmadge, whom Arnall had replaced as governor in 1943, was running for the office again, this time against a surrogate for Arnall, who could not succeed himself. Talmadge's racism was palpable and famous, and his defeat, if accomplished at the hands of Negro voters, would be a racial victory of unparalleled importance. Within days of the Mankin victory, Grace Hamilton was meeting with her colleagues to plan what they would call the All-Citizens Registration Committee.

"I can remember the little group," she recounted years later; "there were just four of us, Bacote [C. A. Bacote], Tommy [Robert Thompson], and Jake [Jacob Henderson]. We met at Jake's house, maps spread all over the living room floor.... It was no one person's idea, it was all our idea.... We put together a very diverse group of people who worked in various organizations and it's the only time to my knowledge, in all the time before or since, when we got the cooperation of church leadership, the fraternity leadership, the business community, everybody. Whites were not really involved. It was something we felt we had to do for ourselves." Indeed, the "masses were in the mood," and the intensity of Atlanta's effort and the unity it generated was matched in other areas throughout the state. The All-Citizens Registration Committee was announced to the public at the Butler Street YMCA on March 6, 1946. "The preliminary work had been done but we wanted a public meeting, a public launching," Hamilton recalled. "It was all cut and dried, everybody knew just what they were going to say. Mr. Dobbs [John Wesley Dobbs] got up and held forth on why we didn't need another organization. They just let him get through and then somebody made the motion, and it passed and that was that." [18]

With Bacote as chairman and David Watson as executive secretary, the All-Citizens Registration Committee moved into high gear. "So many people were involved," Grace Hamilton remembered. "I think that was the heart of the matter, I mean really involved, you know, thinking about how to do it . . . we had a strategy meeting every Saturday down at the League." Thompson, for the League, opened the way to the campaign's success by identifying, through the use of census tracts, all 1,162 blocks where Atlanta blacks lived; 870 volunteers then visited each block urging the inhabitants to register. It was a saturation technique that paid off. "Every house was contacted, not only once but twice," Hamilton recalled. "We couldn't have done it without this widespread group of manpower." [19]

Bacote, writing an account of the campaign for Atlanta University's *Phylon* magazine, added to the story:

> Mr. David Watson was responsible for supervising the activities of all the workers in the field, for arranging mass meetings, for distributing literature, and for watching the progress of registration at the Courthouse . . . 50,000

handbills and 300 placards explaining the registration procedure were distributed. Several thousand stickers with the words "We are registered voters" were placed on home doors. . . . Volunteer workers were stationed at the Courthouse to direct people to the registration office. . . . Car pools were formed to take people to the Courthouse. A speaker's bureau provided speakers at churches, social affairs, public dances. . . . Boy Scouts distributed literature throughout the city.

The *Atlanta Daily World* pushed registration in editorials and news stories, businesses such as the Atlanta Life Insurance Company pushed registration among their employees, and college fraternities and sororities adopted registration as special projects. Baptist ministers Martin Luther King Sr. and William Holmes Borders and most other church pastors of Negro Atlanta devoted sermons to the cause, giving recognition each Sunday to the newly registered in their congregations and transporting members to register at the courthouse. So effective was this drive Hamilton and her colleagues had initiated that crowds became too heavy to handle at the registrar's office; special stations had to be set up throughout the Negro community, and even so hundreds had to be turned away at the end of the day. On May 4, when registration was officially closed, 24,137 Negro voters were on the books in Fulton County alone, up from 7,000 in February. Statewide, thanks to other efforts as successful as Atlanta's, between 118,000 and 134,000 blacks (depending on the estimate's source) were qualified for the franchise, approximately 20 percent of the adult black population, a Negro registration far surpassing that of any other southern state. And nearly 70 percent of the registered Negroes voted on July 17, 1946, in the integrated Democratic primary, the first of the century in Georgia, a vote most probably cast in a block against Eugene Talmadge. It was a vote in vain.[20]

Talmadge lost the popular election, falling ten thousand votes short of the tally for Arnall's surrogate, but he snatched victory from the jaws of defeat thanks to Georgia's peculiar, rural-weighted county unit system. The mechanism that had long decided Georgia elections, the county unit system, placed predominant political power in the hands of white country folk, and it was in these counties, where Talmadge counted on gaining the winning unit votes in the election, that his forces engaged in a systematic preelection purge of the voting lists. The U.S. Department of Justice warned that it would prosecute purgers, the Federal Bureau of Investigation actually made some probes, some purged voters indeed were restored to the rolls, and the total number purged was not massive in relation to the total Negro registrants. But the effectiveness of the Talmadge forays lay in their strategic concentration; Talmadge probably owed his victory to a few small counties with an impressive total of unit votes, where Negroes were eliminated as a force from the voting rolls. With Talmadge in office again (succeeded later by his son Herman), racism again ruled the state. Once developed in 1946, as one historian wrote, "purge techniques were more effective in 1948 and by the mid-fifties had become standard procedure in rural counties." Black registration both in Atlanta and Georgia grew little in the decade after the dramatic surge in 1946. The purge was only one explanation; the Negro's own waning enthusiasm for the ballot was another, for it had failed to deliver the empowerment black leaders had promised. Even the Atlanta school board's apparent capitulation on the bond issue, attributable in part, or so it was thought, to the Negro's newly revived franchise, had failed to bring the promised improvements in Negro schools. Rural Negro voters faced harassment, both legal and illegal, and in the countryside, lynching made a comeback. The result was renewed apathy in the Negro community. The best that could be said in retrospect for the 1946 drive, the same historian thought, was that it "illustrated the ability of the black community to come together to work for racial justice."[21]

8

A Hospital for the Excluded and the "Hidden Agenda"

. . .

ACIAL solidarity and electoral enthusiasm were an inadequate match for the continuing power of white supremacy in the Deep South, and Negroes still found their progress against injustice limited by what the ruling race was willing to allow. Grace Towns Hamilton had a run-in with this reality in her next project at the Atlanta Urban League, the up-front objective of which was a tax-supported hospital for nonindigent Atlanta Negroes. Exposing the poignant facts, as it had done in bringing Atlanta's school inequities to light, the AUL under Hamilton's guidance issued a study in December 1947 called "A Report on Hospital Care of the Negro Population of Atlanta, Georgia," expecting a public enlightened by the shocking chronicle to remedy the injustices. And as was true with the schools, there was much injustice to remedy. Other than the penniless, Negroes had always been barred from white hospitals in the South, even in dire emergencies. In Atlanta, where the nonindigent made up well over half the city's black population, including an economic and social elite of exceptional note, three Negro-owned proprietary hospitals with eighty-seven beds, generally poorly equipped facilities, served these seventy thousand to ninety thousand people. The poorest blacks had always been cared for at Grady Memorial Hospital, the city's public facility, though the three hundred beds set aside for them by 1947 were inadequate to meet the need.[1]

At every level, the health of Atlanta's Negro population compared unfavorably with that of the white population, but shameful as this disparity was, the exclusion of the nonindigent from the city's hospitals was a running scandal largely unknown or ignored in the white world. The cruel reality surfaced only when some known person died for lack of elementary care in an emergency. White consciences were stirred for a time by the fate of Juliette Derricotte, of Athens, Georgia, Hamilton's friend and onetime colleague in the YWCA, who at the time of her death was dean of women at Fisk University. She was injured in a car accident outside Dalton, Georgia, in November 1931. Immediate and skilled hospital attention might have saved her, but Dalton's well-equipped general hospital did not "receive" blacks. Derricotte died in nearby Chattanooga, Tennessee, in a Negro hospital that lacked x-ray equipment. The YWCA and the NAACP investigated and publicized their findings, but the tragedy produced no changes and was soon forgotten.[2]

The task of arousing public action on the facts of medical care was entrusted to a biracial citizens committee of distinguished Atlantans. (Significantly, Hamilton in 1947 received from the Julius Rosenwald Fund, noted for its investment in Negro advancement, a Rosenwald Fellowship [usually amounting to about $1,200] for developing "community organization for intergroup cooperation"; it was meant to further work she was already doing.) R. Hugh Wood, dean of Emory University's School of Medicine, Benjamin E. Mays, president of Morehouse College, and Rufus E. Clement, president of Atlanta University, were among those enlisted in the cause, much to Hamilton's satisfaction. Revealing elation, even as she covered it with characteristic moderation, she summarized her year in a letter to "dear friends" at Christmas 1947: "My own project has been finishing the 'Report on Hospital Care of Negroes in Atlanta.' We hope to send it to the printers this week, and the first Citizens Committee meeting will be held on Thursday. I hope that the committee will want to do a public opinion building program on the needs after the report is released about the middle of January."[3]

As she hoped, the Citizens Committee made a quick and promising start on the immediate objective, a Negro "pay" hospital. Had that hospital been the project's sole goal, it would have been an unqualified success. But the project aimed higher. As Hamilton put it years later, "Our hidden agenda was to provide a means of cracking the door at Grady-Emory." Grady Hospital was a teaching hospital, medically administered by Emory University's School of Medicine, and in 1947, when the Hamilton-AUL project was launched, Emory barred all blacks—it always had—and Grady, though caring for the poorest Negroes, admitted no black interns, residents, or physicians in any of its clinics. The city's Negro physicians could neither practice nor obtain postgraduate training at Grady or in any other hospital in the city. Prevented from developing their talents or keeping up with their profession, Negro physicians shied away from Atlanta, making it difficult to increase the number upon whom the majority of the city's black population depended for medical care. In June 1947 Atlanta had only thirty-seven Negro doctors (twenty of whom were over fifty-five years of age), or a ratio of one to every 3,368 persons, far below the accepted standard of one to each 1,000 to 1,500 persons. The scarcity was both regionwide and threatening to grow larger as the Negro population increased. In the Deep South, all twenty-six medical schools, more than a third of the nation's medical training facilities, were for whites only; even among the seventy-five non-segregated schools elsewhere, only twelve Negroes in 1946 were enrolled among thirty thousand students. Over 90 percent of all Negro physicians were then graduated from Meharry Medical College in Nashville, Tennessee, and Howard University's School of Medicine in Washington, D.C. Given their exclusion from southern institutions and their sparse presence in all others except their own, the number of Negro medical graduates in 1947 barely equaled the number of Negro physicians who died. Hamilton and Atlanta's Negro community were tackling a problem overripe for redress; in return for accepting segregation of the facility, a compromise unwelcome to many, they sought "a pay hospital for Negroes . . . located in geographical proximity to Grady Memorial Hospital" that would have a training program "under the teaching jurisdiction of Emory University." They were even willing to confine Negro trainees to the Negro wards of Grady. It was, indeed, a moderate and just aim, but "cracking the door at Emory-Grady," even ever so little, appeared to be an attack on segregation itself, and white Atlanta in the mid-1940s was not ready for it.[4]

The "pay" hospital for blacks was easily achieved because white Atlanta was at last ready for it, especially inasmuch as federal money had just become available under the Hill-Burton Act of 1946, which appropriated millions to assist states in construction of public hospitals, and more especially because the law, though containing strictures against racial discrimination, specifically condoned separate but equal facilities.

"The people who have the power to bring about changes seem to be interested," Hamilton wrote to an inquirer on December 30, 1947, after the first Citizens Committee meeting. One of those most interested was Hughes

Spalding, chairman of the Fulton-DeKalb Hospital Authority, legal owner and operator of Grady Memorial Hospital. She had wisely also made him a member of the Citizens Committee. Spalding, a leading lawyer in the city and on the boards of two of its most powerful corporations, the Coca-Cola Company and the Trust Company of Georgia, stood at the pinnacle of Atlanta's white power structure. Whether he would have launched the hospital project without prodding from the Hamilton-AUL leadership was never clear; Hamilton said she did not "have any way of knowing, except that he picked up so readily when I talked to him about the idea."[5]

In his own correspondence, Spalding acknowledged that the AUL "initiated" the project, but he also claimed for himself the role of its "chief sponsor," a role Hamilton gladly let him play. "Had he not been in the position he was in, as chairman of the Hospital Authority, even if he'd been in the position of community leadership that he did occupy in general, it might never have come to pass," she recalled. "But he was in a position to pull levers," as Hamilton put it, "and he pulled them from the very beginning." Among other contributions, Spalding's Hospital Authority donated the hospital site, a parcel of land adjacent to Grady, as Hamilton had wanted. As Authority chairman, Spalding cultivated the project among, and won endorsement from, influential entities such as the Fulton and DeKalb County Commissioners—"Sure, build the niggers a hospital," responded DeKalb commissioner Scott Candler—the Fulton County Medical Society, and the city's newspapers and other private opinion molders. He promoted the project in speeches and letters, telling whites, "We have a great responsibility to adequately look after the health of our negro citizens and to make this a better place for them to live in."[6]

He told audiences that the hospital was "a matter of equity, justice and Christian charity," assuring them it also fit within the southern system, that all he sought was that "our Negro citizens ineligible for entrance to the public hospital should have comparable and equal facilities with the other segments of our population." Spalding's devotion to the cause (as he and Hamilton understood it) soon bore fruit. By 1949, all construction money—$1.725 million—was in hand, two-thirds of it federal, the remainder from the state of Georgia and Spalding's Hospital Authority. In recognition of his signal contribution, and after some differences of opinion about who it should memorialize, the new hospital was named Spalding Pavilion and was dedicated and opened for service on May 29, 1952.[7]

However neatly a separate Negro hospital fit into Spalding's scheme of things, however crying the need it met in Atlanta at the time, it amounted to an implicit acceptance of segregation, and the Hamilton-AUL project therefore was not unanimously endorsed by the Negro community, especially its medical members. Hamilton sincerely believed a separate hospital was "a practical step in securing integration in the longer run," but segregation was no longer easy to "sell" in the Negro world. It also must have raised eyebrows at the National Urban League, which enjoined its affiliates to strive for equality, not separateness. If the NUL was disturbed, it never let on, and at this time Lester B. Granger, the NUL's executive secretary, expressed "a very high respect for Mrs. Hamilton's ability" and generally characterized his differences with her as "not only natural but desirable in the kind of free relationship that exists within the Urban League movement." If the NUL did look askance at yet "another Negro hospital as such"—the disapproving words of Dr. W. Montague Cobb, professor of anatomy at Howard University's School of Medicine—its opposition was probably muted in favor of the project's actual, if veiled, effort to whittle away at the segregated walls of Grady-Emory.[8]

· · ·

When G. Lombard Kelly, dean of the University of Georgia's School of Medicine, read the Hamilton-AUL hospital report in 1947, he wrote Hamilton at once, pledging his support for a "common sense solution for this problem" but commenting, "It would be somewhat revolutionary to include Negro trainees in our regularly recognized hospitals." In 1948 in Georgia, Hamilton's goal did in fact approach the "revolutionary," but contrary to her hindsight, it was never a "hidden agenda." Actually, Dr. Charles R. Drew, chief of surgery at Howard University's School of Medicine and probably the most eminent man of medicine in Negro America at the time (he perfected the blood plasma technique that saved thousands of lives in World War II), began as early as 1946 to press just such a course in the South, not only on Dean Kelly but also on the University of Alabama's Medical School. In 1947 he was urging an integrated training program on Paul B. Beeson at Emory University's School of Medicine. Spalding's correspondence on the subject was open and abundant, as was Hamilton's. Writing to Louis T. Wright, a prominent Harlem doctor with roots in Atlanta, after he declined an invitation to speak at the Spalding Pavilion's dedication in 1952, she said, "I believe that we may yet have something here which will help crack the barriers in the medical profession." She replied to the caustic comments of Dr. Cobb at Howard University with assurance that "we expect to continue to press directly for the admission of Negro interns, residents and other staff to the services of Grady, and of course, as directly as we can, for the admission of Negro students to the ranking medical schools of the state."[9]

A stubborn and determined woman once she had set upon a course, she was at the outset, and with some reason, sanguine about its prospects. After all, federal money for the new hospital was granted on the premise that it would teach Negro physicians and allied medical personnel, a premise accepted from the outset both by the Fulton-DeKalb Hospital Authority, Grady's owner, and Emory University's School of Medicine, supervisor of all teaching at Grady. Significantly, such agreements as existed between the Authority and Emory about the training program at Spalding never appeared in a binding contract; the agreement was discussed only in correspondence and written proposals. Speaking for the Hospital Authority, as plans for the new facility were being finalized in July 1948, Spalding wrote: "One of its chief functions will be to train Negro physicians and surgeons. Without this feature it would hardly be worthwhile going on with the subject. As I understand it we have assurances from Emory University that this will be done." Involved in planning the Pavilion from the beginning, Emory had indicated willingness as early as April 1948—"upon proper request"— to assume teaching responsibility at the new hospital. Relying, perhaps naively, on Spalding's "confidence and . . . statements that the necessary arrangements can be achieved," Hamilton wrote exultantly to Channing Tobias, director of the Phelps Stokes Fund and later chairman of the NAACP's Board of Directors, that "it was the first time that Grady authorities have indicated their willingness to proceed with admission of a Negro staff team and Emory University's willingness to assume responsibility is the other encouraging note."[10]

Her hopes were premature, as she might have guessed. Even as Dean Wood of Emory University's School of Medicine told the *Atlanta Journal* in June 1948 that Emory "has assumed responsibility for training the staff of the proposed private Negro hospital," certain faculty members, those most attuned to Negro sensibilities and concerns, tried in vain to get the program off the ground, holding clinics designed to offer postgraduate teaching to Atlanta's thirty-seven Negro physicians, a service supposed to be an integral part of the new training program. Easily the most enthusiastic and sympathetic of the teachers was Hamilton's good friend Dr. Robert P. Grant, and when he left town in early 1950, Negro attendance at these clinics decreased and soon ceased entirely. In 1951, when the new hospital still was under construction, she noted "with some concern" a statement from the

Hospital Authority that "it would be inadvisable and impossible to begin intern and residence training at once." Already the hospital's "purpose," as she (and Spalding, too, apparently) saw it, was under attack. Indeed, Emory drew up plan after plan to implement the promised teaching functions, but it always reneged, pleading lack of personnel or money. By 1953, Spalding himself felt obliged to defend Emory, speciously contending that the teaching program was stalled because Emory's Medical School (led by talented and prestigious professionals in a city "abundantly supplied with knowledge and ways and means in medical education") was "in the dark about . . . how to set it up." In 1958 Spalding would backtrack further, saying the Authority he then still headed had never made a "promise" to start a medical training program at the Pavilion. Dean Wood of Emory by then had already put his finger on the real obstacle. Submitting to the Hospital Authority in April 1954 yet another set of recommendations for the Spalding training program, he noted succinctly: "Eventually ward experience for these interns, already desirable, will prove mandatory. This brings up again the necessity for a policy decision by the Hospital Authority and Emory University as to just how far each institution is willing to go in erasing the color line." So, for nearly six years Jim Crow prevailed and Spalding remained a "teaching" hospital that could not teach. Lacking interns—only one served there in its first three and one-half years of operation, for they resisted recruitment as long as adequate training was unavailable—the Pavilion's service was poor, the patient load accordingly seldom exceeded a third of its capacity, and the facility showed a substantial deficit for a number of years. Closure seemed possible.[11]

Spalding and his Hospital Authority were culpable at least as much as Emory for the failed teaching program, but Hamilton always held Emory primarily to blame. In 1960, making a stern-lipped response to an inquiry about the hospital's history, she wrote: "The Hospital Authority . . . sought and secured federal and state funds to build the Pavilion . . . with the understanding that it would be a 'teaching' unit as Grady Hospital is a 'teaching' hospital . . . and Emory University agreed that the supervision of patient care at the Pavilion and the 'teaching' of Spalding house staff would be conducted as part of the program it conducted at Grady Hospital. When the Pavilion was completed, Emory did not fulfill this commitment." To the same inquirer, Hamilton acknowledged: "The Hospital Authority claimed there were no funds to provide the necessary personnel for patient supervision and teaching." Elsewhere she wrote: "I cannot believe Emory's reluctance to assume the leadership and responsibility for this program is based solely on financial inadequacy. If such were the case, a clear statement of the financial needs involved would be the obvious first step toward securing funds for the undertaking." Emory failed to make such a "clear statement." Even when it was known in the late 1950s that federal funds would be available upon request for the teaching program, Emory refrained from seeking federal money. The sore feelings she held against Emory on this issue remained alive until the end of her life.[12]

She always spared Hughes Spalding from censure on the issue. With him she was understanding, even deferential. When on February 1, 1950, ground was broken for the new hospital and Negroes were neither informed nor invited—only members of the all-white Hospital Authority were present at the event—she spared both Spalding and the Authority from criticism, unlike the *Atlanta Daily World*, which editorialized indignantly against both. Hamilton shied away from confrontation. She wrote Spalding "to express to you especially, and to the other members of the Fulton-DeKalb Hospital Authority the appreciation Negro citizens felt at seeing the announcement in the press yesterday morning that the construction of the Negro hospital had actually begun." When Spalding retired from the Authority in 1959, leaving Hamilton's "hidden agenda" only barely realized, she wrote him stressing the positive: "I will always be especially grateful for the many ways in which you have supported efforts to improve the services for the Negro population and to further the beginnings of training opportunities for Negro medical professionals." In a brief reply, Spalding wrote Hamilton, "I greatly appreciate the cooperation and support which you afforded me over the years."[13]

Hamilton cultivated Spalding because he was one of "the people with the power to bring about changes," and Spalding accepted Hamilton because she had qualities he could relate to—good taste, education, and a moderate approach toward the redress of racial injustice. She was probably the first black woman he had ever encountered on a last-name basis, and he seemed as deferential to her as she was to him. How she became secretary of the Spalding Pavilion's interracial Advisory Board of Trustees was a favored recollection. "In appointing the Advisory Board," she told an interviewer, "he said to me, you can be secretary if you want to be, said I don't really think women have any business being officers in this kind of body, but if you want to be secretary, you can be secretary. And I said, yes, Mr. Spalding, I want to be secretary and that was that."[14]

Hamilton's meetings with Spalding, she remembered, were often "just really visits" in his office, visits during which he would tell her about his

Kentucky boyhood, about the discrimination he himself experienced as a Catholic in the Protestant South. She believed her association with Spalding had influenced his "growth in knowledge and understanding" of the Negro's cause. As evidence, she often cited a visit he made to the AU campus in early 1948 as plans for the Pavilion were taking shape. He had never before set foot in this world-famous center of Negro learning, though it lay near his own place of business in downtown Atlanta. The occasion arose because he had offered to solicit support for the project in white Atlanta and he wanted to inform the Negro community of the results. Hamilton enjoyed relating the story:

> He'd sent out the letters and when he got in a big set of replies, he said where shall we have the meeting and everybody agreed they'd have it in the Board room at Atlanta University. Dr. Mays was there, so was Clement, kind of a diverse group, and the same group that had been carrying the ball at the League, Mr. Whittaker, Mr. Yates and I, were there. And Mr. Spalding said he wanted to share the responses because they'd been so overwhelmingly supportive. So he began flipping them through. He said, "here's one from Scott Candler," who was a wheel in DeKalb County. He said, "by all means build the niggers a hospital." Mr. Spalding was so embarrassed, he flipped that one over fast, went right on, said "here's another from so-and-so." He was just reading it, just reading what Candler wrote. Reading directly.

She told this story more than once in conversations for this book, and she always laughed heartily when she told it. Actually, the story probably revealed as much about Hamilton as it did about Spalding. "That's the only meeting I remember out there," she said. "Shortly after that the Advisory Board must have really come into being, because I remember all the meetings after that occurred in the Board room at the Pavilion." [15]

The Advisory Board of Trustees of the Spalding Pavilion, to which she referred, actually was Hughes Spalding's idea, and it was organized in April 1950, its ten members evenly divided between the races. Hamilton, one of the black five, acted as secretary, but she was in reality the board's catalyzing force and ultimately its mainstay. Spalding at first had wanted to lease the new hospital to "leading Negroes in the community," to "permit the Negroes to take it over, pay for it and operate it, in due course reimbursing the Hospital Authority for its actual cash outlay." Soon abandoning this approach, he then proposed an Advisory Board of Trustees with Negroes in the majority; the evenly divided board that he ultimately created may have been forced upon him by the Authority itself. Hamilton took pride in the board's existence for, as Spalding conceived it in theory at least, its task was to "govern" the hospital. Her feelings probably echoed those of Morehouse president Mays, who said at the Pavilion's dedication: "Distinguished representative citizens sat down together as human beings and planned this project. As a result interracial good will has been generated, interracial respect has been increased, confidence has been strengthened, brotherhood has been furthered, and everybody feels better down in his heart. . . . I believe the advance made in human relations by the two groups planning this project together is far more significant than the physical structure." [16]

Yet the interracial Advisory Board was by no means an independent body. The board was in a real sense Spalding's "baby." He appointed its members, and his correspondence in these years to Hamilton and the board is replete with reminders that the board could act only subject "to the authority and approval of the Fulton-DeKalb Hospital Authority." The board had little discretion, and all too often administrative and policy decisions affecting the Pavilion's operations were made without its knowledge or participation. By 1953, Spalding was complaining about the high rate of absenteeism among Negro trustees at Advisory Board meetings, and he wondered "what shape the Negro Advisory Trustees would be in if Mrs. Hamilton was not a member and if she were not on the job at all the meetings." Nevertheless, he wrote, "I am not discouraged but I think the Negro population and the Negro Trustees should take more interest in this hospital." [17]

Defending the board, Hamilton circumspectly replied, "I feel that we must recognize a human tendency to lose interest in a venture if one comes to believe that it is proceeding without reference to whatever contributions can be made by those who have been asked to assume responsibility. This, I fear, has been the case to some extent with the Advisory Board of Trustees." [18]

Seven years later, in 1960, the board's position was even more ambiguous, as indicated by the growing force of Hamilton's complaint. Spalding by then was no longer on the Hospital Authority, and Hamilton herself had departed the Atlanta Urban League, but she remained on the Advisory Board of Trustees and in a letter pleading with the new chairman of the Fulton-DeKalb Hospital Authority for "greater administrative autonomy" for the Board, she wrote:

> The group of citizens who have given volunteer service to the development of Spalding Pavilion as members of the Advisory Board of Trustees have few reasons to believe that their advisory services are used by the Hospital Authority. Although the members of this group are more intimately acquainted with both the potential and the needs of Spalding Pavilion than any others,

their suggestions, recommendations and/or requests are rarely acknowledged by the Hospital Authority. The Advisory Board has no other means for implementation of its recommendations. Its members have been conscientious and generous in the time and effort contributed over many years to trying to help make it possible for the Pavilion to meet the obligations imposed by its purposes and by the needs of this community.

For such a group to be delegated greater administrative autonomy, under terms which would be defined by the Hospital Authority would seem to be a requirement for sound and creative administration of the Pavilion.[19]

The requested autonomy was not forthcoming, nor was the Spalding Pavilion yet the teaching hospital she had envisioned. Even the Supreme Court decree ending public school segregation, which was everywhere viewed as heralding the end of official segregation in all public institutions, brought no break in the stalled teaching program, leading her to write pessimistically to Joseph J. Johnson, dean of Howard University's School of Medicine: "There seems to be little inclination on the part of either Emory or the Hospital Authority to recognize the fundamentals involved in this situation—the Supreme Court's decision notwithstanding." Yet Martin Luther King Jr. and the modern civil rights movement were already clearly on the horizon, lending indirect aid to her hidden agenda.[20]

Early in 1955, probably emboldened by events of the time, Grace Hamilton struck out anew in behalf of her cause. Since neither the Hospital Authority nor Emory-Grady had lifted a finger to raise funds for the teaching program at Spalding, citing lack of money as the obstacle to its initiation, Hamilton together with key members of Atlanta's Negro law and medical community (aided by a few whites) organized a public corporation whose chief function, as she carefully put it, was to raise "such funds as are needed to conduct a graduate program in surgery [at Spalding] if cooperation of Emory and Grady can be received." With Hamilton once again playing the pivotal role of secretary, the corporation was called the Foundation for the Advancement of Medical and Nursing Education (FAMNE), and pledges amounting to $10,000 were immediately raised from L. D. Milton, a Negro banker, C. R. Yates and J. P. Whittaker, Negro businessmen (both then members of the AUL's Board of Directors and the Spalding Pavilion's Advisory Board of Trustees), and a group of otherwise unidentified Atlanta Negro physicians. If presented the money as a gift—or amounting to the same, as she and her colleagues reasoned—the Authority and Emory-Grady would have little choice but to proceed. And the Authority and Emory did cooperate in the fund-raising, consenting to let it go forward, as

Spalding would later point out with pride, but the "cooperation" carried a price. The two institutions agreed technically to yet another "teaching plan," this one drawn up by Alfred A. Weinstein, white president of Spalding Pavilion's staff and an indefatigable worker in FAMNE's cause, which called for a 40-bed teaching unit at the 130-bed Pavilion, the patients to be drawn from the indigent at Grady Memorial Hospital, and evenly divided among four categories—surgical, medical, obstetrics-gynecology, and pediatrics. But the Authority and Emory-Grady cut the proposal drastically, wanting a "beginning in surgery" only.

"Ten service beds for surgery," plus access to Grady Hospital's outpatient clinics were agreed to, but Negro trainees were, once again, specifically refused the right to serve in the main wards of Grady, even its colored wards, which in practice meant that indigent Negro patients were wheeled from Grady to Spalding for care. It was an impractical, costly, even dangerous, situation and not untypical of the endless anomalies forced upon Negroes under segregation. Many in Atlanta and elsewhere believed the Hospital Authority and Emory University could be successfully attacked in federal court on the issue of the stalled training program, but Hamilton— while acknowledging doubts that funds for a segregated program "will be easily secured"—really wanted to prove that "legal action is not the only means" to accomplish a "change of established institutions." She preferred to think positively, believing "there might be a sympathetic response to support an effort of Negroes to help themselves in this connection." And she was right.[21]

In response to FAMNE's application in 1956, the U.S. Public Health Service granted the Fulton-DeKalb Hospital Authority $40,000 to help finance the first year of the surgical training service, including employment of a chief of surgery at Spalding Pavilion and stipends for two residents. Hughes Spalding, speaking for the Authority and Emory-Grady, assured the Negro community that additional beds for "the three other services" would be made available "should the surgery service work out satisfactorily" and "as qualified and approved Negro doctors become available," ignoring the role such procrastination played, and would continue to play, in creating the dearth of adequately trained Negro physicians in the first place. But more procrastination followed. Surgical training was financed by further Public Health Service grants, but the "other" services were never activated, primarily because no one applied for funding. As Hamilton wrote in 1960, "Despite assurances that federal funds could be made available upon request by the appropriate professional leadership of Grady Memorial Hospital with the sanction of the Authority, such funds have not been sought." Hamilton called the limited program "half a loaf," a mild reaction that masked her real and bitter disappointment. Yet there were pluses in the situation.[22]

If the beginning had to be limited to a single department, surgery was well chosen, for a highly qualified specialist was available to head it. His name was Asa G. Yancey, and he came from a family well established among Atlanta's black aristocracy. Hamilton was elated by his interest in the position; it virtually assured that the surgical program would "work out satisfactorily." Asa Yancey had grown up near the Atlanta University campus, attended medical school at the University of Michigan, and trained in surgery at Freedman's Hospital under Charles R. Drew at Howard University. After serving as assistant surgeon at Boston's Marine Hospital, Yancey had returned South, and at the time Spalding Pavilion was built, he was chief of surgery at the Tuskegee, Alabama, Veterans Hospital. Drew, in continual search for ways to improve the quality and availability of medical training for all Negroes, had groomed Yancey to aid the cause in Atlanta. As early as 1947, he wrote Dr. Paul B. Beeson, of Emory University's School of Medicine: "[Yancey] has the preparation, the personality, the tact and common sense, I believe, to take over a position as an instructor of surgery or assistant surgeon on the colored wards of Grady Hospital in such a manner as to enhance the reputation of the hospital, increase the morale of the patients and make a large step in raising the level of medical care for Negroes as well as doing a therapeutic job of incalculable size on the mental disease which is part of the birthright of all Negroes who must live in the deep South."[23]

Although opposed to segregation "in any form," Drew nevertheless recognized "facts as they are" in the South, and when his eminently sensible proposal fell on deaf ears at Emory University, he nevertheless maintained an interest in plans for what would become the new Negro hospital in Atlanta. Indeed, "The Authority," as Hughes Spalding wrote to Dr. Mays in April 1950, "expected to have the aid of Dr. Drew in working out the set-up and procedures at the new hospital." Sadly, Drew never lived to make his contribution, for he died in a car accident in late March 1950 while on a southern trip that would have included a stopover in Atlanta to discuss Spalding Pavilion with its supporters.[24]

Within days of Drew's death, Hughes Spalding coincidentally told Dr. Mays that he wanted to name the hospital, whose construction had just begun, for Margaret Mitchell, Atlanta author of Gone With the Wind, also recently dead of injuries suffered in an automobile accident. When Spalding asked for Negro consent, Dr. Mays called in the black membership of "the original committee that made plans for the hospital"—the one organized by Hamilton after the AUL's report—and this group unanimously countered with the proposal that it should instead be called the Charles Drew Memorial Hospital. "Dr. Drew would make a better symbol," Mays and the committee believed. Spalding favored Mitchell because, as he wrote Stephens Mitchell, the author's brother, "she originated the idea of the negro hospital with me, what I mean to say is that until after she discussed it with me, it never occurred to me that it was a step that could be successfully taken." Spalding did not press his choice, but he also rejected Drew, who, he wrote Dr. Mays, "was not associated with this community nor with this State and I doubt the wisdom or propriety of naming this hospital for him." Spalding's choice, to say the least, did not reflect well on his sensitivity to Negro history and aspirations; perhaps for that reason, Hamilton, a Spalding partisan, did not remember in her later years that he had ever suggested naming the hospital for Mitchell, though she had faithfully preserved correspondence that fully detailed the episode. In a 1985 interview, when she was still in good physical and mental health, she called it an "interesting" sidelight but one "I don't remember at all." [25]

Yancey was first offered the post of chief of surgery in August 1955, a position that placed him in charge of the surgical training program at Spalding Pavilion. Nearly three years would elapse before he actually went to work at the job, a delay essentially caused by segregation. A segregated program was not to Yancey's liking. In the manner of his mentor, Charles Drew, he accepted it as the only possibility "at this time" for providing "medical education in all spheres for Negro Georgians and Atlantans," but at the outset he was forthright in his view that "the easiest, less expensive and more efficient thing to do is simply admit two Negro interns to Grady Memorial Hospital and carry out all training there." This was not to be, as he was doubtless aware. Even in 1957, with segregation put to rout in public schools, Emory still wanted a teaching program that banned all contact between Spalding's Negro trainees and "students at Emory University." The program nearly foundered once again while Yancey and Emory-Grady "battered back and forth" not only this issue but the equally crucial one of Spalding Pavilion's accreditation. Yancey wanted his trainees to have full and free access to Grady Memorial Hospital's medical library and research facilities, which Emory University was reluctant to give without limitations, and he also wanted firm assurance of Emory's consultative and teaching role in the program. "The main thing was," he later said, "it would be something I could never do, and that would be to come here to pretend to teach and not have a fully accredited program. That would be a disservice to black people and that would be unacceptable."[26]

Years of negotiation in which Grace Towns Hamilton actively participated finally yielded a contract Yancey could live with. "We battered matters back and forth . . . [the Authority and Emory-Grady] participated in various suggestions along with those that were made individually by Grace and myself. . . . So the final decision was . . . we would have an accredited program in surgery, the Boards agreed to it, the American Board of Surgery, the American College of Surgeons, we would use the Emory-Grady library, we would have twelve indigent beds, we would draw patients from the Grady surgical clinics and emergency room, we would have the backing of the Emory surgical staff, for consultative and teaching work and use the research facilities on top of the main building. So that's how we got started in 1958." Weekly lectures for Atlanta's Negro physicians, harking back to the similar but abortive effort in 1948, were also a part of the training program at Spalding and were, as Yancey remembered, "fairly well attended."[27]

Asa Yancey thought the training program, once begun, functioned fairly well because "it carried out our four major efforts—continuing medical education, accredited resident education, high-quality patient care and basic clinical animal research." But its limitations were widely apparent, leading to bitterness in the Negro community and even to support at last from Atlanta's not normally antisegregationist newspapers. In 1962, the *Constitution* editorially doubted that anybody would object "to letting Negro residents and interns treat Negro patients in the Grady wards." The *Atlanta Journal* agreed, writing that "the Spalding Pavilion after twelve years still is not performing the task for which it was created. The few surgical residents are getting limited training of doubtful quality. By keeping them out of Grady, requiring their charity patients to be brought to Spalding, the Pavilion is overcrowded, thereby reducing the quality of service available to private patients at Spalding."[28]

Desegregation, the only answer to the anomalous situation, finally came in June 1965, mandated by a federal court order issued on the heels of the Federal Civil Rights Act of 1964. White society's determination to stand pat on its racial biases had yielded little to the patience and persistence of those like Hamilton and Yancey who hoped separate but equal would lead to "integration in the longer run." Real progress against racial injustice, as Yancey later acknowledged, came only with federal intervention. He said: "They sent a fellow down from Washington and he came in and began to tell the white hospitals [all over the South] the decision was made to abolish segregation in 1954. Here it is 1964, hasn't been done, let's get on with it. Now that's what it amounted to. Some of the black doctors picketed the hospitals, things of that sort, but the main thing was the federal government said, 'okay, it's going to be done.'"[29]

Great changes followed slowly. Yancey joined the faculty at Emory University School of Medicine in 1962, eventually becoming full professor of surgery, then a member and partner of the Emory University Clinic, and finally medical director of Grady Memorial Hospital itself. Grace Hamilton, after entering the Georgia legislature in 1965, was appointed to the previously all-white Fulton-DeKalb Hospital Authority. Spalding Pavilion's surgical training program, finally admitting students of both races, continued until 1972—the "three other services" were never activated—when it was brought to a close largely by changes in medical education decreed by the American Board of Surgeons. The lack of qualified black applicants for the places now available to them in formerly all-white medical colleges became the new challenge, resulting in two new facilities for aspiring Negro doctors, one of them located at Morehouse College in Atlanta. (The Charles R. Drew–Martin Luther King Jr. Medical College in Los Angeles was the other.) By the 1980s, Morehouse and Emory students were training together at Grady Memorial Hospital, while at the same time changing demographics of Atlanta's Negro population, combined with the universality of the new Medicare benefits for senior citizens, lessened Negro dependence on both Grady Hospital and Spalding Pavilion, leading to a veritable battle among all the city's hospitals for black patients of white and black doctors alike. By the 1980s, a patient's insurance, not his or her color, determined the availability of hospital care. Grace Hamilton's father, who died in 1960, was cared for in his last illness at Spalding Pavilion. His daughter's role in Spalding's creation must have been a comfort to him, remembering as he surely did the undignified manipulation required to get his young son a tonsillectomy at Grady Hospital forty years before.[30]

· · ·

In the intervening years, the value of Hamilton's work on behalf of Spalding Pavilion was implicitly recognized by the wider Negro community when she was elected a trustee of Meharry Medical College in Nashville, Tennessee, at a time when Meharry and the College of Medicine at Howard University were still the only training facilities for Negro doctors in the country. She held the post from 1953 until 1984.

And in 1956 two unrelated but not disconnected events occurred in her life. In early June her son-in-law, Charles Benjamin Payne Jr., Eleanor's husband, was graduated from the University of Pennsylvania's School of Medicine in Philadelphia, one of the growing but still sparse contingent of Negroes trained in schools other than Meharry and Howard. Payne was a 1952 graduate of Yale University; Eleanor got her Smith College degree the same year, and they were married in June 1953. While studying medicine in the following years, he drove a cab to support his wife and growing young family. The Paynes, who were divorced in 1970, had four children, one of whom was born in Japan, where Payne served with the U.S. Army between 1956 and 1960.

Grace and Henry Cooke Hamilton attended Payne's graduation exercise in Philadelphia and from there went on to Montreal, where they departed June 18 for a six-week trip to Europe, the first visit either had ever made abroad. The voyage was financed by a travel grant from Atlanta University, and they traveled in a group put together by Oberlin College. For Grace Hamilton, it must have been a reminder of the aborted trip to India more than twenty years before, though this time she was actually making the voyage, but in another direction, across another ocean.[31]

9

A Leave and a Resignation

. . .

B Y 1954, after more than a decade of struggle at the Atlanta Urban League for better education, medical care, housing, and renewed voting power for Negroes, Grace Hamilton felt a need for "time out." Taking an eighteen-month leave of absence, she joined the Southern Regional Council as its assistant director of program planning. Later, she looked back on her work at the council with no pleasure. The primary source of her dissatisfaction was the practices and personality of George S. Mitchell, the SRC's executive director. An economist and former regional director of the Congress of Industrial Organizations – Political Action Committee, Mitchell had held the SRC job since 1948, and Hamilton professed "great appreciation for his leadership . . . and the many things he did" at the council. She always included the council job in her résumé, but otherwise she seemed willing to forget it. "It was a year when she made a mistake," said Katherine Stoney, a fellow staff member during Hamilton's year at the agency.[1]

The Southern Regional Council was founded in Atlanta in 1944 by an interracial group of leading progressive southerners as the successor to the Commission on Interracial Cooperation, which by then was moribund. Hamilton was among the SRC's "organizing group" (though she was not an incorporator), and she served on the original Board of Directors, a position she still held when she joined the paid staff. Initially the council appeared to have better prospects than its predecessor for bringing about meaningful changes in southern race relations. But the Red Scare that hindered the CIC's work after World War I was mirrored in the McCarthyism that swept the country after World War II, and the SRC, which felt duty bound "to warn the Southern people that segregation was on the way out," was soon battling charges of procommunism while struggling to survive with crippled fund-raising capabilities. By 1948, when Stoney became the council's secretary-treasurer, the organization had a $10,000 deficit. Help arrived in early 1954 when the Ford Foundation, anticipating the U.S. Supreme Court's decree ending separate but equal schools, granted the SRC $500,000 to expand its activities in southern states. Mitchell seems to have made the least of the opportunity. Joining the SRC to help develop new state programming aimed at securing community support for the school decision, Hamilton found she had a job without a function. Stoney described the situation:

> She really didn't have anything to do. Because anything she wanted to propose was vetoed or just sloughed off. When he got this money, Mitchell was going to have state secretaries in each state. He hired staff. But first of all he didn't allow enough money to do anything except just have an office and a telephone. And secondly he had no program. He just let the people do whatever they wanted to do. And Grace was trying to get specific.
>
> Mitchell wanted her because she looked good and because she would make a nice presentation as a representative of the council. . . . She was really his symbol. . . . George Mitchell thought she would be a good window dressing. He had no idea she was going to have any influence on what the council did. . . . He was the most paternalistic man I have ever known in my life, paternalistic about women, paternalistic about blacks.
>
> What the SRC needed was somebody with a little practical knowledge. Mitchell made good speeches, he had a great sense of humor and he had done a lot of work with labor and racial causes, but he just was no businessman.[2]

Hamilton herself talked about the experience in 1974 to Jacquelyn Hall, southern historian at the University of North Carolina. "I got very discouraged in those days," she said. "Many of us felt that the only way the Council could really be effective was to strengthen the state groups and the groups at the local level. And in order to do that, resources had to be made available to do some kind of things. And George Mitchell never bought that."[3]

The programs she had been hired to develop for selling southerners on the Supreme Court's school decision were mostly stillborn, but Hamilton persisted, as was her habit when the cause was one she believed in. Toward the end of her council interlude, when she felt most frustrated, she and

C. H. Parrish, another council member, launched within the organization a consultant service for state affiliates and, according to a summary of her year's work which she later submitted at a council meeting, she herself offered part-time advisory services to affiliates in Kentucky, Louisiana, North Carolina, and Tennessee. At Hamilton's urging, the SRC also sponsored a conference of race relations experts in August 1955, and at their urging the council established in November 1955 a Consultant Service Program designed to train state staff, putting John Hope Jr. in charge. The Hamilton-Parrish initiative apparently was the catalyst. But by the time Hope began his work, Hamilton was no longer at the council.

She was seriously alienated one day by a remark by Mitchell, which in his paternalist fashion he doubtless meant in a kindly way. Hamilton told Hall the story: "I was pressing for something to be done that . . . they weren't doing . . . and I thought I had some responsibility for it, as that part of the staff and George said, 'Now, just relax, because you are our symbol of interracial fellowship.' And I said, 'Indeed, I'm not. My days of being a symbol of anything have long since passed.'" Mitchell was "trying to make me feel better," she remembered, but it was a remark she never forgot—or forgave. When her commitment was up, she promptly left the council, returning to the Urban League. "I stayed for the period I agreed to stay for, and that was that," she said. Stoney also departed the SRC not long after.[4]

· · ·

When Grace Towns Hamilton gave notice on June 27, 1960, that she intended to resign as executive director of the Atlanta Urban League, she was fifty-three years old, not old enough to want retirement from active work or financially able to live securely on the reduced income retirement would mean. She had served over seventeen years as the first strong woman executive director in an otherwise male-dominated organization; there is scarcely a recorded trace of the few female executives who preceded Hamilton elsewhere among affiliates of the National Urban League. She had accomplished much at the AUL, and she left an imprint that would be felt for years. Contending with male chauvinism—in her opinion and that of others—had been a continual problem for her. It may even have played a part in her leaving the League.

Not that anyone ever had any hard evidence of such a surmise. Her tenure ended quietly. There was no public sign of the furor that had raged for years beneath the surface of her relationship with the National Urban League and its executive director, Lester B. Granger. When Granger's papers became available for public scrutiny at the Library of Congress, they revealed that she and Granger, whose terms of office roughly coincided, had clashed for years. In the decade following 1950, when Granger spoke of his "high respect for Mrs. Hamilton and her abilities" and characterized their differences as the normal give-and-take of a big organization, the tenor of his communications to and about Grace Hamilton gradually hardened into implacable animosity. In the end, Granger would contend that an "unsatisfactory relationship" existed "between the National office and the Atlanta League" from the beginning of Hamilton's tenure.[5]

Though friends insisted she felt the same way, Grace Hamilton never openly discussed the substance of her disagreements with Granger. She was always guarded in her letters to him, of which few exist among either of their respective papers. In interviews for this book, for example, she implied that there was more accord than discord between them. "I never worked with him closely on League matters but I never thought he was against me in any sense. . . . I never had any feeling we didn't get along," she said. A study of the Granger correspondence indicates, however, that the mutual hostility was so intense that in the end Granger pressed for her removal. It was "a very messy situation which must be corrected either by drastic action at this end or by reversal of attitude at [Atlanta's] end," Granger wrote to Robert A. Thompson just three months before Hamilton's resignation.[6]

They were both strong personalities, stubborn, opinionated, and charismatic. Hamilton refused to compromise if she strongly believed she was right. The same was true of Granger. Each was responsible to a Board of Trustees and though both were inclined to circumvent and bend these boards to their own purposes when they felt the necessity, their respective boards remained loyal to them throughout the storms that beset their relationship. This gave Granger the superior clout—given national precedence over local affiliates—that in the end enabled him to push for Hamilton's resignation and get it.

No hint of this push ever leaked out, and Hamilton denied there was any pressure on her to leave the League. "I never knew of any push if there was one," she later said. "I just came to the point of feeling I was meeting myself coming in the door. I'd done all that I could see that I could do on the major things we were working on at that time." She seemed to prefer papering over the crisis that precipitated her departure from the League in other ways, too. As she remembered it, she worked on as executive director "another year or more" after her troubles with Granger came to a head. In fact, once the crisis erupted, she resigned within three months. The good work she had done in the Atlanta Urban League would surely have safeguarded her reputation from harm had she acknowledged the true story. Apparently she did not think so.[7]

Part of the problem between Hamilton and Granger lay in her personal proclivities. Hamilton was a natural-born leader who thrived on being "in charge" and from the beginning—when she rebuffed W. Y. Bell Jr.'s "oversight" efforts as head of the NUL's Southern Field Office—she held the national at arm's length. "We never did use them for our local things," she remembered. "They didn't do anything for us really, not one thing. We felt the main decisions should be made locally and we had resources for consultants, with the university, with the Atlanta community and so on, and so we didn't need, much less could we afford, to bring them in for that, because they did not, in our judgment, have people particularly equipped to advise us about the things we were doing locally. That was always my position."[8]

When the NUL did offer help, Hamilton tended to reject it. As Southern Urban Leagues came under assault from White Citizens Councils in the wake of the U.S. Supreme Court's *Brown* decree ending public school segregation in 1954, the national organization sought information from affiliates about the nature of the attacks so it might coordinate "a consistently principled defense of the League movement" in the region. Hamilton refused to cooperate—and the AUL board backed her up, authorizing her to treat all such information as confidential—saying that "there were no incidents as far as she had been able to find in Atlanta." But even if "incidents" were to occur, she told Nelson C. Jackson, the NUL's community service director, "she would not like to see the NUL trying to carry out any program in this or any other matter which affected the local Urban League."[9]

By her last years at the AUL, its program bore little resemblance to the national agenda. After she and Thompson in the late 1940s jettisoned employment in favor of housing, other abstentions from staple NUL projects followed. Between 1952 and 1959, the AUL was not represented at the annual NUL conferences, and its representation was resumed only after the Granger-Hamilton discord reached the level of their respective Boards of Trustees. In 1952, Hamilton informed New York that Atlanta would no longer participate in vocational guidance, a major national concern. She pleaded lack of funds. In 1957, she turned thumbs down on two NUL requests for cooperation in soliciting financial support in Atlanta for ad hoc projects aimed at improving race relations. Local money was needed for local projects, she implied. In 1959 Hamilton decided against participation in a new youth incentives program called Tomorrow's Scientists and

Technicians, which provided tuition scholarships to deserving students in scientific and technical fields, and in this same period she declined to join in observance of Equal Opportunity Day, though the Georgia governor sanctioned the event by official proclamation. By the time the NUL created a General Citizens Committee on Employment and Economic Opportunity to promote 1960 census jobs for blacks in Atlanta, the "well-rounded Urban League program" promoted by the national was staffed, to the extent that its constituent programs existed in Atlanta at all, by the Southern Field Office.[10]

Her relations with Granger and the National Urban League eventually foundered, however, not on her deviation from the national's prescribed programs but on her willingness to condone segregation as the price of retaining support of the Atlanta Community Chest. In 1958, the Chest provided 90 percent of the AUL's budget; all sixty-one affiliates of the National Urban League at the time were largely underwritten by their respective Chests. Even dues owed the national organization under its uniform terms of affiliation were "subject to Community Chest action," meaning the Chests had to appropriate the money. With the White Citizens Councils on ever-widening attack and the National Urban League, for all its moderation, regularly smeared as subversive, the AUL's Board of Directors in 1956, under Community Chest pressure, agreed to cease paying dues to the national, and Hamilton cooperated that same year in writing a Chest statement depicting AUL programs as unthreatening to white interests. Later, Hamilton bowed to further demands, agreeing (as she informed Mahlon Puryear of the NUL's Southern Field Office) to "raise no funds within the local community with which dues would be paid," nor (she told Puryear) could she "even permit a receipt for dues paid the national from any source to be part of the files and records of the local office." When in 1957 the local hate groups nevertheless seemed on the verge of persuading the Community Chest to cut off AUL funding, Hamilton and Philip G. Hammer, from the AUL Board of Directors (and always her devoted partisan), held some vigorous discussions, as he later related:

> A big day was coming when the Community Chest Board was to make its final budget appropriations, and we all were preparing for that. We had some strategy sessions. Grace was the master strategist of all times. Three days before the big meeting, Grace got the idea of getting Ralph McGill to write a first-class column on the front page of the *Constitution*. His column was a very influential column in the South. And so I went with Grace to see Ralph, and he said he would be delighted and he was going to take the pitch that the

Urban League was a great conservative force in our community and that it was conserving the town, was making the town work, and should be conserved by all means.[11]

McGill's promised column, appearing on June 25, 1957, was strongly pro–Urban League but also contained the following question and answer:

Q. Does the National Urban League exercise any control over the Atlanta Urban League?

A. No. A volunteer board of directors, composed of local citizens, white and Negro, sets the Atlanta Urban League's program and policies, which are entirely consistent with the customs, laws and traditions of Georgia. The Atlanta Urban League does not follow National Urban League policies and does not support the National Urban League financially.

Though it survived the 1957 attacks, the AUL's Chest support remained precarious. Another editorial, this one unsolicited, appeared in the *Atlanta Journal* of October 13, 1959, reiterating the disclaimers of two years before, saying in part: "Now, as in 1957, the Atlanta Urban League is local. It takes no orders from the National organization and contributes no funds to the same. Its leadership is composed of local citizens and its policy conforms to local pattern and traditions."

Both editorials were reprinted at the Community Chest and distributed locally and, along with Hamilton's blanket ban on payment of local dues to the national body, they became central to Granger's complaint against her.

Hamilton believed that her strategy for retaining Chest support was benign; she was proud to be "one of the few surviving Southern League affiliates with Community Chest support," and she never questioned the soundness of her strategy for keeping that support. But to the National Urban League's executive director, it amounted to "accommodation," "tame submission," and a betrayal of "the fundamental League principle . . . that League activities are to ensure for Negroes the greatest possible degree of equality of opportunity," a principle negated, as the National Board of Trustees later cogently insisted in defense of Granger, by the "customs, laws and traditions of Georgia" to which Hamilton had willingly committed the AUL. Five southern affiliates, subjected to Community Chest pressure, had declined to yield, finding other sources for payment of their dues, some even choosing expulsion from the Chest over submission. Granger felt Atlanta, with its strong black social and economic institutions, could survive a similar principled response. With the pace of racial change quickening in the wake of the 1955 bus boycott in Montgomery, Alabama, and the rise of

Martin Luther King Jr., Granger's patience with the AUL's implicit support of segregation, to which he had never previously objected, at last came to an end. Between 1957 and 1959, five times he brought before the National Board of Trustees what he then was calling "the extremely unsatisfactory relationship" with the Atlanta affiliate, and on December 10, 1959, he took the final step, asking the board to disaffiliate Hamilton's AUL. To Philip Hammer, the action was "sudden and peremptory," coming "out of the clear sky." To Granger it was a confrontation "nearly twenty years in the making." [12]

On January 11, 1960, Granger wrote J. B. Blayton, then chairman of the AUL's Board of Directors, notifying him that "the strong chances are that definite action will be taken [at a January 21 meeting of the National Board of Trustees] on the affiliate status of the Atlanta Urban League." On January 15, 1960, Granger wrote Nelson C. Jackson, an NUL staffer, "If I were asked, I would say bluntly that I do not see any chance of our working through current difficulties as long as Mrs. Hamilton is the executive director." Hamilton was now directly in the eye of the storm. [13]

Fully alert at last to the serious situation, the AUL's Board of Directors on January 18 unanimously declared itself in favor of the national tie and asked for a delay in the "contemplated disaffiliation" until a joint committee of the national and Atlanta boards "shall have an opportunity to meet . . . for the purpose of ironing out mutual misunderstandings and difficulties." Delay was arranged, and a joint board meeting was held in New York on February 29, 1960, at which Granger and Hamilton met face to face in company with NUL board president Theodore W. Kheel and AUL board chairman Blayton, along with NUL board members George O. Butler, Lindsley F. Kimball, and Henry Steeger and AUL board members Hammer and Dr. Harry V. Richardson. General Counsel Lisle C. Carter outlined the "core of the problem existing between the NUL and its Atlanta affiliate," which essentially embodied Granger's complaints that Hamilton had retained Community Chest support in Atlanta at the price of condoning segregation, constituting a violation of fundamental NUL policy, and that the AUL had failed to submit financial statements to national offices as required by the terms of national affiliation and had moreover failed to honor requests from the national office for information and reports about its activities. Finally, as Carter outlined the "problem," the Atlanta executive director "is uncooperative and indeed hostile to the national office." He concluded: "Absent concrete accomplishment at this meeting, the NUL representatives will have no choice but to recommend . . . disaffiliation of the Atlanta Urban

League." The Atlanta Board of Directors was implicated directly in all the charges against Hamilton.[14]

Evidence exists suggesting Hamilton thought the Atlanta Urban League would be better off on its own, and had the decision been hers alone at this point, she likely would have broken the national tie. The Board of Directors, however, wanted to maintain the affiliation, and the three board members who had accompanied her to New York were immediately charged as a subcommittee to devise some means of mollifying the national Board of Trustees. All personally devoted to Hamilton, the subcommittee members produced a statement that was conciliatory on the surface but firmly asserted the Atlanta Urban League's "right to determine for itself what is for the best interest of the Atlanta community . . . and . . . the right to pursue its objectives as it sees fit." The statement was hardly calculated to address the issues central to the Hamilton-Granger conflict.[15]

The catalyst for a change of course in Atlanta occurred on March 17 in New York when the NUL's Board of Trustees, as President Kheel wrote Chairman Blayton in Atlanta on March 23, "reaffirmed its complete dissatisfaction with the existing relationships of the National Urban League with its Atlanta affiliate" and voted unanimously that "unless corrective steps are taken by the Board of the Atlanta Urban League, disaffiliation of the [AUL] will become effective sixty days from the date of our meeting." The deadline thus set was to fall on May 1, 1960.[16]

On March 24, the Atlanta Urban League's board, realizing the original subcommittee was on the wrong track, expanded the latter's membership to include, among others, Jesse Hill Jr., a longtime trustee who was then an actuary at the Atlanta Life Insurance Company. In the decade he had lived in Atlanta, Hill had become a key activist in the civic, political, and civil rights mainstream of the Negro community, and in 1973, he would become president of Atlanta Life, the Herndon institution, which remained one of the largest and most-respected black-owned financial concerns in America. His activist voice by then was resonating in the white community as well. Whether or not Hill was responsible, the subcommittee with him included produced another statement that took a markedly different tone, going out of its way to stress local compatibility with national objectives and implicitly disavowing any future desire to go it alone. After investigating "the allegation of lack of cooperation with the National Urban League and its Southern Field Office," the subcommittee said it was led "to the conclusion that undoubtedly there have been some misunderstanding and perhaps personality differences on both sides of the equation." To prevent similar allegations in the future, the subcommittee promised to "review the past performances of the administration of the Atlanta Urban League" and "recommend . . . steps . . . to improve and strengthen the . . . relationship with the national and regional offices," significantly noting that it would "request and utilize" help in its endeavor from the national and regional offices. The subcommittee also affirmed the "importance of the national projects of the National Urban League," and a letter incorporating this statement, which the AUL adopted unanimously, was sent to New York on April 5, 1960.[17]

If she had left matters as they then stood, Hamilton might have emerged unscathed from the fray with Granger. But in the meantime she had been lending aid to an attack on the national's Southern Field Office, which amounted to an attack on the work of Jesse Hill Jr. himself. Among his many civic responsibilities at the time, Hill was then coordinator of the General Citizens Committee on Employment and Economic Opportunity, the group created by the NUL in late 1959 to promote employment of blacks as 1960 census takers in Atlanta. E. M. Martin, Atlanta Life's president, was the committee's chairman. For professional assistance the Hill-Martin committee had to turn to the NUL's Southern Field Office because the AUL for years had done no work in the employment field. In March 1960, Margaret Davis Bowen, a friend of Hamilton's, wrote to Granger in New York, charging the NUL's Southern Field Office and the Hill-Martin committee with "sponsoring and staffing a 'jim crow' office for the census in Atlanta and 'screening' Negro candidates for supervisory positions." Copies of the letter were sent to the director of the census and to the U.S. president's Committee on Government Employment Policy. Hamilton herself distributed copies to the AUL's Board of Directors. As Granger angrily charged—with some justification—"it was less a letter than an open statement meant to condemn." Granger was no doubt stung by Bowen's charge, which he vehemently denied in a long letter to her, just as Hamilton surely was stung by the "soft-on-segregation" charges she had just faced at the National Urban League. Hill was similarly upset, and in defense of his committee he inserted Granger's reply to Bowen in the minutes of the AUL's Board of Directors meeting of April 21, 1960. Hill went even further, inserting in the minutes a statement that contained harsh words against Hamilton herself:

The gravity and seriousness of this action quite aside from Mrs. Margaret Davis Bowen's complaint and the Citizens Committee reaction is the question of our director giving support to a direct attack upon the National Urban League during our present crisis.

As a member of the Board's committee that spent long hours studying and attempting to draft a reply to Mr. Kheel's letter concerning the preservation of our affiliation, this action strikes me as a directly opposing effort whether intentional or unintentional and likely to seriously hamper our effort in this regard.

The executive director's action completely violates the spirit of cooperation as promulgated by the Board at its last meeting and appears to be in complete defiance of the spirit of the Board's official reply to the National Urban League.[18]

On June 27, 1960, Hamilton gave notice of her intention to "relinquish the position as executive secretary of the Atlanta Urban League," saying she had received an offer from "a national organization with which I have had a long-standing personal association." After September 1, when her resignation became effective, she returned to the YWCA as a community organizer working part-time out of New York. Perhaps, as she said, "I had done all that I could" at the Urban League. Perhaps she knew she could never accept the "reversal of attitude" that Granger (with the backing of the NUL board and now with some support from the Atlanta board as well) was demanding of her. That her departure was in any case encouraged by a "push" is attested by the short sequence of correspondence, all contained in Granger's papers, between Atlanta and New York that followed her departure.[19]

On September 1, 1960, Granger wrote to Robert A. Thompson, who had immediately been named Hamilton's successor: "I have received official verification of Grace Hamilton's resignation which we have been expecting for some time." On September 21, Blayton officially notified the NUL of Hamilton's resignation. On September 23, Granger wrote Blayton: "I want to add this word of mine in appreciation of the influence which you have exerted as chairman of the Atlanta Urban League, to clear up a situation that had become intolerable." On September 26, Henry Steeger, recently named Kheel's successor as president of the NUL Board of Trustees, wrote to Blayton: "I would like to express my appreciation for the fine judgment in leadership you have displayed as chairman of the Atlanta Urban League, in resolving a situation of such grave importance." On October 4, Blayton wrote to Granger: "Thanks for your letter of September 23. Please pass along my thanks to President Steeger for his letter of September 26. Here at the Atlanta Urban League we felt sure that the National Office would approve of our action." [20]

With the Atlanta "situation" finally resolved by Hamilton's departure from the League, it was scarcely a coincidence that in September 1961, Whitney M. Young Jr., after resigning as dean of the Atlanta School of Social Work to succeed Granger at the National Urban League, moved immediately to reduce "local autonomy" among the League's affiliates. "To a good many people," he observed after his new terms of affiliation were adopted by the NUL's 1961 national conference, "the Urban League appears to be 63 or 64 local affiliates with so much local autonomy it is sometimes difficult to identify local activities as part of a nation-wide program or movement. . . . In my opinion this should not be." Under Young's new contract, the national office assumed "more responsibility for the standards of performance of local leagues," and in turn local leagues were "pledged to assume more responsibility for development of total League programs." Young did not specify how the new terms of affiliation would be enforced because Community Chests retained the purse strings, but he did emphatically assert: "We intend to follow them to the letter." [21]

Robert A. Thompson, indeed, soon returned the Atlanta Urban League to the movement fold. Dues ceased to be a contentious issue; Thompson found alternative sources for the funds, including in the first year a personal contribution from his own pocket. Vocational guidance again became a part of the local agenda, as did Equal Opportunity Day, and job procurement also received renewed attention. "Direction and guidance," under Thompson's prompting, was again sought from the national office and its Southern Field Division. Thompson himself meanwhile asserted his own independence by continuing to work on housing, proposing developments, as he wrote Granger in April 1961, that were "planned by Negroes, for Negroes, risk-capital being supplied by Negroes, and coordinated by the Atlanta Urban League." [22]

Grace Towns Hamilton would have found it difficult to live, as Thompson by then apparently did not, with a national organization that bound her closely to its own agenda. But by then she was working once again for her beloved YWCA. And she was soon to enter the legislative years that would be the crowning achievement of her career.

10

Hamilton and the Civil Rights
Movement

. . .

GRACE HAMILTON's resignation from the Atlanta Urban League became effective September 1, 1960. The *Atlanta Journal* had reported the story on August 28, and on August 30, the *Atlanta Constitution* had praised her in an editorial, saying her work at the League "represents 17 years of progress toward racial understanding." Not significant in themselves, these press items are nonetheless noteworthy because they were the first concerning Hamilton ever filed in the newspapers' "morgue," otherwise known as their clipping archive. As one of Atlanta's "preeminent" Negro leaders in her years at the League, she had generated news that was sometimes covered by Atlanta's major white dailies (they came under joint ownership in 1950), but nothing before 1960, apparently, was deemed worthy of recording. It was surely no coincidence that her file, which waxed large in subsequent decades, was initiated just months after the outbreak of direct action in the modern civil rights movement. For that movement also started the process of shredding the veil that separated whites from blacks, and Atlanta's newspapers, long used to blanking out Negro news that lacked a crime angle, were among the first to accord members of the race a more congenial visibility. Hamilton's resignation story in the *Constitution*, for example, was detailed, covering three-quarters of a column. Gone now was the hesitation about the courtesy title. Indeed, no mention was made of her race. It was a far cry from the *Constitution's* four-paragraph "squib" in December 1944 that employed the direct pronoun at painful length to avoid referring to her as "Mrs. Hamilton."

The civil rights movement would also put the Negro into southern politics as never before, and Grace Towns Hamilton would be among the beneficiaries, becoming the first black woman elected to the Georgia legislature—and, indeed, the first black female state legislator anywhere in the Deep South. (Florida elected a Negro woman to its legislature in 1970, Louisiana in 1971, and others eventually followed.) For Hamilton it was an unexpected and climactic new career. "Running for public office was not anything I'd ever thought about," she later confessed, but with the reopening of politics to their race, Negro women no less than men were ready for the challenge. Hamilton preferred to call it public service and she would always look with suspicion on anyone who undertook elective office with less than her own impersonal dedication. She referred to it as her "retirement activity," but for her it was hardly the laid-back pursuit of an average retiree; she worked full-time at the job for the entire eighteen years she served in the Georgia legislature. This new career came relatively late in her life, arriving more by chance than by design, but once in politics, Hamilton seemed a natural.[1]

· · ·

Even as Hamilton moved toward a political career that would place her "among the most successful and influential women in the United States" (in the opinion of one Negro historian), rising militancy among the Negro young was beginning to erode the very old-line institutions that were the foundation of her influence. When on February 1, 1960, several Negro students, denied service at a lunch counter in Greensboro, North Carolina, refused to leave the store, their "sit-in" marked the beginning of a new era in the modern civil rights movement. After Greensboro, civil disobedience, nonviolent resistance, and political reprisal—tactics new to Negro protest—became the weapons of choice in the expanding struggle for civil rights, and the young, with Martin Luther King Jr. in the vanguard, for the first time laid claim to leadership in the fight. Hegemony of their elders, hitherto by common consent the black community's representative in dealing with white power in the South, was shaken as it had not been in the history of Negro protest. Hamilton, as one of this challenged elite, for the next quarter-century would continue to make "significant and lasting impacts on the development of the city of Atlanta and particularly its African-American community" (again in the historian's words), but the forces that eventually would end her career had their origin in the youthful "greening" of the civil rights movement that coincided with her departure from the Atlanta Urban League.[2]

The sit-in phenomenon broke over a region still tightly locked into the caste system. Over the previous century, Negroes had invoked the law, the ballot, economic boycotts, public protests, and marches, but the "scourge of racial segregation and discrimination" remained little changed. Hamilton, like other black leaders, had been willing to work for progress within the bounds of segregation, feeling the civil rights battleground lay not in confrontations but in patient prodding in courts and voting booths. But the gradualism they preached had yielded results that no longer satisfied the young. The legal fall of school segregation in 1954 was a thrilling victory for the courtroom approach, but Negro hopes six years later were largely unfulfilled. School desegregation, where implemented at all, had come only at the point of bayonets, and the Montgomery bus boycott in 1955 had made a national and international figure of Martin Luther King Jr. but had left buses still the only integrated institution in Alabama. Atlanta itself remained basically a Jim Crow city, where a few barriers had been broken but social contact between the races, even at the leadership level, was unheard-of and even dangerous, and residential segregation remained the norm, confining the new availability of desirable housing for Negroes, for instance, patiently achieved under initiatives of Hamilton's Urban League and others, within parameters ultimately fixed by whites.[3]

Militant students, wanting change now if not the day before, by the late 1950s were already taking matters into their own hands, experimenting with sit-in demonstrations at dime-store lunch counters in various cities. Inspired by King's philosophy of nonviolence, they offered no resistance when met with force; yet none of their novel protests had the desired catalytic effect—until Greensboro. Why Greensboro was different no one ever knew, but within a week similar groups were sitting down in protest all over the South, and by October 1960 sit-ins had occurred in more than 112 cities, provoking racial crises nearly everywhere, which highlighted the generational divisions among Negroes as well as those between the races.

In Atlanta, where the dichotomy between young and old was particularly acute, the elder elite, a group exceptional in number and note, managed to mute the militant young for a time by invoking the cause of King, who had returned to Atlanta to lead the Southern Christian Leadership Conference (SCLC) and was then engaged in a tense battle to clear himself of trumped-up tax evasion charges in Alabama. "Flare-ups," cautioned recognized black leaders, would be blamed on him.

By October 1960 the student movement at the Atlanta University complex, the largest and most respected concentration of Negro students in the South, had to their credit one demonstration and a publicized statement of their grievances called *An Appeal for Human Rights*, but they could claim no desegregation successes. Impeccably organized and well-equipped for non-violent combat, their cumulative protest (in the words of King biographer Taylor Branch) "seemed almost trivial in comparison to the non-violent wars of attrition elsewhere." Suddenly on October 19 their restraint came to an end, when, with King among them, students rode the elevator to Rich's Magnolia Room, the elegant top-floor dining facility of Atlanta's leading department store, and staged a sit-in that influenced the nation's history.[4]

Alone among established leaders of either race, as Branch wrote, King had unequivocally endorsed the sit-in protests, praising the students as a mature force in adult politics, but unlike the students he had not yet tested his own nonviolent philosophy outside the safety of oratory. "Fill up the jails," he urged the students, who readily heeded his advice; the Magnolia Room gave him the opportunity, as he said, "to practice what I preached." Arrested under Georgia's newly enacted antitrespass law, King and some eighty students went to jail, refusing bail, demanding revocation of the charges or trial. Frantic manipulations by Atlanta's mayor William Hartsfield (whose long hold on office had lately come to depend on Negro votes) ended in the students' release on their own terms and Hartsfield's promise to begin desegregation talks immediately with the city's downtown merchants. King, likewise absolved of the trespass charge, was nevertheless held in jail on another count, accused of violating parole on an old offense of driving in Georgia with an Alabama license. Sentenced to four months' hard labor on a state road gang, illegally denied bail (though he was willing now to accept it), and transferred to a maximum security prison, King was released on bond eight days later, thanks to the twin effects of gubernatorial intervention and a telephone call to the sentencing judge from Robert F. Kennedy, then managing his brother Senator John F. Kennedy's presidential campaign. Senator Kennedy himself, meanwhile, had made a "sympathy" call to King's pregnant wife, Coretta, a simple act of concern that was proclaimed by his campaign managers in a printed pamphlet quietly distributed nationwide in black churches on the Sunday before election day. In the closest American presidential race of the twentieth century, John Kennedy emerged victorious over Richard M. Nixon by two-tenths of 1 percent of the popular vote, a margin attributed to his commanding majority (70 percent) of the Negro vote. It was a lead comparable to that President

Roosevelt won among Negroes in the depths of the Great Depression. As Branch wrote: "One plain fact shone through everywhere: two little phone calls about the welfare of a Negro preacher were a necessary cause of Democratic victory. . . . That something so minor could whip silently through the Negro world with such devastating impact gave witness to the cohesion and volatility of the separate culture. . . . [That] at the heart of this phenomenon was not just any preacher but Martin Luther King, gave his name a symbolic resonance, [registering him] as someone who might affect the common national history of whites and Negroes alike."[5]

At a time when blacks had helped elect a president, high hopes reigned in the civil rights movement, but in Atlanta, hope was soon dimmed when Mayor Hartsfield failed to broker the anticipated desegregation agreement with downtown merchants. Student demonstrations resumed, and white store owners responded by closing their stores for three months. In an atmosphere combining the students' sense of betrayal with the merchants' stubbornness, the city's plans for a peaceful, limited school desegregation in September 1961 appeared in jeopardy. Pressure built on both sides for a compromise. Black elders, led by A. T. Walden, and representatives of Atlanta's white power structure met secretly at the Commerce Club (strictly forbidden to Negroes) and negotiated an agreement that seemed to promise store desegregation—though the word was carefully avoided—in exchange for a ban—explicitly spelled out—on demonstrations until after school integration was successfully accomplished. Students were dismayed by what they considered an uneven exchange of commitments, but King himself stepped in to quell the discord, and the agreement, though deplored by students and a substantial number of their adult supporters, was finally ratified. It was the first written contract of its kind between the races in Atlanta. When stores not party to the accord remained segregated after September's school integration (which occurred peacefully on schedule), "creating a crazy quilt pattern of discrimination," militant student skeptics and a growing number of young adults were further alienated from the older generation, not excluding King, who had sold them the deplored agreement.[6]

Disenchantment likewise soon set in with the Kennedy administration. In fear of losing the South in 1964, the new president reneged at once on a campaign promise to wipe out discrimination in federally funded housing. He promised—through a speech delivered by his brother Robert, then attorney general, at the University of Georgia—to enforce civil rights statutes but issued no demurrer when Georgia's governor Ernest Vandiver simultaneously announced that the president had given him a pledge never to intervene with force in support of desegregation laws in Georgia. And he disowned congressional legislation to implement the Democratic Party's far-reaching platform on civil rights though he had supported it during his campaign. The new president's strategy on civil rights called for reliance on the law, the voting booth, and presidential appointments. To King and the impatient young, it sounded much like the rejected approach of their elders, for they knew the law offered the Negro scant justice in the South, that ancient fetters still rendered the Negro franchise virtually useless in most of the region, and that Kennedy judgeships had gone to ardent segregationists. Therefore, protests continued and grew in audacity.[7]

When "freedom riders" hit the road in May 1961, seeking to test the Supreme Court's ban a few months before on segregation in terminals serving interstate bus passengers, Attorney General Kennedy maneuvered adroitly to create the Voter Education Project (VEP), a new tax-exempt and well-financed organization designed to channel energies of civil rights activists away from confrontational tactics like the freedom rides and into voter registration work. Housed by the Southern Regional Council in Atlanta and enjoying the Kennedy administration's full support, the VEP ultimately had indeed (as Branch wrote) "far-reaching implications for Southern politics," but when voting rights advocates (mostly affiliated with the Student Non-Violent Coordinating Committee, SNCC, an arm of King's SCLC) met brutality and death as they fanned out over the South, the Justice Department reneged on its promise of full support and protection for their safety, telling them they essentially must look out for themselves. Massive and prolonged demonstrations, meanwhile, had filled the jails with protesters in Albany, Georgia, and when Attorney General Kennedy's Justice Department appeared to favor the city's segregationists, civil rights demonstrations and segregationist resistance further escalated. Kennedy finally mobilized federal troops in behalf of the Negro cause in Oxford, Mississippi, and Birmingham, Alabama, where the violence was greatest. Faced at last with the specter of an endless series of uprisings among black masses and no end of the need for federal intervention, Kennedy asked Congress in early 1963 for new civil rights legislation. A "narrow and limited" voting rights bill was his first offering. But when it languished, Kennedy abandoned the halfway approach and in June 1963 asked Congress for what one chronicler called "the most comprehensive piece of legislation addressing discrimination since Reconstruction." It gave Negroes much of what they had been demonstrating for, an outright end of segregation in all public accommodations.[8]

Fearing Kennedy lacked the will to force the new bill past the powerful segregationists in Congress, civil rights leaders, with King in the forefront, staged a march on Washington in August 1963 to demonstrate the strength of public demand for such a law, a march Kennedy first tried to persuade King to cancel (much as President Roosevelt tried to sidetrack A. Philip Randolph's plan for the 1941 march on Washington), but then, failing in the attempted dissuasion, reluctantly endorsed. Though the march became one of the highlights of the civil rights movement, Kennedy's historic legislation remained unenacted when he was assassinated on November 22, 1963.

In death the martyred president gained credit as a civil rights crusader, but King (according to Branch) thought Kennedy's death "was a blessing for civil rights," as he believed the strong bill President Lyndon B. Johnson soon pushed through Congress would never have emerged under Kennedy's hesitant leadership. Sensing that legal segregation was doomed, that civil rights for the Negro was a cause whose time had come, and knowing the Republican Party (thanks to Negro gains in the fight for freedom) was gnawing away at Democratic hegemony in the South, Johnson used his bona fides as a native southerner and the clout conferred by his years in Congress to strong-arm the Kennedy civil rights bill to early enactment, signing it into law on July 2, 1964.[9]

Though the new law was a signal victory for the civil rights movement, it barely addressed the issue of voting rights. Johnson, whose overwhelming reelection in 1964 demonstrated the potential of civil rights as a vote getter, thought the South needed time to adjust to the realities of integration and accordingly gave a low priority to voting rights. Movement leaders thought otherwise and dramatized the urgency of the issue with renewed demonstrations, the largest and most famous of which occurred in March 1965 in Selma, Alabama, where out of 15,000 blacks of voting age a mere 156 had managed after years of endeavor to get on the voting rolls.

When Selma produced mayhem and murder, Johnson—showing none of Kennedy's aversion to forceful intervention—federalized the Alabama National Guard, ordering its members to protect protesters, who by then had become an interracial throng of thousands, and even as the protest continued presented Congress the proposed Voting Rights Act of 1965. Enacted within months and signed into law on August 6, the new legislation eliminated impediments to the ballot such as the poll tax and literacy tests and, more significant in the long run, required states of the Deep South, including Georgia, to obtain federal approval of changes in their election laws. Coupled with the demise of Jim Crow, this act completed the institutionalization of the civil rights movement's fundamental aims.

The U.S. Supreme Court, in the meantime, had not been unswayed by the strong thrust in the nation toward new justice for the Negro, a thrust it had unsheathed in 1954 when it reversed its own support for separate but equal justice and decided in favor of school desegregation. In 1962 the Court had done another about-face on the issues of malapportionment and unequal districting, old color-blind obstacles to a meaningful franchise, which the Court had always insisted were political in nature and lay beyond reach of legal redress. In a case known as *Baker* v. *Carr*, the Court found the gerrymandered ballot was after all a justiciable issue, and decisions flowing from the new interpretation followed rapidly, all fleshing out the memorable concept of "one man, one vote." First came *Gray* v. *Sanders*, striking down Georgia's county unit system, the state's unique empowerment of rural over urban voters and a device that had become another obstacle to the political emancipation of Georgia blacks. In 1964 came both *Reynolds* v. *Sims* and *Wesberry* v. *Sanders*, the former implementing reapportionment of state legislatures, the latter leading to reapportionment of congressional districts. These decisions shored up the ballot for all people, but their significance was most profound for the Negro, who was now in possession of a franchise freed at last from ancient fetters. Fair districting would finally open the way, for the first time since Reconstruction, to the Negro's return to southern legislative bodies and all other public offices.[10]

The civil rights movement had forged a second Reconstruction, under the spur of young, creative, and daring Negroes disaffected with the caution of their elders, and at mid-twentieth century it seemed this second Reconstruction might redress the failure of the first. For Hamilton, the new national course of events would offer opportunities she otherwise never would or could have dreamed of.

· · ·

Asked in later years by a southern historian if she was surprised by the sudden eruption of direct action in the civil rights movement, Hamilton responded, "I can't say I was surprised, just rejoiced." Her patient and persistent prodding through the years, together with that of like-minded peers, had given her name and the Negro's search for justice some resonance in Atlanta's white community but had scarcely loosened—in fact was not even aimed at disturbing—Jim Crow's hold on the city. Her influence had always been measured by the strength of white leaders' confidence in her moderation. Like her peers, she had worked for greater equality within the segregated system, believing Jim Crow had to be obeyed as long as law required it—"that's the only way you had to work," she was convinced—but she and Atlanta's old-line leadership, having no more love for Jim Crow than the militant students, backed the aims of the audacious young when they set out to topple Jim Crow himself, even though they disagreed with the students' radical methods. Hamilton, for instance, never joined a sit-in or carried a placard in a demonstration. Confrontation, as a friend remarked, "was not her style, she was too much an aristocrat." For her and the majority of her age peers, cheering the protesters remained an exercise on the sidelines.[11]

Perhaps she might have joined black leaders who with white merchants and businessmen negotiated the unique though controversial agreement of 1961 that put a damper on student demonstrations in the interest of peaceful school desegregation in the city. She apparently was not asked, and her exclusion was probably deliberate. For one thing, she was in an interim period of her life, having just departed the Atlanta Urban League, which had long been the base of her leadership role. Her gender also was against her. The white side of the table included die-hards averse to giving equal status to women of their own color; according a like privilege to a black woman would have brought these negotiators to the verge of apoplexy. But students themselves may not have wanted her in this unique conclave. The negotiations were actually undertaken on their initiative, according to accepted accounts, and they chose A. T. Walden, who possessed even wider friendships than Hamilton among influential Atlanta whites, as their representative. When the meetings were broadened to include other blacks, Walden called in only men. Hamilton's moderation was scarcely more pronounced than Walden's, yet young militants appeared to regard her with greater suspicion. An example of their estrangement from Hamilton came to light in 1994 with the publication of a collection of Lillian Smith's letters. A Georgia writer and ardent antisegregationist, Smith in the late 1950s wanted to enlist Hamilton in recruiting young blacks to a more active role in the civil rights cause and sought to use Mozell Hill, then editor of *Phylon*, Atlanta University's review of race and culture, as an intermediary. (Smith probably first met Hamilton when they both served on the board of directors of the Committee for Georgia, a state affiliate of the Southern Conference for Human Welfare, in 1945–47.) Hill cautioned Smith against looking for help from "persons . . . obligated or connected with old institutions and agencies" and pointedly failed to contact Hamilton as Smith had requested. Smith apparently dropped her idea, though the young of their own volition were soon doing just what she advocated.[12]

. . .

Hamilton's unplanned departure from the Atlanta Urban League had left her once again, as in 1941, with time on her hands. Just as then, she returned to the national board of the YWCA, becoming on September 1 the board's Atlanta consultant in community relations with an office at 41 Exchange Place S.E. It was part-time work, requiring occasional commuting to New York. This "Y" connection, like that of the earlier period, was brief; in mid-1961, she gave it up to open her own community relations consulting firm, Hamilton Associates, which operated successfully until 1967.

This independent business venture was never her sole preoccupation in those eventful years, but it did bring her an important client, Eli Ginzberg of Columbia University, for whom she undertook a project peculiarly suited to her persona and skills. Ginzberg was then engaged in a study of the career objectives of middle-class Negro youth, and Hamilton was employed to interview Atlanta subjects. Her interviewing experience dated from the Works Progress Administration project long before in Memphis, Tennessee, and when she needed assistance, she solicited the expertise of her friend Grace Holmes DeLorme. Long a teacher of biology at Spelman College, DeLorme had lately given up teaching for professional interviewing. "I had gotten training on the job so Grace asked if I would like to do the interviews with the young black high school students, and of course I would and that's how it came about," DeLorme remembered.[13]

Hamilton herself interviewed college students at the second- and third-year levels. This project, limited to interviews with Atlanta and New York youths, culminated in a book called *The Middle Class Negro in the White Man's World*, published in 1967 by Columbia University Press. Ginzberg shared his author's credit with the interviewers, including Hamilton, who sent DeLorme a copy of the book with the inscription, "To Grace of God from Grace Amazing." DeLorme remembered: "We would change titles, had a lot of fun, you know." According to its jacket description, the book depicted "Negro youth . . . who are not handicapped by economic and emotional deprivation, who are not absorbed by feelings of hate and resentment for the white man's world . . . who are 'on their way' and the world they expect to find." Except for her age, now past the mid-century mark, Hamilton herself easily fit the description of the book's interviewees. Propelled by the rising tide of social and political change, she too was "on her way."[14]

. . .

When William Hartsfield stepped down as Atlanta's mayor in 1961, Ivan Allen Jr., a self-described "well bred and successful" office supply dealer, won the race to succeed him, largely on the strength of a massive black vote. The last decade of Hartsfield's tenure in the post, extending over twenty-three years, had also been bestowed upon him by his Negro constituency. Registered in numbers close to white voting strength and voting in a bloc, Atlanta Negroes in combination with the city's progressive whites (whose electoral aims for a while after World War II often coincided) had become an invincible coalition. Helen Douglas Mankin was elected to Congress in 1946 from the Georgia Fifth District as the coalition's first victory, a triumph effectively thwarted in favor of her opponent through his unscrupulous manipulation of the county unit system, but in Atlanta proper, where county units were inapplicable, after 1949 no one could become mayor without its support. Blacks by then were well organized as an electoral bloc led by the Atlanta Negro Voters League (ANVL), a bipartisan group of old-line leaders (successor to the Atlanta Civic and Political League and the All-Citizens Registration Committee). Negroes edged back toward the political arena in 1953, when the coalition, in a city-wide Democratic Party primary, elected Atlanta University's president Rufus E. Clement, the first Negro to hold a municipal post since Reconstruction, to a term on the Atlanta School Board. Young militants rebuked Clement for his conservatism, but the Democratic Party's spirited efforts to stop him, plus the vituperation heaped upon him by white supremacists, so outraged the sensibilities of progressive whites that they joined blacks in sweeping Clement into office and with him Walden and Miles G. Amos as members of the Democratic Party's Executive Committee. By the time Allen ran for mayor, the coalition had twice reelected Clement to the School Board post.[15]

Allen was a natural favorite of this interracial alliance. His high status within the city's financial and social elite and the booster spirit that characterized his leadership of the Atlanta Chamber of Commerce in the 1950s made him the darling of the business community, while his moderate statements following the Supreme Court's 1954 school desegregation decision ensured his favor among blacks of the ANVL. Students who disliked Allen for his role as the chief white broker in the controversial sit-in settlement—a deal, indeed, that awaited implementation as the mayoral race proceeded—tried to derail his bid for office, but their support for an Allen rival failed to sway black masses who remained loyal to the ANVL's choice. And when Allen was compelled to face arch-segregationist Lester Maddox in a runoff, even reluctant students came around. In ten of Atlanta's predominantly black precincts, Allen crushed Maddox 17,683 to 95. It was said that the only blacks counted against Allen were those "who pulled a lever on the machine by mistake." Blacks not only voted in a bloc for Allen, they also voted in greater percentages than whites. The potential of black power by 1961 was clearly visible on the horizon.[16]

The mayoral race, Allen would later say, had been initially urged upon him by blacks with whom he had negotiated the sit-in settlement. Grace Hamilton, who had been acquainted with Allen for more than a decade, was not among the negotiators and therefore was probably not among the immediate prompters, but feeling his racial moderation and other qualifications made him an ideal successor to Hartsfield, she quickly enlisted in his campaign, becoming a full-time volunteer.

"When Ivan Allen's first city election came along, that was my first experience with really being involved actively on a political campaign staff," she recalled. "That's when I began to learn about what a city-wide campaign involved. I learned a lot of things and made a lot of friends." Newly arrived in the Hamilton household at the time was a Japanese graduate student from the University of Michigan, Yoriko Nakajima, who was researching the impact of blacks on American politics. Eleanor Hamilton Payne was living in Japan with her children and doctor husband, and Nakajima, who had arrived in Atlanta from Ann Arbor with little money but a desire to know "how the American political system works," was received in the Hamilton home as a surrogate daughter. Grace put her to work at once as another Allen volunteer, and Nakajima, when she later became a professor of political science at Kyoto Seika University in Japan, wrote a book about the experience.[17]

Allen would serve two terms and, he would tell an interviewer years afterward, "Grace Towns Hamilton was one of the mainstays of my tenure." He clearly valued her input along with the racial connection she represented, calling her at the time one of Atlanta's "most capable and most respected citizens." He appointed her to various posts, including an unexpired term on the city's Fund Appeals Review Board and membership on the Citizens Advisory Committee for Urban Renewal. Allen's admiration for Hamilton was forthright and apparently genuine, yet he appears (much in the manner of George Mitchell at the Southern Regional Council a decade earlier) to have made more symbolic than substantive use of her talents. When in April 1966 the mayor made her director of the newly formed Atlanta Youth Council (an outgrowth of recommendations made in 1965 by the Atlanta Commission on Crime and Juvenile Delinquency), charging her with launching the agency's work, he stressed the temporary nature of the appointment.[18]

The *Atlanta Journal* wrote on April 20, 1966: "Mrs. Hamilton will serve as executive director . . . only until the end of 1966 . . . she will be supplied with an assistant who will assume some of the responsibilities of administration and a great share of the research activities that are contemplated." The press announcement of her appointment quoted Allen as saying that "she knows the city and its problems . . . and can get things done." But very little appeared left for Hamilton to do. If Allen was engaged in tokenism, Hamilton never suspected it; had she thought as much, she surely would have resisted as indignantly as she had when she realized the symbolism she represented for George Mitchell. By 1966 Hamilton represented Atlanta's new 137th District in the Georgia General Assembly, and the limited duration of the council position may have been her idea because it accorded with the priority she placed on her legislative duties. Indeed, Allen may have employed Hamilton for her legislative credentials; she made at least one trip to Washington in search of federal funds for the council, a mission admirably in tune with her interests and aptitude.[19]

In his 1971 book *Mayor: Notes on the Sixties*, Allen gave Hamilton indirect credit for his "first awakening to the problems of the Negro." As he related the story, the year was 1947, he was thirty-six years old, and as part of his job as head of the city's Community Chest drive that year he met Hamilton when she came to support the Chest's annual allocation to the Atlanta Urban League. At that point in his life, he wrote, he was a member of "the comfortable white Southern business establishment and therefore had no reason to mingle with the black except on a paternalistic boss-to-lackey basis." Hamilton was nobody's lackey, and to Allen she was a new encounter, "a superb Negro lady" (as he would later call her). When Community Chest directors that year cut from the AUL allocation a $500 item for the agency's national dues, on the grounds it "eventually would be used for Communist purposes," Allen wrote, "They did it against my advice but I don't recall making too much of an issue of it." "The system again," he noted cryptically. When invited to his great consternation to attend the opening fund-raising drive of the Chest's Negro division—a budding politician in a segregationist society, he was loath to attend an all-black affair—his decent impulses nevertheless prevailed and he went, meeting by chance the buxom woman who had attended his mother as midwife at his birth. "The experience that night stayed with me quite a while," he wrote in *Mayor*, "and I remember that a few days later I sat down and wrote out a check for $500 from the Ivan Allen Company to Mrs. Grace Hamilton for National Urban League dues." (Allen's memoirs thus shed more light on the local dues controversy that complicated Hamilton's relations with the National Urban League in her last years with the Atlanta affiliate.)[20]

Allen was a decent man, seized with a need to right white society's wrongs against the Negro, but his racial affinity was culturally conditioned and no easier to shed than his own skin. Barely a year into his first term, he gave young blacks, who had stood against their elders in opposing his mayoral bid, good reason to say, "I told you so." As the Atlanta Negro community, in the wake of World War II, took concerted action to expand black living space on the city's western reaches, an effort in which Hamilton's AUL had been a leader (see Chapter 6), the white establishment lent a helping hand, aiming, to be sure, to increase Negro housing but also to ensure "the preservation and rationalization" of Atlanta's residential separation of the races. Hartsfield, for instance, had cooperated in the mid-1950s in the peaceful transfer of Collier Heights from white to Negro occupancy, and racial transitions occurred in other areas, most without violence. Cascade Heights was less accommodating. It was a more affluent neighborhood, and its residents sent up a cry of alarm at City Hall as transition approached. "Allen set out to save them," closing off the subdivision with barricades at Peyton and Harlan Roads, leaving "entrenched whites on one side, encroaching blacks on the other." The mayor's deed created a sensation. *Time, Newsweek, Business Week,* and other national publications pictured Atlanta, fond of calling itself "the city too busy to hate," as another Berlin, a "divided city" with a wall of its own. Trying to weather the storm, Allen called in old-line blacks who had marshaled the vote that put him in office, offering to rezone a tract of commercial property adjacent to the disputed area (the city, as Allen noted in *Mayor*, had long been dotted with unused commercially zoned plots of land deliberately situated between black and white neighborhoods) in return for cessation of pressures on Cascade Heights. When black elders merely entered a mild protest, young adults from the civil rights movement exerted pressure, forcing the elders to back out of City Hall talks until the "Peyton Wall" was demolished. Allen stubbornly resisted for a while, but, as he wrote in *Mayor*, "The [Fulton County Superior Court] saved me in the end," declaring the barrier illegal less than three months after its erection.[21]

The Peyton Road episode might have made Allen a one-term mayor had he not later mended matters with the black community by going to Washington to deliver an impassioned plea for the Federal Civil Rights Act of 1964. He was the only southern mayor to do so. After that, his reelection in 1965 for a second (his final) term was assured.

But Peyton Road did spell the end for the old black vanguard, forcing it to yield leadership to the Citizens Committee for Better City Planning, an umbrella group of all top civil rights organizations in Atlanta. As historian Alton Hornsby Jr. wrote, "The Walden-led cadre of leaders had not conceded defeat but the 'new blood' had claimed their titles." And a decade later, Atlanta indeed would have a young black mayor.[22]

Grace Towns Hamilton remained a devoted Allen fan throughout her life, as he was of her. In interviews for this book, she often laughed about his Peyton Road blunder, saying it would never have happened if he had remembered William Hartsfield's advice: "Never do anything wrong that they can take a picture of." That it was also a watershed event in the transition between Atlanta's old and new black politics did not figure in her memory of the episode.[23]

As the veil between the white and black worlds began to fade in the 1960s, under impetus of the impious young, Hamilton was increasingly drawn into organizations and projects associated less exclusively with race. Hitherto her influence and acquaintances among whites had been largely a function of her leadership roles in the YWCA, the NAACP (on whose executive committee she had served in the early 1940s), the Atlanta Urban League, the Southern Regional Council, the Committee for Georgia (a state affiliate of the Southern Conference for Human Welfare), and the Highlander Folk School of Monteagle, Tennessee, where, in the late 1940s, she served on the Board of Directors and occasionally led interracial seminars. Now she helped put together or was sought out for organizations working more directly for common concerns of the whole community; the Atlanta Youth Council post was an early example. Since the late 1940s, as head of the AUL, she had served on the Board of Directors of the Atlanta Community Planning Council, an interracial grouping of social agency executives. In 1964, with Mrs. Edward M. Vinson, a former president of the Georgia League of Women Voters, she helped organize Partners for Progress, an interracial women's group aiming to "tap the vast reservoir of good will"

believed to exist in Atlanta for the purpose of promoting "equal opportunity" in business, government, and community affairs. Vinson became
chairwoman of Partners, Hamilton its vice-chairwoman, and among its active members were Rebecca (Mrs. Harry M.) Gershon, who had been on
the Board of Directors of the Atlanta Urban League and was one of Hamilton's dearest white friends (they vacationed together during the 1950s in the
Virgin Islands), Emma Rush Brown, the playmate of her childhood, Coretta
Scott King, wife of Martin Luther King Jr., and Pearl Johnson Clement, wife
of Rufus E. Clement. This racial mixing, limited in scope though it was,
was once unheard-of, but it would grow rapidly in breadth and frequency
in the years ahead.[24]

By the mid-1960s, Hamilton's dedication to public service was legendary
in Atlanta, leading admirers to compare her to the late Eleanor Roosevelt.
While continuing to serve in positions she already occupied, she joined the
boards of the Atlanta Arts Festival, the Committee for International Visi-
tors, the Advisory Committee of the Fulton County Democratic Party, the
Multiple Sclerosis Society, and the Gate City Day Nursery Association,
filling the shoes once worn by her mother.

She was also soon in demand for purposes of state and nation. In 1963
Hamilton had attracted the attention of Georgia governor Carl Sanders,
who appointed her to his Commission on the Status of Women and later
made her a member of the Citizens Conference on Georgia's Judicial System as well as the Georgia Committee on Children and Youth. In 1966 she
was invited to attend a White House conference on civil rights, along with
such race notables as Ralph Abernathy, James Baldwin, Horace Mann Bond,
Edward Brooke, Shirley Chisholm, Kenneth B. Clark, Ira De A. Reid,
Martin Luther King Jr., and A. Philip Randolph. In early 1966 President
Lyndon B. Johnson named her to his Committee on Recreation and Natural Beauty, one of three women singled out for the honor. Hamilton by
then had herself become a race notable. (In Cleveland, visiting her daughter, when the White House called inviting her to the presidential signing of
the executive order creating the committee, Hamilton was amused by her
grandchildrens' reaction to the news: "Will it be on TV?" they asked.)[25]

Amid this state and national recognition, Hamilton experienced "the
most distressing racial incident" of her life, and she immediately set down
the details in a letter to Mayor Allen. Accused of failing to answer a traffic
court summons on a lane violation charge, she was arrested in her home at
8 A.M. July 8, 1964, hauled to court by two policemen who entered her home
"without invitation and practically with force," took her to the jail's rear

entrance, and put her in a cell behind two barred doors to await the court's convening. She pled not guilty to the alleged offense and guilty to a contempt of court charge, explaining her failure to respond to the summons, and was fined $25. The incident was hardly happenstance. Hamilton and her peers typically had blemish-free records, except for an occasional traffic offense, and white supremacists, out to show Negroes who was still boss, often used the traffic courts against them. Martin Luther King Jr.'s incarceration in a maximum security prison on a traffic misdemeanor in 1960 was an example; Horace T. Ward, later appointed to the federal bench by President Jimmy Carter, was excluded from the University of Georgia's law school in 1950, after the U.S. Supreme Court opened graduate schools to all students, because of alleged traffic violations.[26]

"This was a shattering personal experience," Hamilton wrote Allen, "but if it can help make it impossible for this sort of thing to happen to others it will have been worth enduring." Ironically, just the day before she had been asked by municipal authorities to help promote "citizen action to prevent trouble, disorder, dissension and hurt feelings" in the city. What her letter to Allen accomplished besides assuaging her own "hurt feelings" is not known. Then on the threshold of her new career, she doubtless did not dwell on the episode.[27]

11

The Lady from Fulton

. . .

NTERING a Georgia Democratic Party primary cost a candidate $400 in 1965, and on April 16 of that year, the *Atlanta Constitution* reported that "Mrs. Grace T. Hamilton has qualified as a Democratic candidate for the House from the new 137th district." On May 6, the *Atlanta Journal* carried the news that "Mrs. Grace T. Hamilton . . . won her Democratic primary race yesterday and has no Republican opposition in the June 5 general election." Hamilton's only primary opponent was a white industrial management student at Georgia Institute of Technology named James Leland Strange, and she won the race 395 votes to 133. It was a signal event for black women in Georgia and throughout the Deep South. A Negro woman then served in the Missouri legislature, and two others were state legislators in Maryland, but further south of the Mason-Dixon line black women until Hamilton had never before reached the lawmaking level.

This special off-year election, which brought Hamilton and six other Negro Democrats into the Georgia House of Representatives, was in all respects a historic landmark. Breaching the last color bar in the state's legislative apparatus, Georgia voters not only wrote finis to the century-long post-Reconstruction era; they gave the Georgia legislature almost as many Negro members as any state in the Union. Only Michigan and Illinois, with eleven each, had more. The Georgia capitol itself stood in a district represented by one of the newly elected blacks.[1]

The Georgia Senate had lost its lily-white complexion in 1963, when Leroy R. Johnson, a lawyer, former high school teacher, and longtime protégé of A. T. Walden at the Atlanta Negro Voters League, was elected from Fulton County's newly created Thirty-eighth Senatorial District, becoming the first Negro to sit in the Georgia General Assembly since William H. Rogers resigned in 1907 after the state constitutionally disfranchised the Negro race. His victory was the first fruit of a 1962 case, *Toombs* v. *Fortson,* a product of the two earlier suits that year, *Baker* v. *Carr* and *Gray* v. *Sanders.* *Baker* had immediately led Henry J. Toombs of Atlanta and others residing in the state's two most populous counties, Fulton and DeKalb (Atlanta lay astride them both), to file suit for reapportionment of the Georgia General Assembly in which rural voting strength in some cases exceeded that of Fulton County by ninety-eight to one. The federal district court in Atlanta, reluctant to be the first to order general reapportionment, went halfway, holding that Georgia should "have at least one house elected by the people apportioned to population." It pointedly advised the state to "reconstitute the legislature" in a special session to draw up the recommended reapportionment, barring which the court promised further action of its own to "accord plaintiffs their rights." (This court actually retained jurisdiction over Georgia's reapportionment for the next seven years, meaning that every reapportionment devised by the state until 1969 first had to get its approval.) Feeling the heat, the state legislature convened a special session in September 1962 and chose to reapportion its upper chamber. Previously entitled to one seat in the fifty-four-seat Senate, Fulton County was now assigned seven, all to be elected from newly carved districts but by an at-large vote of the whole county, a move patently meant to exclude the election of Negroes. Under Walden's tutelage, Johnson entered the race from the county's new Thirty-eighth Senatorial District, containing seventy thousand blacks in a total population of ninety thousand. Although Johnson won by an overwhelming margin, he had to resort to the court to establish his victory. He would serve twelve years in the Senate. At a time when more and more blacks were elected to public office in Georgia, as elsewhere, a *New York Times* writer called him "the single most powerful black politician in Dixie." In 1964, Johnson was joined in the Georgia Senate by Horace T. Ward, a lawyer, who was elected from the city's Thirty-ninth District, also heavily black. (Unable because of his race to study law at the University of Georgia, Ward graduated from Northwestern University Law School, and when the University of Georgia was finally integrated in 1961, he was the attorney for the admitted students.)[2]

Black political emancipation in Georgia, a halfway measure in 1962, moved nearer completion in 1964 when the U.S. Supreme Court made decisions compelling reapportionment of all congressional and state legislative districts. *Toombs* was immediately reactivated, and the federal district court forthwith directed the Georgia General Assembly to reapportion its lower chamber, which a special House reapportionment committee moved promptly to do, producing a plan approved by the 1965 legislature that redrew the boundaries of two-thirds of the chamber's seats. The court found the plan flawed but approved it as an "interim" measure, stipulating that a new reapportionment must occur in 1967 (this second reapportionment did take place on schedule). The interim plan thus put into effect gave Fulton County an eightfold increase in representation, a number more nearly in accord with its population than ever before in Georgia history. The county had long had only three representatives elected at large, but it was now awarded twenty-four seats, twenty-one to be filled from newly carved districts, the remaining three to be elected from the county at large. A special election, preceded by a May primary, was scheduled for June 1965 to name the upcoming 1966 legislature, and it was this election that sent Hamilton to the state House of Representatives. Her district, the 137th, like all those that produced the new members, was heavily black. According to tradition, her fellow legislators would address her as "the lady from Fulton."

Negro leaders, fully aware of the election's significance, had approached it with caution, choosing a group of candidates who could be perceived, by blacks and whites alike, as eminently suitable. Republican opposition, just beginning to reemerge in the South, was encouraged though none was successful.

Grace Hamilton became a candidate because she ideally matched the criteria. "There was a great effort [in the Negro leadership] to try to find people who were in a position to offer and who would be good members," Hamilton remembered. "We hadn't found anybody from my district. A young lawyer who was going to run himself asked me one day, he said, 'since you've lived in your district most of your life, you know more about it than most people. Why don't you run?' I said I'd think about it. I called Cookie, he was working in Texas [teaching at Prairie View College] that year. I called him up and he said, 'Why not? Go ahead.' And so I did."[3]

Senator Ward also had taken a hand in the selection of candidates, and he remembered: "The original blacks who went into the legislature . . . and on the council and school boards at that time . . . were kind of a pioneer type group who were highly educated or professionals, lawyers and so forth, some of them came out of the civil rights movement, some came out of the community service movement, like Grace. They were sold on that basis. . . . The group that we came out of were maybe overqualified for the job but we were the only ones that could get elected in that day and time, the only ones probably who knew how to get elected . . . [because] we had enough connections to raise a little money and already had some prominence."[4]

. . .

Grace Hamilton's family, professional, and cultural background had prepared her well for this new turn in her life. Her father had single-handedly led an early voter registration drive in Atlanta, and W. E. B. Du Bois, a strong intellectual influence on her thinking, had argued forcefully in the debates that led to formation of the NAACP years before that economic and civic wrongs against the Negro could be righted only when the race regained political power through the franchise. Robert R. Church had schooled her in the importance and techniques of the political process when he was the Negro "Mr. Republican." A. T. Walden had converted her into a "yellow dog Democrat"—as she termed herself—and the rising potential of the Negro vote in Georgia, to which both she and Walden had greatly contributed, had supplied the Democratic political affiliation with significant clout.[5]

Culturally, she had been well conditioned for leadership. "Men and women's roles are not so clearly defined among blacks as in the middle-class white society," she later noted. She also pointed out, "Women in the black community, by and large, have carried much of the burden of community leadership. That's reflected in the work of the church, it's reflected just all through organizations of general community service. Black women, it's nothing unusual for them to carry the burden of leadership and the actual doing of it."[6]

Once elected, she attracted widespread attention, and she tried without much success to keep it all in a neutral focus. She insisted that politics was not a "personal ambition" but rather "a place to put to use things I've learned with my work, an extension of my professional concerns." She stressed that she ran for the legislature "because I realized that working outside of government is uncertain and often futile, that no significant changes can be made without first changing the law."[7]

But eyes persistently turned to her gender and race, and she explained herself frankly. "I hope no one voted for me just because I'm a woman or because I'm a Negro," she told a postelection interviewer from the *Atlanta Constitution*. It was a hope that summed up the political approach that would guide her nearly two decades in the legislature. "I didn't think of myself first as a woman or first as a black," she reminded one and all when her legislative years were over. "I never claimed to be a radical, just reasonable." Racial uplift in itself was always less her goal than "the common good of all." In her view, if all rose, so would the Negro. It was a stance that appealed to establishment whites, but it often baffled and alienated those blacks who believed political means, once reacquired, could legitimately be used to redress ancient inequities between the races. She saw the ballot as a remedy in itself; affirmative action in behalf of blacks was acceptable, though she never stressed it, but she was adamant about the ballot. "My single and continuing interest," she insisted in later years, "has been in making the structure of government more equitable." Occasionally she phrased it another way, speaking of "my long-time and continuing interest in the structure and nature of local government." However she delineated her concern, the stature she achieved as a legislator rested largely on her success in providing Negroes with more electoral representation, in bringing to Atlanta blacks a greater measure of what some of them called "self-government," and when she eventually failed to be reelected it was because younger, more militant blacks believed she had ceased to serve that cause. Her views were always idealistic (even faintly echoing the excessive faith in the good intentions of white society that betrayed—as at least one historian has noted—Georgia's Reconstruction legislators), but they ran deep, they had roots in her family and racial history, and they were, above all, uniquely her own.[8]

Hamilton's political pragmatism contributed to her influence and success in the Georgia legislature, but her elegant personal appearance also helped. She once told an interviewer that she acquired chic by hounding dress sales at Leon Frohsin, a Peachtree establishment catering to well-off women. As in the case of Ivan Allen, Georgia legislators in the early 1960s were still used to dealing with blacks on a "boss-to-lackey" basis; meeting Grace Towns Hamilton was as much a revelation to most of them as it had been to Allen. A young politician who observed Hamilton in her early days in the legislature told the story of the rural white legislator who inadvertently said "yes, ma'am" to her. "He looked a little startled at first—almost as if he'd made a mistake in gender," recounted the politician. "But he quickly recovered and went right on talking. Mrs. Hamilton is just naturally the kind of lady you'd say 'yes, ma'am' to." Said a longtime friend: "From a ladylike, gracious and easy-to-accept token mulatto, she grew into a self-assured spokesperson for all Georgia women."[9]

• • •

Before reapportionment, the Georgia legislature scarcely seemed the forum for developing a black woman's self-assurance. The body had but a single female member in 1965, Janet Merritt of Americus. She and Hamilton would remain the sole women in the legislature until 1973. Only ten women had ever served before them since the first two, Violet Ross Napier and Bessie Kempton Crowell, were elected in 1923, and at some sessions no woman was present. Like other southern legislatures, Georgia's was dominated by small-town and rural white men, most of them older and poorly educated. Before 1962, when Negroes were totally absent, even the state's urban white population had meager representation, thanks to the county unit system. The Georgia legislature was so skewed against city dwellers, more and more of whom were black, that V. O. Key Jr., in his influential 1949 book, *Southern Politics in State and Nation*, entitled his chapter on Georgia "Rule of the Rustics." The legislature's rural bias, the county unit system of elections, and the malleability of the legislature's uninstructed membership "provided an open season for economic pressures from near and far," permitting "a few corporations together with a few skillful politicians" to run the state. Reapportionment circumscribed this rural-corporate power but did not overthrow it, and the Georgia Negro's return in relative force to the halls of political power in January 1966 was more symbolic than real. Georgia had the largest number of black legislators in the South, but as elsewhere, the overall percentage was small and they were—and would long remain—helpless to enact significant legislation, especially laws that benefited primarily blacks, most of whom were urban and poor.[10]

Grace Hamilton did not see the obstacles when she was sworn in as a state representative in January 1966. She forged ahead as if they did not exist.

Renewed power of the black ballot opened up untold possibilities, even—in her view—an end to the legislature's ancient rural-urban hostility. "Georgia is coming closer to the time when we can work together as a group for the common good of all," she said upon election. "We can determine how best to meet the needs of both rural and urban populations without the petty differences which bottleneck plans for the progress of the entire state." She would learn soon enough how utopian her vision was.[11]

Once in the legislature, Hamilton was easily accepted, as demonstrated by the white rural gentleman who had said "yes, ma'am" to her without flinching. "I was graciously and generously received in the Georgia House of Representatives," she later told a reporter for the *St. Louis Post-Dispatch.* "I had no experience of discourtesy. In fact, my fellow representatives gave me the best seat in the House, seat number one."[12]

Hamilton owed her preferential seat, in fact, not to her "fellow representatives," as she mistakenly remembered, but to George T. Smith, the House Speaker. Occupying the most powerful position in Georgia government, the Speaker was elected by the House membership and beholden to no one, not even the governor; he had total authority over all appointments to committees, including the naming of officers; even trips allowed the committees were at his discretion; and the House's exclusive role as originator of revenue and appropriations measures only added to his political clout. Among his other prerogatives was the right to determine all seating arrangements in the House chamber. That Smith held the Speaker's job at the height of the civil rights movement was significant, for he was a liberal in an era when Georgia was dominated by the likes of Lester Maddox, the ax-wielding restaurateur who would ride into the governor's office in November 1966 on a wave of racist reaction to Negro advances. Smith had gone from an impoverished boyhood on a south Georgia farm to become a navy officer in World War II and had used veterans' benefits at the University of Georgia to become a lawyer. In 1959, after ten years practicing law in the small town of Cairo, he was elected to the state legislature, and in 1963 he became Speaker.

One of Smith's earliest moves was to desegregate all public galleries in the legislature's chambers, a move accomplished without fanfare and, as Smith remembered, "without a single incident." But the arrival of Negro legislators on the House floor in 1966 was another matter, presenting Smith, as he put it, with "a delicate situation because there were certain members in the House who would not sit with blacks." Smith resolved the problem with courtesy to all. "I just went down the line and called legislators and said, 'would you agree to sit with the blacks, or by the blacks, or around the blacks?' And I got a group to agree to do it and that's the way I seated them," Smith recollected. Ultimately new Negro members, whom a less liberal Speaker might have seated in a block, "were scattered all over the House," but Smith gave the premiere seat to Hamilton not entirely out of altruism. He wanted to be governor and, as he later confessed, "I just thought, well now I'm going to give her the choice of the number one seat and maybe that'll help public relations between the blacks and me. I asked her if she wanted the number one seat and she said yes." (Smith's calculations only partially paid off; he would be elected lieutenant governor in 1966, a campaign in which Hamilton, as he remembered, "was very active," lose the job in 1970, and fail to win the governorship in 1974. Later he won election to the state's Court of Appeals and ultimately to its Supreme Court.) [13]

His modest self-interest in the seating matter in no way discolored Smith's genuine admiration for Hamilton. "I guess the first time I ever saw Grace in my life," he remembered, "was when she walked into my office to talk about committee appointments." He gave her just what she asked for, explaining his reasons years later: "It was two things. First impression was, she was a lady. The minute she walked into the office, you could tell that. The second thing was, after a few minutes talking to her, you could tell she was intelligent. She had common sense. There were a certain number of people you put on those committees, you filled the vacancies with people who asked for them provided they fit your qualifications. The most significant committee she asked for was appropriations. It was something freshmen legislators just seldom ever got. And I gave it to her." He went on: "She had intelligence, charm, common sense, class and the respect of her peers, and she used all of them to become a very well-liked, effective and influential legislator . . . and she wielded her share of power." [14]

Businesslike in approaching her legislative job, Hamilton first talked to Jack Etheridge, in 1966 chairman of the Fulton County House delegation, about committee requests: "Jack said, 'think about what you're concerned about.' He asked me, 'do you want to be on the committee that raises the money or the committee that spends the money.' I said, 'I want to be on the committee that spends the money.' So I told George T. Smith that my first choice would be appropriations, my second the health and hygiene committee, because that related to my health interest, and third, education. The most significant one was appropriations. We had to choose three. Well, I got all three." [15]

Hamilton's power in the Georgia legislature emanated from her practical approach to race and politics, an approach viewed with dismay by young and militant blacks even though it won her growing confidence among powerful whites. But when influence could further her own purpose of making the structure of government more equitable—according to her notion of equity—she brought all the influence she possessed to bear on the black cause.

Her legislative career peaked between 1969 and 1974, years when the structure of government in Atlanta, under her constant and successful reshaping, aided of course by others, indeed became more equitable. In those same years a second black woman (followed later by others) was elected to the legislature and blacks at last came into their own in Atlanta politics, electing first a vice-mayor and finally the mayor himself. Hamilton had a hand in all these developments.

Upon arrival at the Georgia capitol, she found an issue ready and waiting for her and she grasped it, aware, as an early biographer wrote, that the "respect of one's colleagues would increase if it were possible to secure passage of a bill in the first year." It was a "people" issue that attracted her, naturally; she had been involved with people problems most of her working life. Now new highways pushing through Atlanta were bringing hardship to poor people moved from construction's path, many of them black and lacking means to pay for transferring their goods to new locations. The federal government offered matching funds to meet most such costs, but the Georgia Highway Department had never participated in the program, preferring to use all its funds for roadwork. Hamilton quickly introduced a bill authorizing the state to ante up its matching share, and the measure soon cleared the legislature with strong support in both the Georgia House and Senate.

"She handled it like an old pro," said a legislative observer. "The only ones opposed were those who are against any aid to anybody. Still, there were quite a few of them. I watched Mrs. Hamilton approaching each member, sitting beside him and talking for a few minutes, then moving quietly on to another. The urban members of her own party were already in favor. She concentrated on rural legislators, who might not realize their constituents were as likely as anybody to be uprooted by highway construction. She had all the votes she needed when the bill came up. . . . Her speech for the bill was moving and eloquent, and when she had finished the legislature rose in a body to give her a standing ovation." Hamilton emerged from her initial legislative session as the only black to get a bill enacted into law, and her maiden speech was one of the few she ever delivered (though verification is difficult because no verbatim record is kept). She apparently followed the advice she had early received from Jack Etheridge to "speak little, listen much." [16]

George T. Smith, observing her from the Speaker's rostrum throughout her first legislative session, doubted that she had spoken at all, taking the "ovation" story to be apocryphal. "She never did speak," he said. "She may have but I never did see Gracie in the well the whole time I was there. The man or the woman in the legislature who is most influential seldom gets in the well. You don't place yourself in the position of being embarrassed by some question . . . you're not really prepared to answer. You never show your weaknesses. So you never get in the well. I never did. I figured if I couldn't get a law passed in the back room, then I sure couldn't get it passed down on the floor. And most effective legislators worked that way." As for Hamilton, he said, "There've been very few legislators more effective than Gracie." [17]

"People" issues continued to be the center of Hamilton's concern that first legislative session. With Janet Merritt, her sole female colleague in the House, she cosponsored a successful bill authorizing the Georgia Arts Commission to extend its existing assistance program to music and other performing arts. She also endured disappointment, as when she and Rodney M. Cook, a fellow Fulton County representative, sought to enable Atlanta to enforce repair or demolition of substandard property. Hamilton acidly commented at the time, "Like a lot of the buildings we were trying to destroy or improve, the bill was partly gutted. The right to enforce repairs was removed but the demolition part remained." She nevertheless counted it an achievement that in the first year after the measure's enactment, Atlanta razed three hundred substandard and dangerous structures. [18]

Overwhelming all else at the start of that 1966 session was the Julian Bond issue, whether to seat the militant civil rights activist (son of educator Horace Mann Bond, once a pupil at Atlanta University of Grace's father, George A. Towns), who was among the new black legislators. A few days before the legislature's scheduled convening date, the Student Non-Violent Coordinating Committee, of which Bond was a director, had publicly denounced United States involvement in Vietnam as "murderous aggression," and when asked, Bond said he supported SNCC's position. Charging Bond with "treason," the Georgia House refused to seat him, 184 to 12. He was supported by the black delegation in a solid phalanx and a few sympathetic whites. The *Atlanta World* applauded this "impressive exhibition of [black] union." Hamilton, though her belief in Bond did not grow with the years, on this matter said she believed he had merely exercised his legitimate right to express an opinion about American policy, but she felt compelled to concede that his remarks were "poorly timed." [19]

Hardly had this controversy receded into the courts (which eventually restored Bond to his elected position) than new tension erupted in Georgia, spilling its consequences into the 1967 legislative session. One reaction to the Negro's new political emergence was the revival of the Republican Party throughout the South. In the Georgia gubernatorial race of November 1966, a Republican, Bo Callaway, outpolled the Democratic candidate,

Lester Maddox, a declared racist, but a popular write-in candidate, former governor Ellis G. Arnall, had garnered thousands of votes so neither Maddox nor Callaway had a majority. The decision by law was remanded to the state legislature, which, being heavily Democratic, chose Maddox by a large margin. On this vote, the Negro delegation abstained en masse, leading the *Constitution* to admonish Maddox: "Every Negro legislator, speaking for a race that constitutes a huge minority of his state's citizenry, had nowhere else to go, and abstained symbolically from the making of a future that fills the Negro people with dread and apprehension. These abstentions were a terrible indictment by a great segment of Georgia's people." [20]

Somehow enduring Maddox, Hamilton went on to her next legislative endeavor, but she first had to defend her seat against a militant challenger, Helen Howard, a woman radicalized by the civil rights movement. State legislators normally served two-year terms, but Hamilton and her colleagues from the special 1965 election were compelled to stand again in the regular election of 1966, which was preceded as before by a primary. Howard, Hamilton's primary opponent, was a resident of Vine City, "one of Atlanta's worst slums," and leader of the Vine City Foundation, a group of the area's dwellers who had "banded together to improve their neighborhood." Hamilton was familiar enough with Vine City; she had always had a near view of the area, first from the windows of her father's house on University Place and later from her own home next door. Once after taking up "Sunday painting," she had rendered in oil a rather idealized view of small, colorful houses climbing a Vine City slope with a certain grace and dignity, a painting she framed and kept in her office in the months during 1966 that she worked at the Atlanta Youth Council. It was not the Vine City that Howard knew, and she and her foundation followers picketed Hamilton's home during the 1966 legislative session demanding playgrounds for their neighborhood, a demand Hamilton was unable to satisfy. Howard, Hamilton maintained in a later interview with Jacquelyn Hall, was "just a cat's paw" for the Southern Regional Council, which, Hamilton was convinced, had "put her in the race." Because the SRC was enjoined from direct political action of this kind, this was a serious charge, for which Hamilton offered more surmise than proof. In the decade-plus since she had collided unhappily at the SRC with George Mitchell, who left as director in 1957, the organization had become more focused and militant, in step with the civil rights movement, and some who worked for this "new" SRC had scant use for Hamilton's pragmatic philosophy about racial justice. She was doubtless correct in remembering that many of its people "heartily supported"

Howard. Among the more vigorous supporters would have been Doris Reed, Howard's daughter, an SRC secretary, who was said to have instigated her mother's challenge. The agency also had given Howard space in the November 1965 issue of its magazine, *Southern Changes*, to espouse the cause of the Vine City poor. Hamilton for years was easily aroused to scorn about the Howard challenge and what she perceived as the SRC's role in promoting it. Then and later, she characteristically never could muster any magnanimity toward her political opponents. "Mrs. Hamilton is a politician and I don't need to say any more about it," explained a close woman colleague. "In politics," she added, "you reward your friends and punish your enemies. You may forgive but you never forget." When the votes were counted on September 14, 1966, Hamilton handily overcame Howard at the polls, beating her 690 votes to 343, and for the next eighteen years, her seat, though sought by others, would remain safely in her hands.[21]

· · ·

After she was returned to the legislature, Hamilton's concern turned more and more to the "structure and nature of local government." "People" issues did not disappear from her agenda; she first worked in 1967 for a constitutional amendment providing tax relief for slum owners who improved their property, modeling her effort on an idea then on trial in New York, but when the legislation fell before Republican opposition, she turned to reapportionment, which the House was dealing with again that year under court order. Making the structure of government more equitable now depended on reapportionment, and Hamilton, wanting to lend her talent to the cause, wrote Speaker George L. Smith (who had replaced George T. Smith following the latter's 1966 election as lieutenant governor), offering her services on the "committee studying election laws and the various proposed changes in the code." Smith was not yet ready to put a Negro (much less a Negro woman) on such a politically volatile committee, and Hamilton tactfully accepted his rebuff. But she had her eye on other possibilities.[22]

When the Fulton Country ordinary lost seventeen thousand write-in votes in the chaotic 1966 election and failed to mail out absentee ballots on schedule, resulting in the disfranchisement of additional thousands, Hamilton found an issue needing attention and one suited to her interests and level of legislative experience. Electoral machinery, from the registering of voters to the counting of ballots, had always been entrusted to county ordinaries in Georgia, who in times past—when the Republican Party was moribund in the region—simply abdicated crucial aspects of their authority such as counting votes to Democratic Party officials. The easily manipulated county ordinaries had been the source of much corruption at the Georgia ballot box, and Hamilton in 1967, following the write-in fiasco, wanted to centralize electoral functions in a new County Board of Registration and Elections, to be headed by a supervisor appointed by the Fulton County Commission. Her plan quickly got the green light from the Fulton County delegation, and the House, in accordance with its tradition of accepting any "local" bill approved in advance by the delegation concerned, passed Hamilton's measure creating the new electoral machinery. Difficulties cropped up in the Senate, where the person in charge of registration persuaded lawmakers to let his function remain autonomous and, thus stripped down, Hamilton's measure became law. Not until 1970 was she able to get legislation passed that gave the County Board of Elections the inclusive functions she had originally envisioned. But she had gained her first "restructuring" experience, getting a good taste of the pragmatic maneuvering required for political success in the area where she most desired it.[23]

Hamilton's preoccupation with affairs of the hectic 1967 legislature paralleled another concern, the failing health of Nellie McNair Towns, her mother. In the last months of her life Mrs. Towns was cared for in the Harris Hospital, a proprietary hospital that had long served Atlanta's middle-class blacks. "It was not a nursing home but it was the best long-term care available at the time," Hamilton said. Mrs. Towns died May 11, 1967, at age eighty-eight.[24]

12

The Years of Racial Solidarity

. . .

For Grace Hamilton, the next five years were a time of racial solidarity, a time when she was fully in tune with the aims of her race, and her leadership gained in significance and impact. Beginning with the 1968 legislature, she took on the government of Atlanta in what would be a protracted but eventually successful struggle for a new Atlanta City Charter aimed at making the city's governing apparatus more workable and, for blacks, more representative. She was not alone in the struggle, but in the end she would get most of the credit for its successful outcome.

Of its own volition the city had submitted itself to scrutiny in 1965 by the Public Service Administration (PSA) of Chicago, which came up with a gloomy verdict: "Viewed broadly in a modern professional sense," said the PSA, "[Atlanta's government] would appear to be unmanageable." The problem, as the agency saw it, was that the mayor and the Board of Aldermen were trapped in a tangled skein of executive and legislative authority that weakened the mayor in favor of the Board of Aldermen because the aldermen not only made policy but also administered many of the laws they enacted. The peculiar structure might have cracked before, the PSA thought, had it not been for the personal strength of past mayors and the high caliber of some aldermen, but its viability was increasingly doubtful as the city expanded in size and complexity. The PSA recommended giving the mayor exclusive right to administer laws, the aldermen the sole right to make them.

Between 1968 and 1970 Hamilton mainly sought to implement this PSA recommendation. Mayor Ivan Allen and the Board of Aldermen had had the PSA report for two years but taken no action; Allen did not want trouble with the aldermen, and they did not want to relinquish their prerogatives. Pressure finally wrung from Allen a weak endorsement of Hamilton's aim— she would get the same after 1969 from Allen's successor, Sam Massell— but she was borne along in this campaign mainly by the support of her Fulton County colleagues in the legislature and her own determination.

After introducing what became known as the "strong mayor" bill in both 1968 and 1969 without success, she let the matter rest for a while, then, with characteristic persistence, returned to the attack in 1971 from another direction, seeking this time a total revision of the Atlanta City Charter, a document dating from 1874, whose age and inadequacy she and her supporters considered the primary source of modern Atlanta's "unmanageability." This time she was successful, as she explained in a 1972 interview: "I tried to correct, several times through legislation, matters in the organization of Atlanta's government that everybody seemed to think needed to be changed. These bills didn't pass. It finally occurred to me that the sensible thing to do would be to provide a document more suitable to the times we live in rather than 100 years ago. Therefore, I introduced a bill to establish the Atlanta Charter Commission, which passed." Out of the commission's work would come a new Atlanta city government, one that recognized blacks as never before.[1]

What Hamilton sought was no mere recodification of the old charter; she insisted on "substantive changes," and she wrote into the bill establishing the commission specific authority for this objective. She wanted not only to implement the PSA recommendation; now she was ready to attack the malapportionment and at-large voting that nurtured and perpetuated first the nonrepresentation and then the underrepresentation of blacks in the halls of city government. It was a frank push for "black power," and she used that term in a letter to a student at Morehouse College; it was a push worthy of any of the militant young. She and other blacks thought the charter should be rewritten to reflect and advance contemporary reality, which was that Atlanta's Negroes now constituted 41 percent of the city's electorate, that at crucial points they had voted in greater percentages than whites, and that for years they had cast the deciding votes in Atlanta's mayoral contests and in 1965 had finally managed in an at-large election to put one of their own, Q. V. Williamson, from the city's heavily black third ward, on the Board of Aldermen, the first black alderman since 1870.

Now Atlanta blacks, marching under Hamilton's banner, were out for more, determined, as she put it, "to give the entire populace a real say-so in choosing the governing body of Atlanta." And they now had on their side the U.S. Department of Justice, overseer of the Voting Rights Act of 1965, which had come to see multimember districts, at-large elections, and gerry-mandering as the major hindrances to black empowerment; as Justice had to approve all changes in election laws, including reapportionment plans, blacks were everywhere invoking federal support against white maneuvers to block their advance. Williamson's third ward was an example of the ob-stacles Negroes had faced in Atlanta; not only was it mostly black, it was also the largest ward in the city, having three times more people than the smallest ward, inhabited exclusively by whites. Already in 1969, before the Charter Commission was created, she had put through the legislature a bill making two wards out of the old third, giving the city nine wards, each electing two aldermen by the customary city-wide vote. Hamilton's move met little opposition as the city was by then increasingly swayed by black demands, but in fact her real aim, revealed once the commission went to work, was to shrink the number of aldermen and to elect half of them from redrawn disticts, leaving only six to at-large selection.[2]

The new Atlanta Charter Commission went to work on July 1, 1971, with thirty members appointed by the mayor, the aldermanic board, and the legislative delegations of Fulton and DeKalb Counties. Its mandate was to produce a new charter in eighteen months. Everyone knew Grace Hamil-ton was the project's godmother, but the commission chose to make her its vice-chairman and to name Emmet J. Bondurant, a prominent Atlanta at-torney, as its chairman. If she felt any disappointment, she concealed it with her usual aplomb, saying, "Of course he was an excellent chairman of the commission because he knew, as many of us didn't, we were not lawyers, what was really involved in some of these things."[3]

Exactly a year later, the commission published a first draft of the pro-posed new charter; it held public hearings until October 1, 1972, completed its final draft on December 1, and dissolved on December 31. Atlanta had a new governing document on March 16, 1973, when Governor Jimmy Carter signed the enabling legislation just passed by the Georgia legislature.

Hamilton was proud of the new charter, but it was not all she had hoped for. The first draft had satisfied all her primary objectives, providing At-lanta with a "strong" mayor, as the PSA had recommended, separating leg-islative and executive functions, and placing administrative authority en-tirely in the mayor's office. It also acknowledged racial reality by two new reforms—the Board of Aldermen, renamed the Atlanta City Council, was reduced in size from eighteen to twelve members, eight of them to be elected by redrawn districts and four elected city-wide, and the Atlanta Board of Education's eight members were to be elected half by district and half at large.

The shrunken City Council immediately became the subject of dissent. As Hamilton remembered: "A lot of people got nervous, as people do when there's any change proposed that would increase power or give a different group access to influence, money and so on." Nevertheless, the dissent had to be taken seriously because its sources were both black and white.[4]

The Board of Aldermen had objected vigorously all along to the cutback in number, and now it was joined in opposition by the Atlanta branch of the NAACP, which thought that fewer city aldermen "would reduce the base of representation and thereby reduce the influence of the Negro vote." The NAACP wanted district elections as much as Hamilton, but from more, not fewer, wards. The impasse was resolved by the compromise that left the new Atlanta City Council with eighteen members as before but with twelve elected by districts and only six by the old city-wide system. Hamilton, by now a seasoned and pragmatic politician, accepted defeat on the council's size "because the main thing was to get the bulk of the document through," but she remained convinced that Atlanta needed a smaller governing body, and she pursued this objective with her customary persistence for the remainder of her legislative career. She had achieved a major goal, however, which was "to create a more equitable structure to give the black population more of a chance." It was a chance they quickly seized. On October 16, 1973, when Atlantans, by now 50 percent black, went to the polls in a city election, they not only chose an even number of black and white city councilmen and a city school board with a black majority but also elected their first black mayor, Maynard Jackson, the first black mayor of any large southern city in American history. Over a century of white rule in Atlanta had come to an end and black power had triumphed in the gateway to Dixie. Major credit in the minds of many was due to Grace Towns Hamilton.[5]

Hamilton came to believe that a strong mayor, in the absence of professional management, was not the best answer to the city's problems. Still in the first flush of victory in March 1973, she was filled with optimism and modestly diverted attention from her own role in its creation, focusing praise instead on the commission. "It was a hard-working committee, it wasn't just something that let the staff write the reports. We spent thousands of hours on the job," she later remembered. People such as Sam A. Williams, executive director of Research Atlanta, wanted to keep the spotlight on her, and he wrote her after the charter became effective, saying, "If it had not been for years of work you invested in drafting the legislation, getting the Commission appointed, writing the Charter and finally getting it through the General Assembly, it would not have been done."[6]

• • •

The work of the Charter Commission was only one of her concerns in 1970 and 1971, for she was also much involved with reapportionment. These were the busiest years of her life, and that she could devote "thousands of hours" to the charter when she was simultaneously preoccupied with other major legislative and extralegislative matters (not to mention the attention she constantly had to pay to the day-to-day interests of her district's constituents) was a tribute to her energy, commitment, and indomitable will. There were times, indeed, when the pace fatigued her. "I've taken on too much for one year, I don't have a sense of timing," she ruefully conceded to Reg Murphy of the *Atlanta Constitution* in September 1971, as that year's reapportionment fight heated up. Murphy commented, "Where work is concerned, Grace Hamilton never has a sense of timing."[7]

Overexertion doubtless helped bring on the heart attack she had suffered on March 6, 1969, in the waning days of that year's legislative session. Rushed to Hughes Spalding Pavilion, she was soon transferred to newly integrated Grady Hospital, where Asa Yancey was her physician. What thoughts must have crossed the minds of these two people, who had labored long—and at last successfully—to make the Negro middle-class patient and doctor relationship a routine occurrence at Grady! Even while bedridden, she had busily pursued legislative concerns, discussing with Remer Tyson, the *Atlanta Constitution*'s political editor when he visited her, various proposals for consolidation of Atlanta and Fulton County government, an idea she favored, as she told the newspaperman, if racial gerrymandering could be avoided. A close friend, Helen Bullard, reported that during this "rest" period, Hamilton could be found "sitting in bed like the Queen Mother with work and papers piled all around her."[8]

Discharged with a good prognosis, she was now fully recovered and, ignoring the doctor's admonition to quit smoking, was soon back in the thick of the legislative whirl and busily at work on the charter. She was also pushing her way into the reapportionment struggle, which loomed ever larger in the Negro's fight for more political muscle. In obedience to court order, the Georgia House in 1967 remedied the deficiencies of its 1965 reapportionment, a move that renumbered districts, among other things, putting

Hamilton in the 112th District instead of the 137th. In 1970, the state was compelled to reapportion again in recognition of the population shifts revealed by that year's decennial census, and Hamilton reopened the subject of her committee assignments with House Speaker George L. Smith.

"I knew there was going to be the question of appropriate drawing of lines in terms of the urban areas, as well as in terms of racial representation," she later recollected.

> So the summer before the reapportionment committee was to be appointed, before it was going to work, I went to the Speaker and told him I wanted a change in my committee assignments, that I wanted to get rid of Health and Hygiene, if he would agree, because I wanted a place on the Reapportionment Committee. And George L. said, "Aw, Mrs. Hamilton, I was going to make you vice-chairman of Health and Hygiene." And I said, "I don't need to be chairman or vice-chairman. I want to be on the Reapportionment Committee." So he said, "Well, all right, if that's what you want," and he wrote himself a little note and I got put on it. Without any real trouble. I was the only black person on the committee. And one of three from the urban areas. It was stacked preponderantly away from the urban areas.

Her lost bid for a place on the 1967 committee studying election law changes did not figure by then in her memory at all. In 1971 her reputation in the General Assembly was more secure, George L. Smith obviously thought she posed no threat to the leadership's interests, and neither he nor she apparently remembered the 1967 rebuff.[9]

Hamilton's reapportionment work would put a cap on her legislative reputation, both for better and for worse. The committee had two subcommittees, one on congressional reapportionment, the other on remapping the legislature. In February 1972 Hamilton was made chairman of the former, and in 1975 she would become vice-chair of the full committee, ultimately serving as its chair during her last two years in the legislature. Simultaneously, she chaired a subcommittee of the House Appropriations Committee, and in 1976 she would be elevated to a place on the House Policy Committee, the Speaker's vehicle for enforcing the leadership's agenda, positions she also held for the rest of her House tenure. No black woman in Georgia—or so far as known, anywhere else in the South—had reached such a pinnacle of state political power.[10]

In her appointed slot on the Reapportionment Committee in June 1971, she knew her work was cut out for her, as the predominantly rural-minded body, like the General Assembly itself, was little inclined toward electoral justice for either blacks or city dwellers. "She was very conscientious," recalled Delmer D. Dunn, a political scientist at the University of Georgia who participated in the committee's work. "She had carefully studied the Voting Rights Act, especially its 'Section Five' provision against dilution of black voting strength, and she was determined to make the Committee follow the law." The need for her vigilance was soon apparent.[11]

The committee faced not only the three-pronged task of reapportioning House, Senate, and congressional districts in conformity with the "one man, one vote" command of the Voting Rights Act, but also the necessity to reduce the number of House members, as recently directed by the General Assembly, from 195 to 180. A special ten-day session of the General Assembly commenced on September 24, 1971, and the Reapportionment Committee turned first to the legislative apparatus, producing a House plan that once again changed district numbers, placing Hamilton now in the Thirty-first District instead of the 112th, and dividing up the reduced membership among a nearly equal number of single- and multimember districts. This plan was rejected by the U.S. Justice Department when—duly passed by the General Assembly—it was submitted in November 1971 for federal approval, on the grounds that the potential of multimember configurations had a racially discriminatory effect on voting. Attempting to placate the Justice Department, the committee went back to work in the 1972 General Assembly, converting a small portion of the offending units to single-member districts, but Justice remained unsatisfied and in the absence of an approved plan obtained an injunction against that year's legislative elections. The elections nevertheless occurred on schedule with the express sanction of the U.S. Supreme Court, which temporarily stayed the injunction, reinstating it in May 1973, which sent the Reapportionment Committee back to its labors in the 1974 legislature. A new plan emerged from this session, which, when approved by the General Assembly in February, finally obtained the necessary clearance in Washington. (The only known available documentation of this prolonged procedure is the brief account Hamilton wrote herself and preserved in the papers she gave to the Atlanta History Center.) Once elected from predominantly single-member districts, Georgia's General Assembly began to change color, its black members growing from thirteen in 1973–74 to twenty in 1975–76. (The number had reached forty by 1992.) Among the new legislators in 1973 was the second black woman, Betty J. Clark from the Fifty-fifth District in DeKalb County, for whom Hamilton would become a mentor and close personal friend.

This prolonged foot-dragging on a racially just legislative apparatus had been matched, in the meantime, by even more overt racism within the

Assembly and its House Reapportionment Committee on redrawing the Fifth Congressional District. With Atlanta as its centerpiece, this district had become, as two writers at the Southern Regional Council later called it, "since mid-century one of the South's most volatile and visible political theatres." Hamilton took up her post as chairwoman of the Congressional Reapportionment Subcommittee just as the struggle reached a climax, and from this vantage point she did all she could, with more immediate luck than she had had in the concurrent legislative battle, to influence the outcome in favor of racial justice.[12]

Andrew Young, disciple and friend of Martin Luther King Jr. and then director of the Atlanta Community Relations Council, had nearly captured the Fifth District's congressional seat in 1970, and his good showing, reflecting strong local and national backing from his fellow African Americans and the support of not a few whites from Atlanta's old black-white coalition, raised the hackles of the area's racists. After handily winning the Democratic primary, Young was backed by 43 percent of the voters in the general election, a substantial number of them whites, but he lost out to a backlash Republican, Fletcher Thompson, from suburban East Point, the first GOP representative sent to Washington from Georgia since Reconstruction. Encouraged by this 1970 showing, Young was ready to run again in 1972, and the Assembly's leadership was out to stop him.[13]

Atlanta, which had a population slightly larger than the recognized ideal under the "one man, one vote" requirement, had lost some of its southeastern DeKalb County neighborhoods to the suburban Fourth District in the 1965 reapportionment. Because Thompson was also from a suburban community, Grace Hamilton perceived that the city in 1971 had "two suburban Congressmen . . . effectively denying the core city any representation at all." It was an anomaly she set out to correct on June 21, 1971, when she presented to the Congressional Reapportionment Subcommittee (even before she had become its chair) a detailed redrawing of Georgia's congressional districts. The most newsworthy feature of her plan was a separate district for the city of Atlanta. She told fellow committee members: "The population of Atlanta and sub-populations within the city have generally similar economic and social characteristics . . . they tend to vote differently from voters in the suburbs . . . they are not now effectively represented in the U.S. House of Representatives . . . and they should have the opportunity to elect their own Congressman." Characteristically, she was not trying to secure a niche for a black person. "Race is irrelevant," she insisted, though she acknowledged she "would be happy to send a qualified black Atlanta

to Washington." White Atlanta was generally supportive, though uncon-
vinced by her race-neutral stance, the *Atlanta Journal* conceding without
any apparent alarm that Hamilton's plan "enhances the chances for electing
the state's first [*sic*] Negro Congressman" and the *Atlanta Constitution* calling her plan "an interesting one which merits consideration." Her companions on the Reapportionment Committee, however, were hostile and
soon produced their own scheme, approved in the special session of September 1971, that divided up the city like a giant pizza, carving out its largest
concentrations of blacks and dispersing them, not between two districts as
before, but among three—the Fourth, Fifth, and Sixth. The Atlanta district
was left "hacked and bleeding" (as Reg Murphy wrote in the *Atlanta Constitution*, almost echoing Hamilton), "with nobody representing the city's
view in Washington." Among those gerrymandered into the rural Sixth District, condemning their congressional ambitions to oblivion, were Representative Julian Bond, Senator Leroy Johnson, Maynard Jackson, then Atlanta's elected vice-mayor, and Andrew Young, whose southwest Atlanta
home was removed from the Fifth District by one block. Incumbent Fletcher
Thompson, taking no pains to conceal his elation, was quoted as boasting,
"Well, that gets rid of Johnson, Bond and Young." A Negro housing complex within the shadow of the state capitol was sliced three ways, parts
falling in all three districts, and everywhere they were scattered, black voters became smaller in number than ever before. More than one hundred
thousand blacks were moved in this way from the Fifth District to the
Fourth and Sixth, leaving the Fifth with a population 70 percent white and
30 percent black. As the district had long been no less than 40 percent black
(and was growing darker all the time), it was gerrymandering at its most
blatant, and the plan, enacted into law by Governor Jimmy Carter in October 1971, was taken to court before the ink was dry. Six Atlanta blacks
represented by counsel from the NAACP attacked it before a three-judge
federal court in the Fifth Judicial Circuit. Hamilton was among those testifying against the plan on December 21, 1971. An incensed black community
gave Hamilton credit for leading the "battle for fair reapportionment." As
she told the *Atlanta Inquirer*, a Negro newspaper, her battle plan in a committee bent on legally vulnerable action had been simply to "build a good
court record . . . our efforts to get the proposal amended are on the record."
It proved a sound tactic. She also immediately petitioned the U.S. Justice
Department in a letter dated November 5, 1971, to intervene against the plan;
the Fulton County Democratic Party likewise petitioned on December 13.

Both requests, as well as the court action, were pro forma because changes in Georgia's voting procedures could not become effective without "clearance" from the Justice Department, to which the new plan had already been submitted for review.[14]

The Georgia General Assembly met for its regular session in January 1972, still awaiting Attorney General John Mitchell's response to the proposed gerrymandering; he rejected it on February 11, saying it diluted black voting strength in Atlanta and was drawn with discriminatory intent. Chastised, the legislature on February 29, 1972, adopted a rewritten plan, returning some blacks, including Young, to the Fifth Congressional District and giving it a 44 percent black population. Hamilton tried in vain from the House floor to raise blacks to 48 percent of the new district's population, and she remained convinced that the approved plan was as legally vulnerable as the first. Accordingly, she supported later efforts by C. A. Bacote of Atlanta University and others to persuade the district court, which was still considering the disputed reapportionment, to act against the 44 percent plan. The Justice Department, however, approved it in late March 1972 so the court in May dismissed all action in the matter. Drawing on sympathy generated for his cause in white Atlanta, Andrew Young won the Democratic primary in August 1972, winning nearly twice the number of votes of his nearest competitor, Wyche Fowler, a white who had served on Atlanta's Board of Aldermen. In the general election that followed, Young ran against Rodney M. Cook, beating him with 53 percent of the vote, 20 percent of which came from whites.

Atlanta at last had its own congressman, as Hamilton advocated. Young was the first black to represent a Georgia district in Washington since Jefferson Franklin Long was elected from the Macon district at the height of Reconstruction in 1870, and he would later credit Hamilton with making his election possible. Given her role in the black municipal triumph the following year, it was indeed a time when Hamilton's solidarity with her race had never been greater.[15]

· · ·

As its meaningful political power grew, so did the discord within the black community that would eventually erode Hamilton's ties to her race. Even as she worked tirelessly and successfully to "make the structure of government more equitable," fellow blacks were beginning to look askance at her record. On February 9, 1972, the Butler Street YMCA's Hungry Club, an interracial forum founded by Negroes, invited black elected officials to give "an accounting of their stewardship," coupling the invitation with a charge that three of them—Hamilton, Representative William Alexander, and Senator Ward—devoted too much time to "broad-based" legislation and not enough to efforts to correct specific problems of the race. Alexander apparently answered for all three, saying, "It's true our bills are broad based. They benefit all but are no less relevant to blacks. So don't take the narrow view of what is relevant or not." The *Atlanta Constitution's* account of the meeting indicated that Hamilton offered no response. It was a charge she instinctively felt beneath her, for she believed in the ballot box, not the soap box; besides, she was philosophically committed to working for the common good, believing black and white progress were inseparable.[16]

Blacks might doubt her, but in the white community Hamilton's approach was continually applauded. One white colleague put it this way: "She thought good government had no color," believing her efforts to enhance the Negro's electoral power were "just as good for whites as for blacks." Hamilton was dedicated, as always, to multiracialism, or rather to the absence of race as a consideration in human relations. Achievements of the civil rights era, she was convinced, were not the work of black militants but "the result of increased multi-racial consideration of the problem." So committed was she to multiracialism that she even opposed the formal organization of the Georgia Legislative Black Caucus in 1973, and when it was formed over her objections, and then despite her active participation failed to live up to her expectations, she decided to give it "just nominal support and put my time on other things." Informal gatherings among black legislators were acceptable to her, but formal organization for the pursuit of purely black goals was ideologically offensive. She knew that her race's problems were real, but in the legislature she remained committed to common solutions. She described her approach in interviews for this book: "In the legislature I tended to think you could get further faster by expanding the understanding of the white leadership about the totality of the problem, not acting as if this is just something that affects . . . blacks. I had a responsibility, I thought, to contribute to the education of the people that deal with resources for the poor." Broad-based legislation focusing on the "structure of government," therefore, remained at the center of Hamilton's concerns for the rest of her legislative years.[17]

• • •

Never afraid to tackle a hornet's nest, she proposed in 1970 the consolidation of Georgia's 159 counties so none would have fewer than ten thousand people, a move that would have eliminated 79 counties in a fell swoop. She noted: "Some of these counties have more trees than people, and in most of them government is the biggest industry—the sheriff, county commission posts and smaller offices. This type of industry is a drag on the taxpayer, not a boon." The bill "didn't fly"—to use one of her favorite metaphors—but it indicated the statewide scope of her concerns.[18]

Despite her preoccupation with governmental restructuring, she managed in the early 1970s to join the growing struggle to legalize abortion. In 1968 a new law permitted abortion in Georgia under highly controlled and limited circumstances and, though even such restricted choice was a rarity in America at the time, Hamilton and Representative Kiliaen Townsend, a Fulton County white Republican, introduced bills in the 1970 and 1971 legislatures that went further, freely sanctioning abortion in the first twelve weeks of pregnancy. Georgia's 1968 law was meanwhile before the courts, in one of the many legal maneuvers of the national pro-choice movement. Hearings held on the Hamilton-Townsend bills were rendered moot on January 22, 1973, when the U.S. Supreme Court in *Roe* v. *Wade* legalized first-trimester abortions nationwide and simultaneously reinforced that finding with a decision in the Georgia case, *Doe* v. *Bolton*, striking down all the state's early abortion restrictions.[19]

In 1971 Hamilton also aided Representative John Greer of Fulton County, a close personal friend, in getting the legislature to approve a sales tax increase in Atlanta to finance a city-wide rail and subway system, but when the system under the Metropolitan Atlanta Regional Transportation Authority finally became operative, Greer rather than Hamilton would be most closely identified with its creation.

In 1971 Hamilton was named Atlanta's Woman of the Year in the Professions, the first Negro ever honored in that competition, which had been an annual city event since 1943. She typically refrained from acknowledging the racial singularity of the honor in her acceptance speech at the awards banquet, choosing to remark on its other innovative aspect. "I rejoice," she said, "that work in the political process was regarded by the nominating committee as a profession."[20]

In January of that year, life came full circle for her when she was appointed by the Fulton County Commission to the formerly all-white Fulton-DeKalb Hospital Authority, the body with which she had worked closely during the days of segregation in bringing about the creation of the Hughes Spalding Pavilion. "We can't think of a better qualified person," commented the *Atlanta Journal.* "There is the tact and intelligence as usual, but there is also the knowledge accumulated over a quarter century's study and worry of the problems faced by this authority."[21]

In 1972 she was elected to the executive committees of both the Fulton County Democratic Party and the Georgia Democratic Party, posts she would occupy for the next six years; she was also named that same year Georgia Speaker of the Year by student debaters of Emory University in recognition of her work on behalf of "abortion, the new Atlanta Charter and fair reapportionment in Georgia." Her alma mater, Atlanta University, on whose Board of Trustees she had served since 1953, in 1969 had chosen her its Alumnus of the Year. These were only the earliest of many awards and honors Hamilton would receive during and after her years in the legislature.[22]

· · ·

Hamilton might have slackened her pace once the Atlanta Charter and the Fifth Congressional District were reshaped to her liking, but she seemed incapable of slowing down. "She turned loose one problem and just picked up on another," a colleague remembered. In 1974, with "good government" as ever her overriding aim, Hamilton "picked up on" the Fulton County Commission, which was responsible for governing the portion of the county outside Atlanta and the last remaining all-white governing entity in the metropolitan area. The commission was racist and generally incompetent, and it was the constant butt of jibes in Atlanta newspapers, which often described commissioners or depicted them in cartoons as "pompous," "pious," and a "round-the-bend gang." Commission chairman Goodwyn (known as Shag) Cates was the target of especially pointed abuse. Hamilton apparently shared this media opinion, considering the commission under Cates a bastion of county cronyism. She was not alone in attempting to restructure this ailing body, but her growing political skills and influence plus the unflagging attention and respect paid her in the media assured her an effective voice. She had learned well how best to use her assets.[23]

Restructuring the commission, like the legislative reshaping then also under way, became a long, drawn-out controversy, embroiling the commission for the next four years in court challenges, legal hassles, and legislative maneuvering that left none of the active participants untouched by the fray, including Hamilton. She would, in fact, come close to losing her seat in the legislature as the result of a challenge not unrelated to the fray, and as a more direct consequence she would be deprived of the seat she highly prized on the Fulton-DeKalb Hospital Authority. It was scarcely a coincidence that the erosion of her racial solidarity began precisely in this period of the commission affair.

The three-member Fulton County Commission, elected since 1952 by plurality vote, was brought under a new local statute in 1970 requiring winners to gain a majority, which figured heavily in the new commission dispute. In the 1973 legislature, where Grace Hamilton was absorbed in launching the rewritten Atlanta Charter, Senator Paul D. Coverdell, an Atlanta Republican, authored local legislation—bitterly opposed by the commissioners—that enlarged the body to seven members, leaving three to be elected at large and four new members to be chosen from districts, two of which were drawn to include populations nearly 90 percent black. When Hamilton finally studied the Coverdell legislation at the outset of the 1974 legislature, she considered one "white" district seriously malapportioned against blacks and immediately introduced legislation to remedy the defect. Race was not the main issue between Hamilton and Coverdell. He was not antiblack, but he was even more pro-GOP; he was among southern Republicans in that period who thought reapportionment could serve his political party as well as the Negro cause, and this sometimes involved working with blacks and sometimes against them. His strategy in 1974 was anti-Hamilton, and he deftly maneuvered to win legislative approval of the malapportioned district boundary he preferred, which just happened to favor the GOP. Hamilton retaliated at once, formally complaining, with her colleague Representative J. C. Daugherty, to the U.S. Justice Department, urging its intervention to compel fairer reapportionment.

Influenced no doubt by the Hamilton-Daugherty entreaty but required to make its own evaluation, the Justice Department on May 22, 1974, cleared the law's broad purpose but objected to its at-large component, saying (as had become its custom) that at-large seats unconstitutionally diluted black electoral strength and even more so when combined, as here, with majority voting. The ruling arrived in Fulton County just as the deadline approached for candidates to qualify for the next commission elections. With the Coverdell-sponsored law thus mooted by Justice objections and replacement legislation blocked in the General Assembly (where the Senate was much swayed by incumbent Commissioner Cates and his allies), the impending contest appeared likely to have no governing statute. Into the breach stepped the Fulton County Board of Elections, which, in an exercise of doubtful legality, ordered the three at-large commissioners to run under the old plurality requirement, leaving the four new commissioners alone to be chosen under majority voting. It was an idea nobody much liked, not even Commissioner Cates, and certainly not Hamilton, who was so certain it was not only racially discriminatory but also illegal that she, joined by Daugherty, petitioned Justice to seek an injunction against the election. Justice did not oblige. Just hours before the qualification deadline, however, on June 17, a three-judge federal panel held the Coverdell law unenforceable, said the Board of Elections acted without authority, and turned over to Judge Newell Edenfield, a panel member, the task of devising an "interim" basis for conducting the election. Edenfield's plan, "drafted most hastily" the same day, adopted essentially without change the Board of Elections' "plurality" idea, stipulating that it was for "one time and one county only." He also directed "the next session of the Georgia General Assembly" to produce "a final and constitutionally acceptable remedy . . . for the entire controversy." Confusion reigned, and it would get worse before the situation improved, but the 1974 elections occurred as scheduled on August 13, yielding a new seven-member commission with two blacks among them. Cates and his fellow incumbents squeaked through thanks only to the "old" plurality provision, gaining nowhere near the majority win of their new colleagues and leaving the media with grounds for new contemptuous thrusts against them.[24]

· · ·

Although the election defused the commission controversy, the legislature still faced Judge Edenfield's demand that it find a "constitutionally acceptable remedy" for the problem, and this became Hamilton's immediate objective in the 1975 legislature. Beginning anew seemed to her the best solution, and accordingly she soon tossed in the hopper a bill reducing the just-elected commission's life to two years instead of the prescribed four, restructuring some of the designated district lines for what she considered better racial balance, and proposing a referendum to ratify her approach. The Fulton delegation in the House sided with her, assuring passage if the matter came to a full House vote, but her bill was stymied when the Senate refused even to consider it. With the legislature still at loggerheads, even the federal courts seemed unable to agree on what should be done. A solution nearly identical to Hamilton's was proposed by Judge Edenfield himself in June 1975, but the Fifth Circuit Court of Appeals in 1976 stayed the plan (thus throwing into limbo Hamilton's own proposed statute) and, pointing to the election of blacks under the Coverdell law in 1974 as proof of its nondiscriminatory effect, ordered the commission to submit that law anew for clearance at the Justice Department. This time Justice approved it.

Hamilton, continuing to find fault with the Coverdell law, in 1977 proposed constituting the commission in another way, dividing its seven members among six districts with the seventh to run at large for the chairman's post, a plan she thought fairer to blacks. It "didn't fly," and the revived Coverdell law became the statute governing the 1978 election. "Shag" Cates by then was no longer on the commission, having had himself appointed by the commission as Fulton County tax assessor, and all survivors of the "Shag Cates gang" were defeated for reelection. Michael Lomax, a black who had moved to Georgia from California in the 1960s, in November was elected as one of the at-large commissioners. "The politics of racism," commented Bill Shipp in the *Constitution*, "may be fading fast."[25]

· · ·

The personal fallout Hamilton endured from the commission affair shook her temporarily but left her basically unscathed politically. On February 5, 1975, the "new" commission had voted unanimously, with Henry D. Dodson, one of the black commissioners, abstaining, to renew Hamilton's appointment as a member of the Fulton-DeKalb Hospital Authority, a post she had held since 1971 and considered "one of the highlights of her career as a public servant." She was notified by mail of the reappointment.[26]

Suddenly on February 19, the commission rescinded the reappointment, removing her from the authority by the same unanimous vote as before, Dodson again abstaining. They gave Hamilton the gate, said the commission, because she had not actively pushed for state funds to help Grady Hospital, a palpably false charge because her efforts on behalf of the institution had been unremitting from her seat on the House Appropriations Committee but had been long blocked by the legislature. No one doubted the real reason was her move to shorten the current commission's life. Hamilton personally blamed Cates. Public reaction was swift and all pro-Hamilton.

"An outrage," cried the *Atlanta Constitution*. "A damned outrage," shouted her friend, Representative John Greer, and Speaker of the House Tom Murphy said the commission made "a bad mistake" in firing Hamilton because "she really worked for Grady." The Georgia House went to bat for her, passing a resolution expressing admiration for her work on the authority, which it presented to her with a standing ovation. A month later, in what the *Constitution* called a "Tribute to Grace," the Assembly voted special financial help for Grady. The outpouring of support led neither to passage of her commission curtailment bill nor to her return to the Hospital Authority, a post she never held again.[27]

In perhaps a more telling outgrowth of the commission episode, Hamilton had to contend with the animosity of Henry Dodson, depicted by the *Constitution* as one of the "Shag Cates gang," when in the 1976 Democratic primary she suddenly faced the most formidable opponent of her legislative career, Georgia Blackburn Jones, a well-regarded placement director at Clark College. Dodson had his own bone to pick with Hamilton, for he maintained that the district lines she drew in her bill restructuring the commission—bottlenecked in the Senate, a fact he failed to acknowledge—put him in a politically impossible position, and he was bent on "taking a shot at her." He "tooled around the 31st district," a *Constitution* reporter wrote, in the car provided him by the commission, putting up signs and shaking hands for candidate Jones. "I want Sister Grace to know how it feels to know that somebody wants your job," Dodson explained. But he was not the only one of Hamilton's black colleagues siding with Jones, for some who sat with her in the legislature gave Jones money and otherwise pushed her election bid. Hamilton fought the challenge with her usual campaign strategy, spending little money, never taking to the streets, sending out brochures that informed her constituents of her legislative activity in the previous two years, and then sitting back in expectation of the usual victory.[28]

Her expectation was fulfilled, but just barely; she won the August 10 primary by 944 votes against 824 for Jones. So close was the tally that a recount was legally required if Jones requested it, which she did, but the recount, held on August 16, made no change in the outcome. In 1978 Jones switched her party affiliation to Republican and ran against Hamilton in the general election, a contest Hamilton won more easily than the first, gaining 81 percent of the vote to 18 percent for Jones. Until her last year in the legislature, Hamilton never again faced opposition in either primary or general elections. In this same 1978 election, Henry Dodson was turned out of his seat on the Fulton County Commission.[29]

13

Waning Solidarity, Growing Power

. . .

WHILE pouring her energy into revamping the Atlanta and Fulton County governments, Grace Hamilton remained firmly committed to city-county consolidation, a controversial goal she shared with others who were likewise convinced that metropolitan Atlanta was a single unit with common problems easier to solve in a unified government. Other cities such as Jacksonville in Duval County, Florida, and Columbus in Muscogee County, Georgia, had tried it successfully, and she had supported merger based on these models—provided gerrymandering could be avoided—since soon after she entered the legislature. It remained her goal, though a failed one, until the end. Opposition from whites fearing absorption in the city had always shot it down; now it was opposed as firmly by blacks who feared they would be outnumbered by whites in a city they aspired to govern.

Even as she labored conscientiously to provide her race an equal share in the city and county government, she supported a plan, launched by Mayor Sam Massell in 1972, that would probably have blocked the triumph of black power in the city, though that was not her purpose in supporting it. Massell was elected to office in 1969 along with a black vice-mayor, Maynard Jackson, by a coalition of black and Jewish voters, a variant on the city's old black-white voting alliance. Soon he was seeking to annex more whites into the city both to enhance the city's financial health and not incidentally his own reelection chances should he have to oppose a strong black candidate like Jackson. He carefully crafted a plan for two cities, empowering Atlanta to annex north Fulton County, an affluent, mostly white area that would have converted Atlanta's population again to majority white, leaving south Fulton County, a rich industrial area, to be incorporated into a separate municipality. Blacks, knowing as well as Massell that affluent whites would do more for the city's tax base than the mass of lower-income blacks still flocking into Atlanta from the rural South, were conciliatory and offered Massell a trade — their support for his annexation scheme in return for his delaying the expansion until after the October 1973 elections. Grace Hamilton's name was among those on this compromise offer. In this form, the Massell plan went to the state legislature, which had to approve all such local matters but normally did so without debate under its "local courtesy" custom, provided the matter had the consent of two-thirds of the local delegation concerned. Duly approved by the Fulton County delegation, including all black members, the Massell plan was transmitted to the House, where it was unexpectedly brought up for debate and amended to make the annexation effective four months before the 1973 election. The House voted twice for annexation on these terms. Five out of its twelve black members voted "yes" the first time, only two on the last count. Hamilton voted affirmatively each time. But Senate inaction killed the measure that session.

Aware of the ire he had stirred in the black community, Sam Massell compounded his problem by going before the interracial Hungry Club in September 1972 to urge the Negro leadership to "think white," to accept the reality that a majority black city would be less and less able to pay the bills and to relinquish hopes of taking over City Hall. Blacks did not buy Massell's line. When his plan came up again in the 1973 legislature, it was approved as before through white support, in which Hamilton again joined. This time it might have won Senate approval but for a procedural dispute between the bill's sponsors and arch-segregationist Lester Maddox, then Georgia's lieutenant governor and thus president of the Senate, who refused to call up the bill for a vote. "Maddox has just elected Atlanta's first black mayor," said one Atlantan. Even if enacted, Massell's plan might not have won clearance in the Justice Department, which had just turned down annexation in another southern city as a dilution of black voting strength. Massell at the Hungry Club had doomed his reelection chances; Jackson, the strong black candidate he feared, succeeded him as mayor in 1973.[1]

Hamilton's little-noticed vote on the 1972–73 annexation plans echoed oddly in the years when her racial solidarity seemed unquestionable. Yet she believed a county-city merger would offer better government to both races, and what she regarded as principle, as always, was her first priority. "Black at all costs," she later commented, "violates my basic philosophy." Black power to Hamilton meant black influence wielded effectively in a biracial context, and she did not consider her vote for Massell's twin-city a betrayal of her own real objectives.[2]

. . .

Atlanta and Fulton County continued to function as a governmental hodgepodge, the business of equalizing tax and service burdens giving rise at times to a virtual city-county war, and Hamilton moved forward with characteristic persistence in search of a solution. Favoring consolidation but knowing the obstacles to its advance, she resorted in 1974 to the trusty legislative holding action, proposing a blue-ribbon citizens' committee to study Atlanta–Fulton County relations. When Maynard Jackson, by then Atlanta's mayor, joined with the Fulton County Commission in shooting down the idea (forming instead a joint study commission of their own), Hamilton was so stung she persuaded the House of Representatives to create a special legislative group (called, not unexpectedly, the Atlanta–Fulton County Study Committee) which she headed, to delve into the perennial troubles and recommend a basis for legislative action. In fact, the county-city conflict had been mulled over by more than 120 study groups in the previous decade with no results. Typical of the stalemate, Hamilton, for all her influence, could not even get a consensus bill out of her committee.

By late 1976, the deadlock between county and city was a serious economic detriment to the area, and influential Atlantans, apparently including Hamilton, importuned Governor George Busbee to bring state leadership to bear on the problem. When Busbee responded on March 3, 1977, by naming an extralegislative body, called the Atlanta–Fulton County Study Commission, giving it twenty members, a professional staff, and ten months to come up with results, he crippled its potential by specifically excluding consolidation from its agenda, citing "the emotional and highly controversial nature of the issues involved." Of the twenty members, thirteen were white, the remainder, including Hamilton, were black. Twelve came from the city and seven from other parts of the county while one resided part-time in both areas. A fair sample of the community, this group in December 1977 produced recommendations for division of the most disputed services, for example, giving water, sewage, and the library to the city, while centralizing tax collections in the county. The recommendations became the model for a legislative package approved in the 1978 legislature and submitted to a state referendum (because constitutional amendments were involved) in November 1978. Bill Shipp, associate editor of the *Atlanta Constitution*, was caustic, saying, "Those esoteric schemes to streamline the governments of the city and county simply aren't going to fly." Like Hamilton, he favored consolidation, the "forbidden" remedy. The commission's proposals did indeed crash in the referendum of November 6, 1978. Neither this "esoteric scheme" nor any variant was ever again resurrected during Hamilton's tenure in the legislature; the city and county struggled lamely to patch over their relationship, and Hamilton turned her attention elsewhere.[3]

· · ·

Once Hamilton considered a goal worthy of her political agenda, she clung to it stubbornly, as, for instance, her belief in a downsized Atlanta City Council. During her long and productive work in 1972–73 on the new Atlanta City Charter, biracial pressure compelled her to bow on the issue, and the council continued with eighteen members instead of the twelve she thought desirable. Its members evenly divided afterward between the races, the council had revealed itself a flawed body, in Hamilton's opinion, a view fully shared by Atlanta's mainstream media, which regularly referred to it as "large and unwieldy," "parochialist," and "a miserable failure." Hamilton was critical but less blunt, saying, "I have felt many things would be easier and improved if the group were smaller because that would tend to cut down on the provincialism of the members." At about this time, she wrote in a confidential memo that she put in her files: "The new Charter is not working as intended by the [Charter Review] Commission and some reform is not only desirable but necessary if the City of Atlanta is to stay out of serious trouble."[4]

Apparently Hamilton did not circulate this memo, but in 1980 she resumed the struggle, introducing a bill to cut back the council to twelve members and add new strength to the mayor's administrative powers (already greatly expanded under the 1972 charter). Both Atlanta's white newspapers immediately sprang to her aid, writing repeated editorials with such admonishing headlines as "Reorganize Council," "Trim City Council," and "Pass Hamilton Legislation." "Free Hamilton's Bill," cried a *Constitution* editorial when Representative J. S. Billy McKinney, head of the Fulton delegation's subcommittee on the city of Atlanta—required to approve the bill before it could even reach House consideration—held the bill in captivity, refusing to let it come to a delegation vote. Hamilton, now possessed of her own well-honed legislative know-how, pried her bill from McKinney's grasp and took it to the delegation, where it was soundly defeated, ten to three. Only one other black joined her and her friend John Greer in voting affirmatively. McKinney, who in 1948 had served as one of Atlanta's first black policemen, spoke effectively against it, warning fellow delegates that it was being pushed by the Atlanta news media and the "downtown power structure" to "castigate" the biracial City Council which he and others contended was doing a good job. The council's even racial balance would be disturbed, he also insisted, while playing down voter registration figures compiled by Hamilton and disseminated in Atlanta news stories that seemed to belie that possibility. Hamilton owed her stunning defeat on the issue to what the *Constitution* called McKinney's "heated opposition."[5]

Hamilton's solidarity with her race, scarcely wavering in the earlier 1970s, was crumbling noticeably, and Billy McKinney was among her ardent enemies. "Philosophically we just had different ideas about black people . . . and where black people need to go," he later explained. "We don't get anything out of this legislature, period," he said. "And what little we get we fight for very hard. It's frustrating to serve in this body. Such small numbers. Other people with such overwhelming power and . . . not to be able to do anything for your constituents. Very frustrating." When in 1981 Hamilton attempted to remove the council's power to draw its own election districts—a power she said was reserved by the Georgia constitution to the legislature and illegally granted the city in the new charter she had been instrumental in writing—McKinney again led the charge that brought down her efforts. McKinney had been among those working quietly for Hamilton's opponent, Georgia Jones, in the 1976 Democratic primary. "We came close to getting her," he remembered. After 1981, his animosity would be open, bitter, and effective, part of a growing anti-Hamilton movement.[6]

• • •

Political peers might be giving her a hard time, but in the early 1980s, Grace Hamilton's honors and awards continued to multiply and her reputation in Atlanta among both whites and most of her fellow blacks seemed totally secure. In May 1976, in a bicentennial tribute, *Atlanta Magazine*, an organ attuned to the white establishment, singled her out as one of two hundred "city shapers," placing her with Ellis Gibbs Arnall, Georgia's reform governor of 1943–46, Martin Luther King Jr., Bobby Jones, the golfer, author Margaret Mitchell, and Coca-Cola magnates Asa Griggs Candler and Robert W. Woodruff. For an Atlanta Negro woman whom the *Constitution* had reluctantly addressed with the courtesy title mere decades before, Hamilton had joined exalted company. Yet another tribute came to her in October 1981 that probably meant more, this one from Atlanta University, on whose Board of Trustees she continued to serve (now as vice-chairman), which made her the first recipient of the Towns-Hamilton award for public service, a prize established to honor her and her late father, George Towns, on the occasion of AU's 116th anniversary. "Her voice shook with emotion as she expressed her thanks for the honor," wrote an *Atlanta Constitution* reporter who covered the event. This award was presented to her again before the Georgia House of Representatives on March 12, 1982, by two of AU's white trustees, John Griffin and Jack Etheridge, the latter a former Fulton County representative. In October 1983, Hamilton and John Greer— who between them had served forty-one years in the Georgia General Assembly—were honored by the Democratic Party leaders of Fulton County at a reception, where Barbara Couch, a House colleague, called Hamilton "the most effective woman legislator the state has ever had," and Lieutenant Governor Zell Miller sent a note praising her as "a class act." Also in 1983, the Atlanta Urban League gave her its Distinguished Community Service Award, but if the League was extending a peace offering, belatedly apologizing for its part in ending her own AUL leadership over two decades earlier, Hamilton chose not to acknowledge the possibility. "I can't imagine why they gave it to me," she said afterward. "I'd had so little involvement with them in recent times." And on February 29, 1984, the Georgia House of Representatives unanimously accepted a resolution "commending [Hamilton] and expressing to her its gratitude for her many contributions to her state and country." She owed this tribute to her friend and fellow Fulton County representative G. D. Adams, whose resolution was ostensibly motivated by the desire to praise Hamilton for cooperating with the Georgia *Living History* project, for which she was then recording her experiences as a legislator. Adams doubtless also wanted to show Hamilton's opponents, then quietly closing in on her, the extent of her support in the legislature. Emory University, a mainstream institution, may have had the same effect in mind when at its commencement exercises on May 14, 1984, it awarded Hamilton an honorary Doctor of Laws degree.[7]

· · ·

White flight to Atlanta's suburbs by the turn of the decade had cut Fulton County's population relative to the state as a whole, and the reapportionment that followed the 1980 census forced the county to yield five seats in a state House of Representatives that contained a constant 180 members, reducing it from 24 to 19 members. Population shifts likewise compelled realignment of the state's congressional districts in response to the one man, one vote command of federal law. This recarving of the political pie, which actually occurred in 1981–82, would be no less contentious than the previous decennial remap, and Grace Towns Hamilton would be actively involved from the outset. It would pit her decisively against young, more race-conscious blacks who saw her philosophy and her remarkable power in the state legislature as an unacceptable hindrance to their conception of racial advance. It was young against old, literally a battle to the finish, and it would play a role in bringing an end to Hamilton's long legislative career.

The political context of the struggle was not dissimilar to the 1970 reapportionment when Hamilton stood solidly with her race. African Americans (as they were soon to rename themselves) represented 30 percent of the state's population in 1980, yet for all their advances, they held only 15 percent of the seats in the lower house of the Georgia Legislature and only 10 percent of the seats in the Senate, and at that time no Georgia black was in the U.S. Senate. Andrew Young, who in 1977 was named the U.S. ambassador to the United Nations, had been succeeded as congressman in the Fifth District by Wyche Fowler, the prominent white politician he had bested in 1972. Blacks continued to push against these limits, aiming for the clout greater numbers might bring, while the white legislative leaders sought with their usual intensity to minimize black political ambitions. Hamilton had opposed the leadership in the 1970s, using her growing influence to bring new color to state power, but by 1980, though she contended forcefully that her aims remained the same as ever, she was firmly entrenched as a member of the state legislative leadership and, it seemed, more and more in tune with its aims.

Other factors affected this struggle. The U.S. Justice Department, for example, was now saying that a "sure" black district had to have a population 65 percent black, and shrewd Republicans, keener than ever to profit from the demand for minority representation, were agreeing to black demands for greater numbers in specific areas in a collaborative effort to enhance their chances in adjacent territory. This had already happened in Texas; Georgia, which had a glimpse of the phenomenon in 1971, would see more of it in 1981. Just as important, in the eyes of younger blacks, was the rising racial polarity in metropolitan Atlanta; a few more African Americans had won at-large offices, feeding off the old black-white coalition, but Andrew Young's white backing, relatively strong when he was elected to Congress in 1972, had been cut in half by the time he departed for the United Nations. Alton Hornsby Jr., a young historian at Morehouse College, would soon be writing of "the Second Reconstruction betrayed."[8]

Hamilton was nearly seventy-five years of age when the reapportionment struggle peaked in 1981; her memory was not as sharp as it once had been, but this posed no handicap to her work and the energy she poured into it remained as abundant as ever. Her unprecedented power in the state legislature had even augmented with her age; in matters small and large, she got special consideration. When a valid parking space was unavailable at the state capitol, "she parked right on the curb, she didn't care whose parking place it was, Miss Grace parked it there and everyone knew just to let her park where she wanted," House Speaker Tom Murphy remembered. "She'd been in my place a time or two and I just told my driver to park somewhere else and let Miss Grace have it, she was that good a leader." Speaker Murphy had in 1980 provided Hamilton with a secretary, Betty Buchanan of Griffin, Georgia, when he made her head of a House Appropriations Subcommittee on Human Services, essentially concerned with overseeing federal welfare payments. Such help normally was reserved for committee heads. (When in 1983 Hamilton took the helm of the House Congressional and Legislative Reapportionment Committee, Buchanan returned as Hamilton's full-time assistant.) Her long years at the state capitol had taught her "how to use the system," a close legislative colleague remembered. "That's how she got the things done she wanted, doing favors for other legislators and calling in her chips when she needed a favor in turn." Hamilton enjoyed her power, yet it isolated her. Only one other black had been added to the nineteen-member Reapportionment Committee by the time Hamilton took its helm, and the same was so on the House Policy Committee, where she had been joined by Representative J. C. Daugherty. She remained aloof from the Black Caucus, paying her dues but attending no meetings. And she lately had had difficulty finding a black she favored over a white for public office. She had helped Andrew Young win his congressional seat in 1972, but in 1981 when he resigned his U.N. post and returned to Atlanta to make a successful bid for mayoralty, she supported Sidney Marcus, white leader of the Fulton County House delegation, who ran against him. Bradley Hubbert, a successful young businessman, ran for a post on the Fulton County Highway Board that required legislative consent and won against the opposition of Hamilton, who supported his white opponent. And when Marcus died soon after he lost the mayoral race and a replacement was sought to head the delegation, Hamilton supported a white, G. D. Adams, against her old friend Representative Daugherty, a defection for which Daugherty never forgave her. (He refused to be interviewed for this book, saying he had no time for any matter concerning Grace Hamilton.) Even her husband, by now in ill health and confined to home much of the time, had begun to feel she "thinks too white," one close friend revealed. There is little doubt that the white power structure both in Atlanta and in the state legislature used Hamilton as a buffer against the abrasive demands of the radical young among her race, but there is also no doubt that Hamilton gave them nothing she did not wish to give. As she put it, "They supported what just happened to be my position." Knowing Hamilton thought of herself as a bridge between the races, Julian Bond was once asked if Hamilton allowed herself to be walked on. "To be walked on? No, I can't imagine Grace Hamilton ever being walked on." Hamilton herself put it more simply: "I try to be true and honest to what I believe is the best course." And in defense of the "best course" as she conceived it, Hamilton could be a fighter of steel will and icy determination. The Black Caucus was about to see her in action.[9]

Legislative reapportionment was the first bill out of the hopper when the Georgia General Assembly met in special session August 24, 1981, to recarve the state. Metropolitan delegations such as Atlanta–Fulton County's (Augusta in Richmond County and Macon in Bibb were others) cooked up their own mini-pies, and upon arriving at a plan acceptable to two-thirds of their members presented it to the House Reapportionment Committee, which in turn dispatched it without change to the Speaker of the House who used his great power to ram it through the chamber by unanimous consent. It was a custom "that had never been deviated from," said Linda Meggers, then (and in the 1990s still) director of the Georgia Reapportionment Committee Unit, which worked closely with both House and Senate Reapportionment Committees.[10]

Dividing up Fulton County's reduced delegation was at the heart of Hamilton's conflict with the Black Caucus—she was at odds with all of them— and at-large representation was the sticking point. Multiple-member districting had always worked to black disadvantage, but Hamilton consistently believed in "providing for the overall view" and even while working to reduce at-large voting in support of greater black numbers in the early 1970s had demanded electoral slots on the Atlanta City Council and the Fulton County Commission whose incumbents would look out for "the welfare of the whole." By early summer 1981, as head of the Fulton delegation's subcommittee on reapportionment, Hamilton had devised what became known as "the 17–2 plan," under which seventeen of the county's state representatives would be chosen from districts, and the remaining two would be elected county-wide. Satisfying her principles, Hamilton promised that her plan would also preserve in the forthcoming legislature the same racial proportions as in the last, meaning it would produce eight blacks and eleven whites instead of the previous ten-to-fourteen ratio. The Black Caucus meanwhile huddled with Republicans seeking to augment their own numbers, and together they agreed to eliminate at-large representation, creating instead nineteen single-member districts, eleven of which, they figured, would go to blacks (probably all Democrats), five to whites of the GOP persuasion, and the remaining three (probably) to white Democrats. Hamilton's subcommittee met on July 14 and after approving the "17–2" configuration sent it on to the full twenty-four-member delegation, which met on July 16 and by an exact but unexpected two-thirds majority voted it down, agreeing instead to the plan of the black-Republican alliance.[11]

Thwarted, Hamilton was a formidable if quiet-spoken foe, as Barbara Couch, the House colleague who admired her, recalled: "She could stick a knife in your back and you wouldn't even know you were bleeding until you were dead." First, she wrote a concise, well-reasoned statement of her position on the matter and submitted it for the record to the Legislative and Congressional Reapportionment Committee, of which she was then vice-chairman, saying her plan, contrary to Black Caucus contentions, had future potential to increase black numbers and that the victorious proposal served the cause of conservative Republicans to the probable detriment of black aspirations. As it happened, among her companions on the "17–2" plan was John Greer, a fellow member of the House Policy Committee, who feared his political survival was jeopardized by the black-Republican plan. Some believed Hamilton put "pal over principle" on "17–2," advocating it because of Greer, a charge that may have had some merit. With her views properly recorded, Hamilton then went into action behind the scenes, working with fellow leaders to rout the alliance and reinstate her own plan. Linda Meggers later recounted the next development:

> So Miss Grace went to the Speaker and talked to him about it. And he called in Joe Mack Wilson [Reapportionment Committee chairman] and Mr. Wilson said, you know, my hands are tied. If I do that, then what am I going to do when others come in? We can't do it in the Committee. So it was decided that it would be done on the floor of the House, as a floor amendment. It was usually agreed on beforehand . . . the chairman knew ahead of time which ones he was going to object to and which ones he was going to let go. He was determined that Mrs. Hamilton's amendment would not be objected to, so therefore it was going to pass. The Speaker was going to see to that. So we passed it on the floor of the House. . . . The Black Caucus was furious.

Hamilton's had been the only black vote for her amendment. More of the same would follow. Caucus anger flared to new heights when she was again the lone black voice against their floor amendments to create more single-member districts in rural areas of south Georgia.[12]

Parliamentary maneuver, like war, gains by surprise attack, and Hamilton gave her opponents no advance notice of her floor intentions. She fought in defense of principle; Caucus members saw it as a double-cross, an old woman determined to have her own way. Having abided by the rules, the Caucus had confidently expected to carry the day and thus had given scant heed to the district lines laid out in Hamilton's plan. One Caucus member, Robert A. Holmes, was stunned to find himself in the Thirty-fourth District instead of the Twenty-eighth, which he had been elected to represent, and to maintain legal title to his office was forced to leave home and family and rent an apartment within his "new" district. "Getting" Holmes was not Hamilton's intention—she was just determined to draw "clean" lines, Meggers said—but once legalized, as far as she was concerned her plan was written in stone. Holmes, however, was, like Hamilton, a fighter.

"The Wider View Regained" was the title of a supportive editorial appearing a few days later in the *Atlanta Journal*, which praised "the redoubtable Rep. Grace Hamilton" and the House of Representatives for "correcting the mistake" foisted on the county by a "gang" of "narrow, self-interested blacks and Republicans." Elated, Hamilton on September 28, 1981, sent to the U.S. Justice Department a file of news clippings along with her floor remarks on behalf of the "17–2" amendment, saying she hoped it "would be useful" in its evaluation of the state's redistricting package. Justice was already deluged with pleas for intervention against the plan from the Black Caucus, the NAACP, and an interracial coalition of Georgia legislators (including white Democrats) but found fault with only minor aspects of the overall carving job and in early 1982 approved it, turning the plan into law.[13]

Returned to the 1983–84 legislature by an impressive electoral margin from the Twenty-eighth District, where he was now a "renter" resident, Holmes persuaded a sufficient number of his colleagues to support a "precinct swap" with the Thirty-fourth District so he could return home. Technical revisions of district lines occurred often in the months after any decennial remap, and Holmes, armed with the required consent of two-thirds of his delegation (he did not ask Hamilton), had his revision made by amendment to a Senate bill, thus bypassing the House Reapportionment Committee, which Hamilton now headed. The amended bill was passed by a lopsided majority in the House over Hamilton's furious objections.

Accusing Holmes of gerrymandering and violating her committee's "established procedures," she persuaded Governor Busbee to veto the "Holmes home bill," as it came to be called. Again Hamilton acted on principles which she felt should govern the drawing of district boundaries; Holmes considered it a gratuitous insult. "For philosophical and other reasons she opposed the Caucus on reapportionment, but this was clearly aimed personally at Bob Holmes," he later insisted. And soon after the veto, Holmes was among the growing Caucus contingent laying plans to "get" Hamilton at the ballot box. Only after she departed the General Assembly, indeed, was Holmes legally able to include his family home in the district he represented in the state legislature.[14]

. . .

Even as the Holmes episode fueled anti-Hamilton sentiment, she was providing the Black Caucus with new reason to promote her downfall.

When in 1971 Hamilton tried to get Atlanta its own representative in Congress, she had not sought to create a sure seat for either race. She had insisted only on a district that included an intact city, for she had a high respect for municipal boundaries. In 1981, she was as opposed as ever to a seat in Congress made to order for a black. "In matters of the operation of an elective democracy," she later said, "it does black people no favor to be condescending and say that you provide for their representation on a different basis than is provided for everybody else because I think that's very dangerous." She also put it another way: "It seemed to me going beyond the cause of justice to say that you have to have a disproportionate number of black citizens when you are trying to establish a one-man, one-vote principle." Justice's contention that only districts 65 percent black or more were likely to send blacks to Congress was an idea Hamilton flatly rejected.[15]

Young Black Caucus members in 1981 saw the matter differently. Convinced that the Fifth Congressional District Andrew Young once represented would never go black again as long as it remained majority white, they set out to convert the district into a "sure" seat for their race. Backed by the entire Caucus (Hamilton excluded), Senator Julian Bond and Representative Al Scott (members of their respective Reapportionment Committees) devised a district incorporating the heaviest black sections of inner Atlanta, south Fulton County, and neighboring southeast DeKalb County; the latter two areas had become heavily black in the preceding decade. It was a grouping of homogeneous populations that Bond called "fair and just and right . . . but unpopular." To overcome the latter flaw, the Caucus again invoked the support of Republicans, who readily obliged because the

black plan lifted numbers of their race, most of them committed Demo-
crats, from the neighboring Fourth District, leaving it a sinecure for the
GOP. As in the 1973 reshaping of the Fulton County Commission, Senator
Paul Coverdell played a key role in this black-Republican alliance.

Percentages weaved back and forth between the House and Senate as
Bond and Scott demanded a district with more blacks than they expected
to get, hoping a compromise would give them the 65 percent they actually
desired. Bond fared better than Scott, managing to wheedle out of the Senate—unexpectedly aided by Senator Thomas Allgood, the maverick majority leader who called himself "in racial terms a staunch Georgia liberal"—a
new district with a whopping black majority of 69 percent.

In the House, Scott was up against the unabashed racism of Joe Mack
Wilson, chairman of the Reapportionment Committee, who had never
learned to say "Negro" and was also scornful of the GOP. "The only thing
worse than niggers is Republicans," he remarked to a member of the committee as tension mounted in the special session. Legislation to benefit
blacks, to him, was "nigger legislation," and he had opposed most of it.
"I'm not going to draw a nigger district if I can help it" was another of his
choice remarks. That Wilson tore into Scott's plan was not surprising;
what seemed unusual was the support he got from Hamilton, but again it
was Wilson who accepted her objectives, not she who supported his, or so
she reasoned. Hamilton did not want a Fifth District cut to measure for a
black or one that dismembered Atlanta; she did want a black population in
the Fourth District sufficient in number to wield some political influence,
and the Fifth District agreed to by the committee she and Wilson headed
contained a population that was 52 percent black and otherwise suited all
her criteria. Afterward she was one of its key defenders, finding it easier
to tolerate Wilson's racism than the district desired by her black peers. "I
didn't object to working with [Wilson]," she later commented, "because
I think a state legislature has all kinds of people in it and you have to
work with them. What he said was no more than the kind of disparaging
remarks that some members of the House make all the time. Even in my
conversations with Joe Mack he made them. You have to regret that, but
that's his nature and he's probably not going to ever be any different." The
bill favored by Wilson and Hamilton was soon approved by the full
House.[16]

When it was dispatched to a conference committee with the Senate, the
"sure" black district idea came under blistering attack from Atlanta's white
media. Bill Shipp, associate editor of the *Constitution*, inveighed against

Julian Bond's "plot to draw a ghetto district" and tore into "Julian Bond and the new separatism." Dick Williams in the *Atlanta Journal* called it "the apartheid gerrymander plan for Atlanta," and Hamilton called it the "Johannesburg plan," an epithet she would employ in describing the Fifth Congressional District for the remainder of her life. Jim Wooten in the *Journal* tried to bring some understanding to Bond's purpose, saying his plan "acknowledges the reality that within metropolitan Atlanta two separate and distinct communities exist . . . blacks have political power, whites economic . . . and peaceful coexistence, not racial brotherhood, is the true state of affairs." Hamilton did not want any part of Bond's purpose. One of her friends once said she was Atlanta's only real integrationist and Bond's analysis of the racial picture, however realistic, was bound to be anathema to her.[17]

As conferees tried to produce an acceptable compromise between the districts devised in the House and Senate, they labored without advice from blacks. Hamilton, the natural choice for the conference committee, was not asked to participate. Its members were dictated by the General Assembly's leaders, who thought the presence of blacks would impede agreement. This judgment, evidently arrived at behind Hamilton's back (since she belonged to the leadership), may have privately offended her, but it failed to diminish the enthusiasm she continued to bring to the defense of her committee's positions on the new district. At one point her enthusiasm was excessive.

Compromise was elusive, and five reports were presented to the two chambers, which often worked late into the night, before a sixth was finally approved, providing a district with a white majority of registered voters but a total population 57 percent black. The fourth conference report passed the House by one vote, or so it seemed until two Black Caucus members— Holmes and Douglas Dean—reported to Speaker Murphy that Hamilton had voted "yes" on the machine of her colleague Representative Daugherty, who was absent. A recount was called, and this time the report failed. Hamilton at once acknowledged her "grave error," calling it a "thoughtless act" and insisting lamely, "My recollection of the whole evening is foggy." She later explained that she and Daugherty had often by agreement voted each other's machines. He had given her no proxy authority that evening, and her enthusiasm had clearly exceeded her better judgment.[18]

Once signed into law by Governor Busbee on September 23, the 1981 congressional reapportionment was sent to Washington for Justice Department review. Black Caucus members, joined by the NAACP, immediately filed formal objections, which won a more sympathetic hearing than their concurrent complaints against legislative reapportionment. On February 2, 1982, Justice refused to clear the Fourth and Fifth Districts as drawn, saying the plans worked unconstitutionally to dilute potential black voting strength.[19]

The state leadership exercised its prerogative under the Voting Rights Act and in March 1982 petitioned the U.S. District Court in the District of Columbia for forthright approval of its disputed districting and, even in the absence of certification, proclaimed the plan the guiding statute for the upcoming fall elections. Nineteen Black Caucus members and three citizens, already accepted as intervenors in the case, joined the Justice Department in seeking an injunction against this action, which was granted May 24, 1982, by a three-judge panel appointed to decide the contested districts. State elections were officially postponed when the U.S. Supreme Court immediately refused to stay the injunction.

The three judges heard the congressional case in Washington, D.C., between June 28 and July 1, 1982, and from the beginning the two blacks on the panel, Harry Edwards and Aubrey Robinson (the third was a woman, June Green), seemed partial to the views of the Georgia Black Caucus. Grace Hamilton was the lone black testifying in Washington on the state's behalf, which she did at the request of Georgia attorney general Michael Bowers.

"They asked me to testify and as a committee vice-chairman I had a responsibility and I said I'd be glad to help out," she remembered. "The state leadership was for a better plan, not as good as it could have been but it was better than the Johannesburg plan." To the Black Caucus solidly arrayed against her, Hamilton was thumbing her nose at them again, and anger among some of them continued to mount.[20]

Georgia generally had a hard time before the panel; even Mayor Young of Atlanta refused on the stand to support, as he had been expected to do, the importance of preserving the city's boundaries in the new Fifth District. "There's nothing sacred about keeping the city in one district," he said. "It is more important that the Fifth District not in any way be designed to discriminate against the black citizens of the State of Georgia." Young had insisted in a deposition for the court that "a candidate for the 5th district . . . in the present district and under present circumstances . . . could be discriminated against on the basis of race." On the stand Hamilton got less than a warm reception from Judge Robinson, who questioned her use of the word "Negro," asking if she was talking about "blacks." She replied, "I've been an American Negro all my life." Robinson responded, "Would the same hold true for 'colored' if you happen to slip into that?" Back home, the *Atlanta Journal,* quick as ever to spring to Hamilton's support, said editorially, "We don't know what such matters have to do with the merits of the case, but we catch the possible drift of [the judge's] thinking and we think Grace Hamilton deserves better treatment than that."[21]

On July 22, 1982, the court found "the Fifth District was drawn to suppress black voting strength in Georgia," adding that "a cohesive black community" was "divided to prevent a black majority." The state was ordered to redraw the lines within twenty days, which the legislature—once the U.S. Supreme Court refused to stay the command—proceeded to do in a special session convened on August 3. On Sunday, August 8, opposition to a "sure" black seat for an Atlantan having collapsed, the legislature stamped its okay on essentially what Julian Bond and Al Scott sought at the outset— a district containing a population 65 percent black, of whom nearly 60 percent were registered voters.[22]

Judge Edwards, author of the court opinion accompanying the order, delivered direct, almost scathing, criticism at the state leadership, singling out for special rebuke Speaker Murphy, Lieutenant Governor Zell Miller, the Senate leader, Joe Mack Wilson, and Hamilton. Murphy and Miller were accused of contradictory testimony amounting to a cover-up of their own racial bias, Wilson was flatly called "a racist," and Hamilton was labeled "a pawn for the House leadership . . . during the 1981 reapportionment process." With seeming approval, the judge also noted that "she has been characterized as an 'Aunt Jane,' the female equivalent of Uncle Tom." (This characterization, accepted as a finding by Edwards, had been offered in depositions for the court by both Randall and Holmes, the representative Hamilton had drawn out of his home district, stubbornly blocking his legislative effort to return.)[23]

Outrage erupted at once in Atlanta. Durwood McAlister in the *Journal* accused the judge of a "gross . . . injustice." Grace Hamilton, he insisted, "is nobody's Aunt Jane. She is a black leader of immense dignity and strength whose steel spirit and quiet eloquence have won battle after battle for black rights." A *Journal* editorial decried the judge's "cavalier treatment of Rep. Hamilton, a figure of legendary integrity and courage in Atlanta." These observations were true enough, and nobody really acquainted with Hamilton believed she was a "pawn," knowing her principles were her own. But the *Journal* vitiated its pro-Hamilton stance by simultaneously coming to the defense, albeit lamely, of Joe Mack Wilson, saying, "We were unaware the law defined racists by name." It did not elaborate, but the "possible drift" of its thinking was easy to catch. Among the city's black newspapers, the *Atlanta Inquirer* was elated by Edwards's forthright language, running its account of the opinion under the heading "Court Lashes Racists." Noting that Hamilton was among those lashed, the paper may have tried to contact her but said she "could not be reached for comment." Since Hamilton was no recluse, often sitting by a telephone at home, the paper likely wished to spare her what it might have thought would be embarrassment.[24]

Stalled state elections, except for the Fourth and Fifth Congressional Districts, were put back on track August 13 by the three-judge court, but when the new reapportionment plans were approved August 24 in Washington, elections in the disputed districts were postponed until November in the interest of fairness to electors and electorate. Julian Bond, chief designer of the new Fifth District, announced on August 30, as expected, that he was running for the seat, but, equally unexpectedly, he dropped out of contention on September 18, citing lack of money for the race, thus relieving the white incumbent, Wyche Fowler, of any serious black opposition. In the delayed general election of November 30, Fowler's popularity with both races won him 81 percent of the vote; a meager 13 percent went to his nearest competitor, Representative Billy McKinney, who had run as an independent. Fowler would win yet another congressional term in 1984, leaving the post in 1986 to wage a successful race for the U.S. Senate. Julian Bond that year at last made his bid to succeed Fowler in Congress but lost out to John Lewis, a close comrade from the civil rights days. Bond's black following remained strong. For a district designed for and by blacks, the strange fact was that Lewis's winning margin came from his overwhelming support among the district's white precincts. As Grace Hamilton expected, the new Fourth District in 1984 turned out its longtime Democratic congressman, Elliott Levitas, in favor of a Republican, Pat Swindall.[25]

14

A Landslide Defeat

. . .

B Y 1984 Hamilton was in her seventy-eighth year and had begun thinking about retirement, but she gingerly sidestepped a decision, wanting what she called "one last go-round." That she was politically vulnerable had not occurred to her. In hindsight, she was sure she would have
run "one more time" even if she had been fully aware of all she faced. There
was, after all, ample reason for confidence. She had been in the General Assembly longer than any other woman before her. As the *Atlanta Journal*
wrote admiringly, she had become "an institution in the House of Representatives." The paper's approval, as she was aware, reflected both the respect and affection she had gained in the dominant white society and the
widespread pride her accomplishments inspired in the black community.
True, she had come close to defeat at the hands of Georgia Blackburn Jones
in 1976, but otherwise she had always won without ever making a real campaign or delivering a political speech on her own behalf, understandably if
ungraciously saying once that she thought political speeches useless, a lot of
them amounting to "rousing the rabble." Never had she spent more than
$1,500 on any election, $400 of that going for the Democratic Party's filing
fee, and she had never sought endorsements though they had come to her
unsolicited.[1]

Aloof but confident, therefore, Hamilton in early July 1984 again filed
for reelection, forking over the $400 fee demanded by the Democratic Party
for candidates in its August 14, 1984, primary, which even amid a rising

Republican Party still was tantamount to the general election in Georgia. Her impending troubles, if not suspected by Hamilton, were very much on the mind of some of her friends.

Andrew Young, respectful of Hamilton despite the public support she had given his opponent in the 1981 mayoral race, did not want to see her humiliated by electoral defeat at the end of a praiseworthy career in public service and tried to persuade Martin Luther King III, a resident of Hamilton's Thirty-first District, to talk to her about letting him run in her place. Young King evidently disliked the idea, for he never approached Hamilton. Another concerned friend and adviser would later say:

> I think Grace offended a lot of blacks when she testified in Washington on reapportionment. She was seen as a traitor to the black cause. Grace is elitist, one of the Atlanta old guard that's constantly under challenge from the young. . . . She was hurt by her age. Couple that with the fact that she is not a mixer, physically, doesn't do what the average politician does which is walk the streets and visit the churches. What we should have done was to get a delegation from the black community to go to her and say, "We sure do appreciate the contribution you have made. You are one of our mentors and we will always revere you for the high standards you have set and so forth." And then say, "We really think you are going to be in jeopardy if you run again because of certain factors and what we want to do, whether you run or not, is to honor you with a big banquet." Then the banquet will either help propel her back into office or else she will decide on her own to step down and let somebody else take her place.[2]

For one of her political savvy, Hamilton's failure to detect the risk she faced was a remarkable oversight. Another friend, who pitched in to try to save her in the end, later explained, "I think she knew she was at risk, but how much she knew is questionable, because to be scared you have to have your ear to the ground, and frankly I don't think Grace had her ear to the ground." But as she found herself facing what the *Journal* called "her most formidable set of challengers to date," she must have known this election would be unlike any other. In a story centered on Hamilton, the *Journal* listed her opponents alphabetically: Larry Dobbs, a thirty-nine-year-old businessman who had the backing of his cousin, former mayor Maynard Jackson, and certain anti-Hamilton members of the Black Caucus; Sandra Robertson, thirty-six, a Chicago native who had migrated south a decade earlier and was serving as director of the Georgia Citizens Coalition on Hunger; and Mable Thomas, a twenty-six-year-old graduate student in public administration at Georgia State University.[3]

Thomas had just returned from the Democratic National Convention where she had served as a Jesse Jackson delegate, having won more votes for the post than even popular former mayor Jackson, and she quickly became the challenger to beat. Thomas was known to the legislative Black Caucus because she had sandwiched in among her many political pursuits a stint at the Georgia capitol as an intern on the staff of Senator Julian Bond. "She's a terrific woman," said William C. Randall of Columbus, then Caucus chair, in a later talk about the election. "We knew her and liked her but if she hadn't decided on her own to enter the race, we'd have found someone else, Dobbs or Robertson would have been acceptable too." Caucus members out to topple Hamilton soon were giving Thomas their undivided aid and support.[4]

With enthusiasm, energy, and determination—a replica in her disciplined determination of Hamilton herself—Thomas set up headquarters near where she had grown up in Vine City, at an address just down the hill from Hamilton's own quiet residence on University Place. Though Thomas actually lived outside the district, she had faithfully maintained her voting residence in Vine City and staffed it with old and young from the district's numerous public housing projects while she tooled about the neighborhoods in an old Impala plastered with signs urging votes for "Able Mable," proclaiming to all, "It's Time for a Change," and occasionally echoing the Caucus charge that Hamilton had worked against increasing the black presence in Congress and the state legislature. Thomas financed her campaign with her own savings and contributions from friends and supporters—indeed, from some of the same sources who also gave to Hamilton. Jesse Hill, for instance, gave money to both, though significantly, perhaps, his contribution to Thomas was nearly twice the sum he gave to Hamilton. Banks and political action committees also made like contributions to both, though the latter groups gave Hamilton the bigger share. As Thomas went about arousing people and drumming up support, Hamilton neither could nor wished to match her tactics. Liking campaigning no more than ever, she also was concerned with her husband, Cookie, whose health was failing, giving her the ideal excuse to stay at home, which is what she wanted to do anyway. So she sent voters her usual brochure, detailing her legislative record, and waited for what she believed would be the usual favorable outcome at the polls.[5]

It was not to be. Thomas, who had entered the race a long shot, emerged with 1,401 votes to Hamilton's 1,170, with Dobbs and Robertson trailing far behind with 755 and 570 votes respectively. Since neither she nor Thomas won a majority of the votes cast, for the first time in her political life, Hamilton had to face a run-off, called for September 4.

Awakened at last to her vulnerability, Hamilton called in a dozen friends, and more people, including some she did not know, quickly gathered round as the run-off approached. "There were a lot of people out there who wanted to help Grace," remembered Representative Georganna Sinkfield, who had entered the legislature from the Thirty-seventh District in 1983. She and her husband, Richard, a lawyer, were among those rallying earnestly to Hamilton's side. The Black Caucus had stood solidly against Hamilton on the 1981 reapportionment fights (Sinkfield was not yet in the body), but it was far from solidly united against her reelection. "There were probably more that liked her than otherwise," said Sinkfield, who herself surveyed Caucus sentiment on the matter. As proof, two ten-year veterans of the legislature, Betty J. Clark and Lorenzo Benn, joined the Sinkfields in trying to salvage the Hamilton campaign. Money was no problem; Hamilton collected and spent a total of $11,600 in this effort to hold on to her office, all of it coming, mostly in small amounts, from friends, acquaintances, banks, and political action committees. It was nearly ten times what she had ever amassed and spent before.

Her Caucus opponents meantime diligently aided Thomas, giving her money toward the $7,000 she eventually paid out for her campaign and circulating through the district a flyer attacking Hamilton for "helping whites to keep blacks down," a reference to her actions on the 1981 reapportionment. The flyer made another point, one particularly stinging to Hamilton, charging her with persuading a freshman legislator to cast the deciding ballot with her against Representative Daugherty's bid in 1982 to head the Fulton County delegation in the House of Representatives. As the other charges were merely a recitation of the facts (even if they omitted the context of her motivating principles), Hamilton could do little but fume about the "impropriety" of this "interference" in her district, but Daugherty had been her special friend. She had opposed him as a delegation chairman for what she considered good reasons—mainly his failing health, she said—and she "greatly regretted" the strained relations between them. "All during the campaign I tried to reach him," she later recalled, "did everything I knew, left messages with his office, with his wife, went by his office, and he never returned my call. I finally said to hell with it. And that was that." She also approached Marty King, though she knew nothing then of Andrew Young's earlier intercession, because she thought (certainly not without some self-interest also in surrounding her campaign with the aura of King's name) that the young King might benefit from some political experience, but she could reach only Coretta King, who promised to give her son the message. Young King never returned her call.[6]

Because the time between primary and run-off was short, the Sinkfields and the growing cohort of volunteers pulled out all the stops, inheriting from Congressman Wyche Fowler, a primary winner and a devoted Hamilton friend, the use of his vacated campaign headquarters, a special boon because her husband's illness made Hamilton's home unsuitable as a working site for a crowd. Busily they "signed" Hamilton's district, reerected signs as fast as they were taken down (combating the standard tactic of all political opposition), blanketed the area with leaflets, and rang doorbells. At the urging of Richard Sinkfield, who had been designated her campaign manager, Hamilton appeared at churches because, as another volunteer-friend said, "That's where you find the multitudes." Bad luck plagued their efforts. When Georganna Sinkfield and Clark called a press conference to demonstrate that the Black Caucus was at best divided on Hamilton, a dozen media people showed up but no report reached print or television, whereas the opposition press conference, a counter-Hamilton move, received good coverage. At Richard Sinkfield's behest, Hamilton sought endorsement from the African Methodist Episcopal Church's Ministers' Union, only to find when she got it that they had also endorsed Mable Thomas.[7]

Thomas was ahead of Hamilton on another crucial matter. Before Hamilton volunteers were aware of it, Thomas had forged a "piggyback" alliance with Richard Lankford, a popular black candidate in a hotly contested county-wide race for sheriff against a longtime white incumbent. Piggybacking was a valuable campaign mechanism for getting voters to the polls, especially the poor, lame, elderly, and blind, who seldom made the effort, and Thomas's capture of the Lankford connection gave her what some, including Richard Sinkfield, thought was the key to the election's outcome. Lankford's stance was otherwise neutral between Thomas and Hamilton; Hamilton herself might have teamed up with him if she had been the first to seek him out. "We never were able to put together anything like that group," Richard Sinkfield recalled. "If one candidate has that mechanism and the other candidate doesn't," he said, "it's almost a foregone conclusion who's going to win the race." Hamilton, Georganna Sinkfield later remembered, "was never there, in essence she was like a phantom, a name ... it was the nonexistence of a campaign that defeated Grace Hamilton." Julian Bond, whose ambivalent relations with Hamilton did not prevent his praising her as "a healer, a communicator and a bridge builder," reached the same conclusion: "She could still have been here in the legislature," he said in 1986, "but she created her own defeat." [8]

. . .

On September 4, 1984, Mable Thomas, a half-century her junior, claimed Hamilton's seat in the Georgia House of Representatives, winning 2,502 votes to Hamilton's 1,013. Hamilton lost decisively in fourteen of the district's seventeen precincts. She did not even carry 2-H, her home precinct centered around Atlanta University. It was what the *Atlanta Journal* called "a landslide defeat."

The *Journal* reported the next day that a "bitterly disappointed" Hamilton had "hinted at possible legal action" and was charging Thomas with a variety of forbidden electoral tactics. Enraged, Hamilton was certain a case could be made against Thomas for residing outside the district she had just been elected to represent, but the law clearly permitted anyone to maintain a voting residence apart from his or her domicile, and Richard Sinkfield, Hamilton's lawyer in the matter, feared the legal ambiguities would jeopardize a court challenge and put her once again on the losing side. Reluctantly Hamilton accepted his advice to abandon legal redress. "It nearly broke our friendship," Sinkfield remembered, "but it was the best thing I ever did for her." The Board of Registration and Elections called for an examination of returns in three precincts, but nothing ever came of the probe. [9]

Self-criticism not being Hamilton's strong point—a virtue indeed enjoyed by few—she long remained convinced her defeat was illegally contrived, and she seemed heedless of the possibility that she was leading blacks where they no longer wanted to go. Publicly she showed a good face and talked good sense. For example, on September 16 the *Atlanta Journal-Constitution* published her letter thanking the Thirty-first District "for the opportunity and privilege of serving as their representative for the past 18 years," and on January 22, 1985, she told an interviewer for the same paper, who wanted to know how she felt as the Georgia General Assembly convened without her for the first time since 1966, "I'll tell you what I really feel, no effort of any individual ever gets lost but I don't have any sense of 'Gee, isn't it awful that I'm not down there.'" But privately she remained bitter, never wavering in her hostility toward those she held responsible for her loss. In interviews for this book, Hamilton was relentlessly scornful of Thomas, whom she never met and to whom she never conceded the election, derided Holmes as a man "who doesn't have the truth in him," labeled Randall a zealous self-promoter, and expressed a special contempt for the Black Caucus as a whole, calling it "a special interest group, pure and simple . . . a group obsessed with trivia." She accused her adversaries of "sour grapes," calling them "individuals who have not been able to achieve anything of significance in the legislature," and occasionally she turned on her district's many "poor and ignorant . . . who are easily exploited," blaming them for her defeat. Few escaped her ire in those bitter days.[10]

Her many friends and admirers remained steadfastly loyal, and in the early days after her defeat, letters poured in from the faithful, but she seemed inconsolable. Betty Clark, whom Hamilton had mentored with care and concern upon Clark's arrival in the Georgia legislature in 1973, felt Hamilton's reaction was understandable. "You don't get over that kind of thing, a defeat like that after all those years of service, I know I wouldn't," Clark afterward remarked.[11]

The Atlanta media continued to shower her with devoted attention. After pleading for her reelection, the *Atlanta Journal* followed her defeat with an editorial headed "Grace Hamilton—Victor!" Said the *Journal*: "Mrs. Hamilton's career went well beyond her 'first black' status. She was first, period." Friendly interviews with Hamilton continued to appear periodically in the *Journal-Constitution*. The Georgia House of Representatives, having just commended her by resolution in February 1984, unanimously commended her again in February 1985, "paying tribute to our former colleague, Grace Towns Hamilton, for her personal and political influence in supporting and sponsoring legislation which has substantially improved the quality of life for our citizens and contributed to Georgia's position of leadership in the new South." Whereas the 1984 resolution originated with Adams, a white, the 1985 tribute was sponsored by Lorenzo Benn, the black colleague who had worked hard for her reelection. Clark, Adams, and Speaker Murphy were also sponsors.[12]

Eventually, her private rage subsided, and on April 8, 1986, in one of the last interviews for this book, she was able to say with apparent conviction: "The Lord works in mysterious ways. Since I didn't have enough sense to know when enough was enough, the good Lord took a hand."[13]

15

The Last Years

· · ·

SHORN of the public office at which she had been uniquely successful, Grace Towns Hamilton lived on another eight years, overseeing the care of her ailing husband before his death, guiding the search for a suitable depository for her papers and effects, collecting numerous accolades and awards, and finally battling her own illness and decline.

She never was sure why she lost to novice Mable Thomas, or so she publicly maintained, and coping with the defeat long exacted a personal toll. She smoked more than ever, her own way of dealing with stress, and concerned friends hovered near, doing what they could to cheer her. Betty Jean Weltner, former wife of Georgia Supreme Court judge Charles Weltner, brought her the *New York Times* on Sundays, and Father Austin Ford and Osgood O. Williams Jr., a young attorney known as "Buz," who with his father, Judge Osgood O. Williams Sr., also had long been Hamilton's close friends, paid regular visits to her hilltop home. They usually found her seated by the telephone, perhaps talking with callers, a cigarette never far from hand. The living–dining room area, pleasantly cluttered with family pictures and the accumulations of a busy professional life, was her work space. Her husband, now compelled to wear a pacemaker, was mostly confined to the adjacent bedroom, though from time to time he strolled in, clad in his plaid bathrobe, for a chat with his wife. The house's wing that accommodated her husband's no-longer-used billiard table was packed nearly to the ceiling with her legislative papers, carefully stashed in cardboard boxes. Rosa Edwards, a practical nurse, looked after Cookie Hamilton's needs and, when he felt up to it, took him for a drive in the family's 1978 Chrysler. Hamilton herself had sometimes acted as her husband's chauffeur, but she was not a good driver, dealing poorly with the traffic congestion that had grown heavily in their area, and the afternoon rides were finally delegated exclusively to Edwards. Otelia Samples also came in to help with cooking and other household chores.

In October 1985 Cookie Hamilton was well enough to accompany his wife to Cleveland, Ohio, for the wedding of their granddaughter, Lisa Carolyn Payne, to Peter Lawson Jones, but in 1986 she went alone to the wedding, also in Cleveland, of grandson Charles Benjamin Payne III to Wanda Smith.

· · ·

Loyal legislative colleagues believed Hamilton's experience could still serve public purposes and sought to find a place for her as a consultant at the state capitol. Rumors circulated during the legislative sessions of 1985 and 1986 that she was already at work, but they were unfounded. The only public post she filled after her legislative defeat was an unpaid position on the Georgia Advisory Committee to the U.S. Civil Rights Commission (USCRC), a position she assumed in January 1985 and held until January 1987. She probably was recommended for the work by Georgia governor Joe Frank Harris or attorney general Michael Bowers because the commission's authority required it to work through state leaders in making appointments and it normally did so. For a time it appeared the job would be foreshortened; the U.S. House of Representatives in July 1986 defunded the commission, but new money was finally provided and as of 1994 the commission still was a functioning agency.

The USCRC, originally founded to promote compliance with the Civil Rights Act of 1957, was a fact-finding agency, and the state advisory committees (SACs) acted as its eyes and ears at the grassroots level, sending in studies and reports devised with aid from the commission's regional offices. The commission lacked enforcement authority, but the moral stature of its earliest chairmen, Father Theodore Hesburgh and Arthur Flemming, gave clout to its findings. By November 1983, when it was reorganized by President Ronald Reagan to reflect his cautious, conservative view of civil rights, opinion was widespread that its best and most productive years were in the past. To remake the commission in his own image, President Reagan put at the helm two men, Clarence Pendleton, a black whose experience included a stint with the San Diego Urban League, and Morris B. Abram, the Georgia lawyer who aided the Atlanta Urban League's housing drive when Hamilton headed the agency and had since joined a New York law firm, figuring prominently (as he had in Georgia) in causes involving civil and human rights. Named chairman and vice-chairman respectively, Pendleton and Abram shared Reagan's aversion to measures such as affirmative action on behalf of minorities and school busing to achieve desegregation. The commission under their direction was soon embroiled in feuds with more militant civil rights advocates and their supporters in Congress. The threatened demise of the commission in 1986 was only one of their bitter encounters.

The Georgia SAC, like its counterparts elsewhere in the country, after the 1983 reorganization had eleven members, including a chairman, all appointed by the USCRC, but as its traditional fact-finding projects were largely carried out by the commission's regional offices, SAC meetings were devoted primarily to routine business and planning issues, rarely attracting a quorum of its members. Hamilton, one of three women on the new Georgia SAC, was immediately elected its secretary (committee members elected officers other than the chairman), and she was faithfully among the four or five attending SAC's periodic meetings through mid-1986. Her papers contain not only the meetings' minutes but also the meeting notices as well as reports developed under SAC's imprimatur both before and after her service in the post. In her files, for instance, she kept a report on the SAC-sponsored community forum in 1982 called "Perceptions of Hate Group Activity in Georgia," a lengthy 1986 briefing memorandum, "Women and Minorities in the Georgia Media," and a summary of another community forum held June 8, 1987, after she had left SAC, "Bigotry and Violence in Georgia." As the federal commission staff acknowledged, SAC reports such as these were often outdated when published and of uneven utility, and the absence in her files of SAC minutes during the last six months of her term probably indicates Hamilton's waning interest in the agency's work. No indication exists to show what input, if any, she had in the SAC report on the Georgia media, the only one completed during her term.

Hamilton's appointment to the Georgia committee had won immediate attention from Vice-Chairman Abram, who made laudatory remarks at the USCRC meeting in San Diego on January 10, 1985, where her appointment was confirmed, praising "whoever it was who first suggested her name," calling her one of his own "heroes and mentors," and saying she "clearly symbolizes, in her life and work, the standards of civil rights as I learned them and as I would like to see them practiced in the country." He sent a copy of his remarks to the *Atlanta Constitution*, which published excerpts on January 27, 1985, and the report was so framed that a reader might have gleaned the impression that Abram himself was responsible for the appointment. In fact, Abram doubtless would have hesitated to sponsor Hamilton for the committee post had he been aware how sharply her views differed from his own on affirmative action. "I believe absolutely that affirmative action is a good thing," she said in 1986 in an interview for this book. She even supported quotas, strictly anathema to Abram. "I think it perfectly legitimate to establish goals in terms of numbers and levels of positions to be filled by minorities," she said in the same interview. That Abram claimed Hamilton as a "hero and mentor" seemed ironic, too, for he had been unwilling when racism still ran high to jeopardize his political ambitions in Georgia by addressing her openly as "Mrs. Hamilton."[1]

· · ·

Hamilton's premature departure from SAC was influenced by reasons other than a loss of interest in the agency, for by mid-1986 her famous energy, once inexhaustible, was on the wane and her agenda had veered from public to family and personal concerns. Her husband's heart condition was worsening, and her own health seemed on a downhill slope in tandem with his decline.

In this period she decided to yield to the importuning of friends, black and white alike, who wanted her to give the complete collection of her professional papers to the Atlanta Historical Society. As she had always intended to place them at Atlanta University, the decision to make the deposit elsewhere hardly could have lessened her emotional stress at this time of transition in her life. She believed strongly in the worth of her papers, seeing in them, as Celestine Sibley wrote in the *Atlanta Constitution*, "an extremely valuable bonanza for students of five decades of Atlanta history," and she yearned to have them securely placed in her lifetime. Jane Maguire Abram, a personal friend of Hamilton's and former wife of Morris B. Abram, agreed with her objectives, convinced that "what happened in Atlanta affected the social fabric of the entire nation . . . and unless carefully documented, the days of our years will be as ephemeral as water dripping out of sight." Jane Abram was soon leading fund-raising for the Grace Towns Hamilton History Project (GTHHP), an interracial group of Hamilton sympathizers who rallied in search of a solution to her dilemma. Important to the group's work were not only Abram but also Judge Williams and his son, Buz, James A. Mackay, a former congressman from Georgia's Fourth District and then president of the DeKalb County Historical Society, George Berry, an Atlanta real estate developer who at that time was commissioner of the Georgia Department of Industry and Trade, and coauthor Jean B. Bergmark.

Removing the papers from Atlanta University was not the project's initial intention, for all concerned were aware of Hamilton's commitment to the institution. In 1950 she had begun donating noncurrent records and papers to what was then called AU's Trevor Arnett Library, where they joined the collections of her father and mother, Professor George A. Towns and Nellie Towns, and those of such notable organizations as the Neighborhood Union of Atlanta, the Southern Education Foundation, the Commission on Interracial Cooperation, the Southern Regional Council, and the Institute of Black World Archives. Her own collection by 1980 occupied one hundred linear feet of shelf space, and sufficient processing had been done to make them useful to Sharon Mitchell Mullis (later Sharon Mitchell Sellers) when she wrote a doctoral dissertation in 1976 on Hamilton's early public career. This progress had come to a halt in January 1982 when AU merged all its library and archival holdings (though retaining legal title to them) with Atlanta University Center's Robert W. Woodruff Library, a merger that led to staff reductions and curtailed work on many collections, including Hamilton's. She immediately withheld delivery of further papers, and when this biographical work began, with its peculiar need for cataloged records, her collection was divided between the library and her home. The problem weighed on her mind.

The GTHHP, moving to her rescue, at first sought to convert the old Towns home into a museum that would serve as the desired depository but could not implement the idea (the home was sold in 1989 to Morris Brown College). The Georgia Department of Archives, meanwhile, had talked about acquiring the papers but this interest soon flagged. Minnie H. Clayton, head of the Woodruff Library's Division of Special Collections and Archives, had drafted a proposal aimed at keeping the collection intact at the Atlanta University Center. The project's leaders, in firm possession of Hamilton's confidence, appear to have given little consideration to the Clayton proposal, for even before it was presented Jane Abram and Buz Williams had already approached the Atlanta Historical Society (AHS), which responded favorably and with enthusiasm when queried about its interest in Hamilton's papers.

The AHS was finally seeking to create new holdings on the rich history of the city's black population which it had hitherto ignored, and Hamilton, tired and anxious about the matter, was said to have willingly changed her mind about her papers' disposition. Perhaps she believed white Atlanta's new interest in black history had to be encouraged, but whatever emotional trauma it may have triggered within her, on November 17, 1986, she signed a letter giving all her "papers, correspondence, newspaper clippings and miscellaneous items of memorabilia" to the Atlanta Historical Society (soon to be renamed the Atanta History Center). Her only condition was that AHS archive the collection with funds to be raised by the GTHHP. At this point, AHS was acquiring only those papers Hamilton still held in her home. As the project felt money could best be found for archiving the whole collection, including the part held by AU, Hamilton soon persuaded Luther S. Williams, then president of Atlanta University, to relinquish its library holdings, which he did by letter on December 18, 1986.

By January 1987 the AHS had in hand the entire Hamilton collection, and the GTHHP's spirited search for the $35,000 the AHS estimated it needed for the archival work was accomplished by mid-July. The Herndon Foundation best represented black interest in the project, giving $2,500, though individual African Americans made smaller contributions. The largest contribution came from the state of Georgia, Governor Joe Frank Harris giving $7,500 from his discretionary fund, and the bulk of the remainder came from white monied sources. Ivan Allen Jr. jump-started the drive by pledging $5,000 and promising more in case of a shortfall, but the campaign was so successful that he was relieved of his commitment and his final contribution was $1,000. Other sizable sums came from the J. B. Fuqua Foundation ($3,000), the Coca-Cola Foundation ($2,500), the John and Mary Franklin Foundation ($2,500), Josephine J. Heyman ($2,500), the Metropolitan Atlanta Community Foundation ($1,000), and a $1,000 anonymous gift in memory of Rebecca Gershon.

Processing the papers was turned over to William Richards, director of Library Archives at AHS, and Rosa Dickens, an African American archivist, who began work in September 1987, completing the entire project in a single year and "under budget," according to Richards. The Grace Towns Hamilton Collection was officially opened to public use on September 28, 1988, at a reception which Hamilton attended in a wheelchair guided by her faithful friend Father Austin Ford. Getting a viable depository for her papers, the last major goal of her life, had been accomplished, and guests at the reception gave her a standing ovation.[2]

· · ·

The months when Hamilton was thus satisfactorily disposing of her papers coincided with her husband's final illness and the first major break in her own health. Her sister, Harriet Towns Jenkins, a retired nurse who had long worked for Planned Parenthood in Brooklyn, New York, had just joined the household to help care for the ailing couple when in December 1986 Cookie Hamilton was taken to Hughes Spalding Medical Center (the former Hughes Spalding Pavilion), a trip from which he never returned. He died there January 2, 1987, at the age of eighty-seven.

His life and work as a teacher and researcher were celebrated at a service January 5 in the First Congregational Church, still the church of choice of Atlanta's black elite, and the church where both the Hamilton and Towns families had deep roots. "Dr. Cookie," as the *Atlanta Daily World* called him in its January 9 obituary, was movingly eulogized by Hugh M. Gloster, president of Morehouse College, who had been Cookie's student at LeMoyne College in Memphis and later his colleague on the faculty there. Later still they were reunited at Morehouse College, where both occupied administrative positions. Cookie's pastimes—bridge, billiards, and tennis—and his delicious rendition of Sunday morning waffles got equal recognition in Gloster's tribute, along with his accomplishments in teaching and research. He was buried in South View Cemetery beside members of his wife's family.[3]

Cookie Hamilton's marriage to Grace Towns had been a successful but unusual relationship, an affair of the heart that gradually became a congenial arrangement of parallel lives. From 1970 to 1976, when Grace was busiest and most active in the Georgia legislature, Cookie, who had retired from Morehouse, was mostly away from home, occupying one-year teaching posts in Texas, South Carolina, and Georgia. He was more race-conscious than she and was known to be irritated by what he considered her inclination to think too often that "white is right." Yet, as their daughter said, after years of trying to understand their relationship, she had given up. "They had something working for them . . . and I don't have to understand it. It works!"[4]

Four months after her husband's death, Hamilton broke her hip getting out of bed one morning and was likewise taken to Hughes Spalding Medical Center, where she was also diagnosed with a possible stroke. Her sister, Harriet, had by mutual agreement become a permanent part of her household and, in the health crisis that now beset Hamilton, was her constant companion. Daughter Eleanor visited from her home in Shaker Heights, Ohio, when possible. Friends and flowers arrived often. In August doctors declared her ready for release, and she was sent to Wesley Woods Geriatric Hospital near Emory University for recuperative therapy, where just before her scheduled departure she fell again and had an identical fracture of the other hip. Again she was treated at Spalding and again she went to Wesley Woods for therapy. These multiple fractures and the apparent stroke took their toll, and during the next years her physical and mental health slowly but steadily weakened.[5]

• • •

Meanwhile, the accolades poured in. Grace Hamilton in her lifetime received more recognition from her fellow Georgians, black and white, than any woman before her, except perhaps Margaret Mitchell, the legendary author. Even after she left the state legislature, indeed even after she was bedridden and had lost much of her grasp on reality, awards and honors never ceased. They came so steadily that after Eleanor Payne moved permanently to Atlanta in November 1990 to assist in her mother's care, she felt compelled to call a halt to the adulation, saying for Hamilton's sake "no more."

Hamilton's professional résumé at the end of her legislative career listed twenty-five awards and honors between 1965 and 1984. Some of these awards already have been enumerated here, and some were more significant than others. After her legislative years, the tributes were of a more lasting kind, as if both blacks and whites wanted to make sure her name would not be forgotten.

In May 1985 the American Jewish Congress, founded in 1918 to fight discrimination in America by litigation and legislation, gave Hamilton its prestigious Phoenix Award at a dinner in her honor and announced that evening that the award thereafter would be called the Grace Towns Hamilton Award. The award has since continued to be given annually to persons dedicated to human rights and social betterment in the Atlanta community.

In 1988, Emory University, now generously honoring blacks in marked contrast to its stubborn resistance to racial change in years past, inaugurated a lecture series bearing Hamilton's name, a move meant to promote Emory's African American Studies Program. This lectureship was the idea of Delores P. Aldridge, who had been director of the program since 1971. Aldridge frankly confessed that she proposed Hamilton's name on the lecture series as a means of facilitating fund-raising for its support, but if the honor was more apparent than real, it was nonetheless permanent. The first lecture in October 1988 was delivered by Yvonne Brathwaite Burke, a veteran of California politics who had represented her Los Angeles district in both the California Assembly and the U.S. House of Representatives. Hamilton was present, again in a wheelchair, at the well-attended event, but her attention wandered and she was unable to withhold expressions of discomfort during the lecture. It was the only lecture in the series she was ever able to attend. Other distinguished African Americans arrived annually in Atlanta to speak in the series, including Julius Chambers, director of the NAACP Legal Defense and Educational Fund; Jewel L. Prestage, Honors Professor of Political Science and dean of Benjamin Banneker Honors College at Prairie View A&M University, Prairie View, Texas; Alton Hornsby Jr., professor of history at Morehouse College; Judith Jamison, artistic director of the Alvin Ailey Dance Theatre; Andrew Billingsley, professor of sociology at the University of Maryland; Andrew Young, by then, after long years in local, national, and international politics, the vice-chairman of an international engineering and environmental consulting firm in Atlanta; and Julian Bond, who had left Atlanta to become Distinguished Scholar in Residence at American University in Washington, D.C., and a member of the history faculty at the University of Virginia.

Going further, Emory University in 1990 created a chair in Sociology and African American Studies, naming it for Grace Towns Hamilton and designating Delores Aldridge its first occupant. Aldridge's successor in the African American Studies Program was Rudolph Byrd, a Texas native with Atlanta connections, whose academic credentials included a doctorate from Yale University in American Studies.

In 1989 Hamilton paid her last visit to the Georgia capitol, this time to be present at the unveiling of her portrait painted by Tokuya Kaneko, which now hangs in the inner lobby (or cloakroom) of the House Chamber.

And in October 1992 the Georgia Legislative Black Caucus, moving to heal the breach that had grown between the group and Hamilton in her last years, voted unanimously to create a Grace Towns Hamilton Leadership Award for "individuals who have made significant contributions to their communities . . . and provided examples of good citizenship and service to mankind." This posthumous honor was suggested by Michael Thurman, 1992 Caucus chair, and among its energetic supporters was Georganna Sinkfield, who had looked to Hamilton as a mentor when she entered the legislature a decade before. Hamilton, in Sinkfield's view, was a "pioneer stateswoman" whose influence in the legislature had been—and was likely to remain—unequaled among African Americans, and Sinkfield had eagerly awaited an opportunity to promote Hamilton's public reinstatement in Caucus favor.[6]

· · ·

After the portrait unveiling, Hamilton seldom again left her home. She was well attended by a rotating group of nurses, sitters, and helpers, including some, like Otelia Samples and Rosa Edwards, who had served the family since the early illness of "Dr. Cookie." Edwards retired soon after his death, and her place was filled by Mary Sallie Hughes, a nurse and former political activist who came out of her own retirement to help care for Hamilton, whom she much admired. Daughter Eleanor and, on occasion, sister Harriet also remained on call. On March 21, 1991, her condition having worsened, Hamilton was taken to Briarcliff Nursing Home, where she remained until the end of her life. Buz Williams, whom Hamilton had appointed executor of her estate, recalled his part in the decision. "I mentioned to Grace that I thought it was time to go to a nursing home and she replied without hesitation, 'I think you're right.'" The family reluctantly agreed.[7]

At Briarcliff Hamilton's life seemed to come full circle, for also among its patients was Emma Rush Brown, her childhood friend, but for these two, it was a reunion too late. They were both too ill even to talk to each other. Hamilton's memory failed completely, and at the end she did not remember those closest to her, even her daughter. On June 18, 1992, fifteen months after her admission to the nursing home, Hamilton died there in her sleep, alone, at 4 A.M. She was eighty-five.

The *Atlanta Constitution* ran on its front page a lengthy obituary with a two-column-wide photo. The writer was Celestine Sibley, the *Constitution*'s popular columnist who had long been a Hamilton friend and admirer.

On June 20, a memorial service was held, as it had been for her husband, at the First Congregational Church. Eleanor Payne wanted no "eulogy," and in accord with her wishes, her cousin Theodore G. Towns, former professor of chemistry at Fisk and Howard Universities and at the time senior research chemist at Pittsburgh Plate Glass Industries, Inc., presented "remembrances." He spoke of her "towering" presence as he knew her from his earliest childhood. "By her stature she was Grace, grace personified— it wasn't a walk, it was a glide; the children—me, my brother, my cousins, her grandchildren—weren't 'snatched' away from anything, we were 'swooped' up. . . . Her gestures were large, yet delicate; powerful and purposeful, yet gentle." Father Austin Ford, as he had at her husband's funeral, gave the prayer. It was summer, and many of Hamilton's friends were away; death had also claimed some of them, but among those who did appear were U.S. senator Wyche Fowler and Fifth District congressman John Lewis, Judge Charles Weltner, John A. Griffin, former director of the Southern Education Foundation in Atlanta, and columnist Sibley. Mable Thomas, who had captured Hamilton's seat in the state legislature, was also there, the closest she and Hamilton ever came to a public meeting. The paucity of blacks at the funeral service was noted in the *Atlanta Daily World*'s obituary, which quoted one of those who came as saying, "The Church should have been packed with blacks, she paved the way for so many." Always her admirer, the *World* called her "a stateswoman."

Hamilton was buried at South View Cemetery alongside "Dr. Cookie" and other family members. Pallbearers, representing family and friends with whom she had engaged in numerous political and social endeavors, were William H. Alexander, George J. Berry, Hugh M. Gloster, Lee J. Price, R. Edwin Thomas, Horace T. Ward, Osgood O. Williams Sr., and Asa G. Yancey. Honorary pallbearers were her old cohorts, the Fulton County delegates to the Georgia General Assembly, many of whom were present at the funeral with their spouses. It was the kind of interracial gathering she spent her life trying to convert into a cultural norm.

Epilogue

. . .

GRACE TOWNS HAMILTON was a controversial figure, a legend in her own time, whose legacy was better appreciated by blacks than by whites. The white world adored and glorified her, clothing her in virtue without flaws. The black community viewed her with greater ambivalence, seeing blemish as well as the best and came closer to discerning the real and important person she was, probably because she was truly one of their own.

Her own generation took pride in her accomplishments and the status she won in the white world without apparent cost to her principles. The militant young eventually rejected her less because they were unaware of her real contributions—as many whites maintained—than because she had stood aside as they fought the terrible battle against segregation, and finally because she had grown old. They knew well enough she had used her influence to wrest from whites electoral gains that gave them a measure of political power in Atlanta and Georgia. Mable Thomas, sensing Hamilton's vulnerability and wanting change, captured her seat in the state legislature, but Thomas had voted for her time and again. Julian Bond, who fought her to the finish on the 1982 reapportionment issues, still appreciated Hamilton as "a healer, a communicator and a bridge builder." Georganna Sinkfield recognized the feet of clay that led to Hamilton's downfall in the state legislature but revered and honored her just the same. Alton Hornsby Jr., the Morehouse College historian who had himself been among the militant young, spoke in 1990 on the legacy of Grace Hamilton, and he may have summed it up best when he said: "A political leader who changes his stances to fit the times is often called a politician in the dirtiest sense of the word. One who refuses to change, who remains with her lifelong ideals, is often called reactionary and stubborn. But such a person may also be seen as possessing both honesty and integrity. It is because . . . of this probability that we remember and honor the legacy of Grace Towns Hamilton in the city of Atlanta today." [1]

Notes

. . .

Introduction

1. GTH interview with LNS and JBB, April 23, 1984. George Alexander Towns's papers include the jottings on his ancestry and history of his father's enslavement, Atlanta University Center's Woodruff Library Archives; Sharon Mitchell Mullis, "The Public Career of Grace Towns Hamilton, a Citizen Too Busy to Hate" (Ph.D. dissertation, Emory University, 1976), 34–35, 60; Mullis, "George Alexander Towns, Educator," profile published in *Dictionary of Georgia Biography*, 2 vols., ed. Kenneth Coleman and Charles Stephen Gurr (Athens: University of Georgia Press, 1983), 2: 994; Kenneth M. Stampp, *The Peculiar Institution: Slavery in the Ante-Bellum South* (New York: Vintage Books, 1956), 196, 358–59; Joel Williamson, *The Crucible of Race: Black-White Relations in the American South Since Emancipation* (New York: Oxford University Press, 1984), 40–42; Williamson, *New People: Miscegenation and Mulattoes in the United States* (New York: Free Press, 1980), 1–4, 112–17; Copy of George Washington Towns will, certified by Bibb County, Ga., Ordinary on March 9, 1962, provided by GTH for authors' files.

2. GTH interview with LNS and JBB, April 23, 1984; Margaret Mead and James Baldwin, *A Rap on Race* (New York: Dell, 1971), 6–7; Williamson, *New People*, 42, 53–56, 96, 137–39; Stampp, *Peculiar Institution*, 350–61.

Chapter 1: Genesis

1. Charles Crowe, "Racial Massacre in Atlanta, September 22, 1906," *Journal of Negro History* 54 (1969): 166–68; John Dittmer, *Black Georgia in the Progressive Era, 1900–1920* (Urbana: University of Illinois Press, 1977), xi; Nancy J. Weiss, *The National Urban League, 1910–1940* (New York: Oxford University Press, 1974), 4; Eric Foner, *Reconstruction: America's Unfinished Revolution* (New York: Harper & Row, 1988), 602–4; Clarence A. Bacote, "The Negro in Georgia Politics, 1880–1908" (Ph.D. dissertation, University of Chicago, 1955), 1–36; Joel Williamson, *New People: Miscegenation and Mulattoes in the United States* (New York: Free Press, 1980), 62, 112; John Hope Franklin, "History of Racial Segregation in the United States," in *The Making of Black America*, ed. August Meier and Elliott Rudwick (New York: Atheneum, 1969), 2: 3–13; Jacqueline Jones, *Soldiers of Light and Love: Northern Teachers and Georgia Blacks, 1865–1873* (Chapel Hill: University of North Carolina Press, 1980), 56, 200–201; W. E. B. Du Bois, *The Souls of Black Folk* (1903; rpt. New York: Avon Books, 1965), 282.

2. David Levering Lewis, *W. E. B. Du Bois, Biography of a Race* (New York: Henry Holt, 1993), 252–53; Clarence A. Bacote, *The Story of Atlanta University* (Atlanta: Atlanta University Press, 1969), 86–97, 239; W. E. B. Du Bois, *The Autobiography of W. E. B. Du Bois* (New York: International Publishers, 1968), 222–23; Sharon Mitchell Mullis, "The Public Career of Grace Towns Hamilton, a Citizen Too Busy to Hate" (Ph.D. dissertation, Emory University, 1976), 14; Crowe, "Racial Massacre in Atlanta," 168.

3. Dean Rowley, "George Alexander Towns: A Profile of His Atlanta University Experience, 1885–1929" (M.A. thesis, Atlanta University, 1975), 82; Margaret Mead and James Baldwin, *A Rap on Race* (New York: Dell, 1971), 6–7; Mullis, "Public Career of Grace Towns Hamilton," 51, 67–70.

4. Du Bois, *Souls of Black Folk*, 284–319; Genealogy table of Towns family as made available to authors by Grace Towns Hamilton; Williamson, *New People*, 24–25; Rowley, "George Alexander Towns," 4; Profiles of George Alexander Towns and George Washington Towns in *Dictionary of Georgia Biography*, 2 vols., ed. Kenneth Coleman and Charles Stephen Gurr (Athens: University of Georgia Press, 1983), 2: 994–97; Booker T. Washington, *Up from Slavery* (New York: Avon Books, 1965), 29.

5. Du Bois, *Souls of Black Folk*, 284, 287, 292–94, 303.

6. John Hope Franklin, *From Slavery to Freedom: A History of Negro Americans*, 5th ed. (New York: Knopf, 1980), 123–29; Kenneth M. Stampp, *The Peculiar Institution: Slavery in the Ante-Bellum South* (New York: Vintage Books, 1956), 60–73, 200–201. George Alexander Towns's notes on history of his father's enslavement are included in his papers, Atlanta University Center's Woodruff Library Archives.

7. Franklin, *From Slavery to Freedom*, 229–30, 234; Edmund L. Drago, *Black Politicians and Reconstruction in Georgia* (Baton Rouge: Louisiana State University Press, 1982), 111–20; Roy F. Nichols, *The Stakes of Power, 1845–1877* (New York: Hill and Wang, 1961), 164.

8. Du Bois, *Souls of Black Folk*, 221–39; Franklin, *From Slavery to Freedom*, 230–38,

242–50; Jones, *Soldiers of Light and Love*, 52–53; Nichols, *Stakes of Power*, 169; Drago, *Black Politicians and Reconstruction in Georgia*, 35–36, appendix; Bacote, "The Negro in Georgia Politics," 524–25.

9. Franklin, *From Slavery to Freedom*, 236–37; Jones, *Soldiers of Light and Love*, 58–59, 62, 85–93; Langston Hughes, Milton Meltzer, and C. Eric Lincoln, *A Pictorial History of Blackamericans*, 4th rev. ed. (New York: Crown, n.d.), 198–217; Drago, *Black Politicians and Reconstruction in Georgia*, 98.

10. Jones, *Soldiers of Light and Love*, 58, 61–62, 76; Drago, *Black Politicians and Reconstruction in Georgia*, 51–52, 66, 93–94, 112–16, 122–24, 160; Du Bois, *Souls of Black Folk*, 231, 238, 287, 313–14; Dittmer, *Black Georgia in the Progressive Era*, 14–16.

11. Du Bois, *Souls of Black Folk*, 306, 333–34; Franklin, *From Slavery to Freedom*, 137; Stampp, *Peculiar Institution*, 325, 334–40, 361–82; Jones, *Soldiers of Light and Love*, 67, 133; Williamson, *New People*, 20; Mullis, "Public Career of Grace Towns Hamilton," 35–36.

12. Jones, *Soldiers of Light and Love*, 11–13, 135; Joe M. Richardson, *Christian Reconstruction: The American Missionary Association and Southern Blacks, 1861–1890* (Athens: University of Georgia Press, 1986), 22, 37, 75–83, 109–11, 123, 127, 134, 145; Du Bois, *Souls of Black Folk*, 267–68.

13. Bacote, *Story of Atlanta University*, 3–30, 37, 44, 70–76, 86–94, 121; Jones, *Soldiers of Light and Love*, 135, 198.

14. Ridgely Torrence, *The Story of John Hope* (New York: Macmillan, 1948), 127–28; James Weldon Johnson, *Along This Way* (New York: Viking Press, 1934), 65; Du Bois, *Souls of Black Folk*, 267; Bacote, *Story of Atlanta University*, 30, 37.

15. Dittmer, *Black Georgia in the Progressive Era*, 151; Richardson, *Christian Reconstruction*, ix, 22, 123–40, 243–50; Jones, *Soldiers of Light and Love*, 4, 6, 9, 12, 16–20, 26, 50–51, 66–70, 84, 92–93, 135–39, 142–43; Bart Landry, *The New Black Middle Class* (Berkeley: University of California Press, 1987), 33; Carter G. Woodson, *The Miseducation of the Negro* (1933; rpt. New York: AMS Press, 1973), 6–7, 33.

16. Johnson, *Along This Way*, 65–66; Bacote, *Story of Atlanta University*, 70–76, 86–99, 236–39.

17. Rowley, "George Alexander Towns," 4–8, 11–12, 18; Mullis, "Public Career of Grace Towns Hamilton," 34–40; Bacote, *Story of Atlanta University*, 44–45, 238, 256–57; George Towns's teacher contracts contained in his professional records folder, George Alexander Towns Papers; Johnson, *Along This Way*, 103, 105, 119.

18. Johnson, *Along This Way*, 65–66.

19. Jones, *Soldiers of Light and Love*, 137–39; Dittmer, *Black Georgia in the Progressive Era*, 153–54; Johnson, *Along This Way*, 66–67, 70–71, 83, 105; George A. Towns, "Sources of the Traditions of Atlanta University," *Phylon* 3 (1942), as quoted in Rowley, "George Alexander Towns," 10, 21, 35; Mullis, "Public Career of Grace Towns Hamilton," 40.

20. Johnson, *Along This Way*, 3–5, 45, 66–68, 78, 83, 100, 103; Rowley, "George Alexander Towns," 17, 18, 45–47, 88.

21. Bacote, *Story of Atlanta University*, 37, 226; Mullis, "Public Career of Grace Towns Hamilton," 61; *Atlanta Journal-Constitution*, December 1, 1985, for reproduction of AU's 1894 class photo.

22. Franklin, *From Slavery to Freedom*, 258–67; Franklin, "History of Racial Segregation in the United States," 3–13; Foner, *Reconstruction*, xxv; Johnson, *Along This Way*, 158, 165–70; Mary White Ovington, *The Walls Came Tumbling Down* (New York: Harcourt, Brace, 1947), 58; Bacote, "The Negro in Georgia Politics," 26, 301.

23. Johnson, *Along This Way*, 122, 137–39, 141–44, 302–3, 309; Rowley, "George Alexander Towns," 21–23, 26–31; Bacote, *Story of Atlanta University*, 130–31, 134, 178–90; Lewis, *W. E. B. Du Bois*, 3, 217–18; Miles M. Jackson, ed., "Letters to a Friend: Correspondence from James Weldon Johnson to George Alexander Towns," *Phylon* 29 (1968): 182–98; *Atlanta Daily World*, January 25, 1950, article on his Harvard experience in George Alexander Towns Papers.

24. Lewis, *W. E. B. Du Bois*, 177–78; Vivien Beavers interview with LNS, January 24, 1986.

25. Mullis, "Public Career of Grace Towns Hamilton," 49–50; Rowley, "George Alexander Towns," 36; GTH interview with LNS and JBB, April 23, 1984.

26. Harriet Towns Jenkins telephone interview with JBB, September 11, 1989; GTH interview with LNS and JBB, April 23, 1984; Bacote, *Story of Atlanta University*, 8, 10–11; Vivien Beavers interview with LNS, January 24, 1986.

27. Anna DeRosa Byrne and Dana F. White, "Atlanta University's Northeast Lot," *Atlanta Historical Society Journal*, Summer–Fall 1975, 155–58.

28. Dittmer, *Black Georgia in the Progressive Era*, 165, 180; Drago, *Black Politicians and Reconstruction in Georgia*, 159.

29. *Atlanta Independent*, September 3, 1910; Rowley, "George Alexander Towns," 29–31, 34–36; Mullis, "Public Career of Grace Towns Hamilton," 42–43.

30. Du Bois, *Souls of Black Folk*, chap. 3, for Du Bois's first telling salvo in his battle with Booker T. Washington, esp. 240–42, 245–48, 251; Dittmer, *Black Georgia in the Progressive Era*, 157, 169–74; Ovington, *The Walls Came Tumbling Down*, 100–107.

31. George Towns's correspondence with Bumstead contained in George Alexander Towns Papers; Stephen R. Fox, *The Guardian of Boston: William Monroe Trotter* (New York: Atheneum, 1971), 61–62; Bacote, *Story of Atlanta University*, 148.

32. Franklin, *From Slavery to Freedom*, 263–67; Bacote, "The Negro in Georgia Politics," 400, 431, 433–38, 440–41, 455–60, 479–95, 498–500; Crowe, "Racial Massacre in Atlanta," 166–68; Dittmer, *Black Georgia in the Progressive Era*, 94–104.

33. Torrence, *Story of John Hope*, 133–35; Dittmer, *Black Georgia in the Progressive Era*, 174–75; Johnson, *Along This Way*, 314–17; Mullis, "Public Career of Grace Towns Hamilton," 47.

34. Associated Press dispatch in Towns Papers.

35. Du Bois to Towns family, December 22, 1960, letter shown to LNS by Grace Towns Hamilton from her personal files.

36. Horace Mann Bond remarks in Towns Papers; Bacote, *Story of Atlanta University*, 401–8.

Chapter 2: Growing Up Negro in the Progressive Era

1. Sharon Mitchell Mullis, "The Public Career of Grace Towns Hamilton, a Citizen Too Busy to Hate" (Ph.D. dissertation, Emory University, 1976), 67; GTH interview with LNS and JBB, April 23, 1984; Anna DeRosa Byrne and Dana F. White, "Atlanta Univer-

sity's Northeast Lot," *Atlanta Historical Society Journal*, Summer–Fall 1975, 155–59; "Beauty of Mansion Undimmed," *Atlanta Constitution*, January 26, 1986; Dean Rowley, "George Alexander Towns: A Profile of His Atlanta University Experience, 1885–1929" (M.A. thesis, Atlanta University, 1975), 80–82.

2. W. E. B. Du Bois, ed., *The Negro American Family*, as quoted in Byrne and White, "Atlanta University's Northeast Lot," 156.

3. Ibid., 160–74; *Atlanta Independent*, September 3, 1910.

4. GTH interview with Carole Merritt, curator of Herndon Home Museum, July 28, 1988, transcript on file at the museum; Eleanor Hamilton Payne unrecorded conversation with JBB.

5. Clarence A. Bacote, "The Negro in Georgia Politics, 1880–1908" (Ph.D. dissertation, University of Chicago, 1955), 467–68; John Dittmer, *Black Georgia in the Progressive Era* (Urbana: University of Illinois Press, 1977), 8–22; John Hope Franklin, *From Slavery to Freedom: A History of Negro Americans*, 5th ed. (New York: Knopf, 1980), 266–67; John Hope Franklin, "History of Racial Segregation in the United States," in *The Making of Black America*, ed. August Meier and Elliott Rudwick (New York: Atheneum, 1969), 2: 10–13; James Weldon Johnson, *Along This Way* (New York: Viking Press, 1934), 64–65, 84–85; Mullis, "Public Career of Grace Towns Hamilton," 24, 27, 31.

6. Rowley, "George Alexander Towns," 41–42; Dan Durrett and Dana F. White, *Another Atlanta, the Black Heritage*, pamphlet published in 1976 by the Atlanta Bicentennial Commission, 3–4; Dittmer, *Black Georgia in the Progressive Era*, 13, 20–21; Mullis, "Public Career of Grace Towns Hamilton," 28.

7. GTH interview with LNS and JBB, April 23, 1984; GTH interview with Carole Merritt, July 28, 1988; Clarence A. Bacote, *The Story of Atlanta University* (Atlanta: Atlanta University Press, 1969), 44–45.

8. GTH interview with LNS and JBB, April 23, 1984.

9. Mullis, "Public Career of Grace Towns Hamilton," 29–30, 70–71; Bacote, *Story of Atlanta University*, 29–30, 143–44, 169.

10. GTH interview with Carole Merritt, July 28, 1988; Rowley, "George Alexander Towns," 30–31.

11. Mullis, "Public Career of Grace Towns Hamilton," 51–55, 65–66; Bacote, *Story of Atlanta University*, 10, 59; *History of Gate City Free Kindergarten Association*, pamphlet contained in Mrs. G. A. (Nellie McNair) Towns Papers, Atlanta University Center Woodruff Library Archives; quotation from Gate City Day Nursery Association pamphlet, taken from Gerda Lerner, ed., *Black Women in White America: A Documentary History* (New York: Pantheon Books, 1972), 509–12.

12. "A Brief Tribute to Mrs. G. A. Towns," by Frankie V. Adams on behalf of Gate City Day Nursery Association Board of Trustees, in Nellie McNair Towns Papers.

13. Mullis, "Public Career of Grace Towns Hamilton," 51, 67, 68; GTH interview with Carole Merritt, July 28, 1988; GTH interview with LNS and JBB, April 23, 1984.

14. Mullis, "Public Career of Grace Towns Hamilton," 68.

15. Genevieve Pou, "Grace Hamilton: The Case for Commitment," *Atlanta Magazine*, June 1967, p. 28; Mullis, "Public Career of Grace Towns Hamilton," 69–70.

16. GTH interview with LNS and JBB, April 23, 1984, with LNS October 20 and 24, 1985; Dr. Asa G. Yancey interview with LNS, April 18, 1986.

17. GTH interview with LNS, October 24, 1985.

18. Bacote, *Story of Atlanta University*, 143, 169–71; Grace Holmes DeLorme interview with LNS, January 24, 1986.

19. Annie Ruth Simmons Hill interview with LNS, January 30, 1986.

20. Mary White Ovington, *The Walls Came Tumbling Down* (New York: Harcourt, Brace, 1947), 100–112; Nancy J. Weiss, *The National Urban League, 1919–1940* (New York: Oxford University Press, 1974), 40–46.

21. Dittmer, *Black Georgia in the Progressive Era*, 181, 186–91; Johnson, *Along This Way*, 300–301; Franklin, *From Slavery to Freedom*, 323–25.

22. Dittmer, *Black Georgia in the Progressive Era*, 186–87; Franklin, *From Slavery to Freedom*, 339–41, 347–50; Johnson, *Along This Way*, 319–26.

23. Franklin, *From Slavery to Freedom*, 347; Dittmer, *Black Georgia in the Progressive Era*, 201, 208–9, 210; Morton Sosna, *In Search of the Silent South* (New York: Columbia University Press, 1977), 119–20.

24. Mullis, "Public Career of Grace Towns Hamilton," 71–73.

25. Bacote, *Story of Atlanta University*, 276; Harriet Towns Jenkins interview with LNS, June 26, 1985; George A. Towns Jr., letter to parents, February 26, 1960, shown to author LNS by Grace Towns Hamilton from her personal file.

26. Dittmer, *Black Georgia in the Progressive Era*, 153–54; Mullis, "Public Career of Grace Towns Hamilton," 72–73.

27. Dittmer, *Black Georgia in the Progressive Era*, 152–53, 159–60; Annie Ruth Simmons Hill interview with LNS, January 30, 1986; LNS interview with source demanding anonymity for quote on GTH's racial bias.

28. Mullis, "Public Career of Grace Towns Hamilton," 74–79; Grace Holmes DeLorme interview with LNS, January 24, 1986; Gladys Gilkey Calkins, "The Negro in the YWCA: A Study in the Development of YWCA Interracial Policies and Practices in Their Historical Setting" (M.A. thesis, George Washington University, 1960), 38–67, 105.

29. Mullis, "Public Career of Grace Towns Hamilton," 74–76.

30. GTH interview with LNS and JBB, April 23, 1984; Dittmer, *Black Georgia in the Progressive Era*, 22.

31. Annie Ruth Simmons Hill interview with LNS, January 30, 1986; Harriet Towns Jenkins interview with LNS, June 26, 1985.

32. Wenonah Bond Logan interview with JBB, September 14, 1985.

33. Mullis, "Public Career of Grace Towns Hamilton," 79; Bacote, *Story of Atlanta University*, 169–71, 269–71, 293–95, 332–35, 407–8; Rowley, "George Alexander Towns," 95; Harriet Towns Jenkins interview with LNS, June 26, 1985.

Chapter 3: A Rude Awakening in Ohio

1. Genevieve Pou, "Grace Hamilton: The Case for Commitment," *Atlanta Magazine*, June 1967, p. 28; Sharon Mitchell Mullis, "The Public Career of Grace Towns Hamilton, a Citizen Too Busy to Hate" (Ph.D. dissertation, Emory University, 1976), 78; GTH interview with LNS and JBB, April 23, 1984.

2. John Hope Franklin, *From Slavery to Freedom: A History of Negro Americans*, 5th ed. (New York: Knopf, 1980), 316–17; Lillian Hervey Jackson, letter of December 9, 1985, describing Negro proscriptions in Columbus in the 1920s in files of LNS; Alexa Benson

Henderson, *Atlanta Life Insurance Company: Guardian of Black Economic Dignity* (Tuscaloosa: University of Alabama Press, 1990), 120; GTH interview with LNS and JBB, April 23, 1984.

3. GTH interviews with LNS and JBB, April 23, 1984, and October 16, 1985.

4. Mullis, "Public Career of Grace Towns Hamilton," 98, quoting Wenonah Bond Logan.

5. Franklin, *From Slavery to Freedom*, 346–47, 350.

6. GTH interview with LNS, April 24, 1984.

7. Gerda Lerner, ed., *Black Women in White America: A Documentary History* (New York: Pantheon Books, 1972), 488.

8. Grace Gilkey Calkins, "The Negro in the Young Women's Christian Association: A Study in the Development of YWCA Policies and Practices in Their Historical Setting" (M.A. thesis, George Washington University, 1960), 24.

9. Ibid., 24, 26, 30, 34, 38, 39–46, 50–51, 53–54, 56, 62–65, 81–82, 84.

10. Ibid., 27, 28, 30, 38–40, 89, 105; Clarence A. Bacote, *The Story of Atlanta University* (Atlanta: Atlanta University Press, 1969), 127, 242; Leslie Blanchard, *The Student Movement of the YWCA* (New York: Women's Press, 1927), 9–12.

11. Anne Arnold Hedgeman, *The Trumpet Sounds: A Memoir of Negro Leadership* (New York: Holt, Rinehart, and Winston, 1964), as excerpted in Lerner, ed., *Black Women in White America*, 489–91.

12. Ibid., 489; Lillian Hervey Jackson, letter of December 9, 1985, describing YWCA building in Columbus in 1927, in files of LNS. Mullis, "Public Career of Grace Towns Hamilton," 81–83.

13. Calkins, "The Negro in the Young Women's Christian Association," 37, 54–55; Lillian Hervey Jackson, letter of December 9, 1985.

14. Mullis, "Public Career of Grace Towns Hamilton," 81–84; Hedgeman, *The Trumpet Sounds*, as excerpted in Lerner, ed., *Black Women in White America*, 490.

15. Lillian Hervey Jackson, letter of December 9, 1985, in files of LNS.

16. GTH interview with Carole Merritt, curator of Herndon Home Museum, July 28, 1988.

17. Mullis, "Public Career of Grace Towns Hamilton," 84; Bacote, *Story of Atlanta University*, 328–30.

18. Anthony M. Platt, *E. Franklin Frazier Reconsidered* (New Brunswick, N.J.: Rutgers University Press, 1991), 62–81.

19. Bacote, *Story of Atlanta University*, 329; GTH interviews with LNS, April 24, 1984, and October 24, 1985, with LNS and JBB, October 16, 1985.

Chapter 4: The Depression Years: To Memphis and Back

1. August Meier and David Lewis, "History of the Negro Upper Class in Atlanta, Georgia, 1890–1958," *Journal of Negro Education* 28 (1959): 128–39; Sharon Mitchell Mullis, "The Public Career of Grace Towns Hamilton, a Citizen Too Busy to Hate" (Ph.D. dissertation, Emory University, 1976), 84–86; Tribute to Henry Cooke Hamilton by Hugh M. Gloster, President of Morehouse College, at Hamilton's funeral, First Congregational Church, Atlanta, Georgia, January 5, 1987, copy in LNS files; E. R. Carter,

The Black Side: A Partial History of the Business, Educational and Religious Side of the Negro in Atlanta, (Atlanta: N.p., 1894); W. E. B. Du Bois, ed., *The Negro Artisan: Proceedings of the 7th Conference for the Study of Negro Problems, Atlanta University, May 27, 1902* (Atlanta: Atlanta University Press, 1902); Stephen Birmingham, *Certain People* (Boston: Little, Brown, 1977), 212, 219–21, 224, 237–38.

2. Reverend Benjamin Bickers telephone interview with LNS April 14, 1986, transcript in LNS files.

3. GTH interview with LNS, April 24, 1984, and October 20, 1985, and with LNS and JBB October 16, 1985; Anthony M. Platt, "Racism in Academia: Lessons from the Life of E. Franklin Frazier," *Monthly Review* 42 (September 1990): 29–40; Jacqueline Jones, *Labor of Love, Labor of Sorrow: Black Women, Work and the Family from Slavery to the Present* (New York: Basic Books, 1985), 4; Jeanne L. Noble, "The American Negro Woman," in *The American Negro Reference Book*, ed. John F. Davis (Englewood Cliffs: Prentice-Hall, 1966), 526; George W. Lee, *Beale Street: Where the Blues Began* (New York: Robert O. Ballou, 1934), 29–30.

4. Eleanor Hamilton Payne interview with JBB, May 14, 1984; GTH interview with LNS, April 24, 1984.

5. Clarence A. Bacote, *The Story of Atlanta University* (Atlanta: Atlanta University Press, 1969), 4; GTH interview with LNS, April 24, 1984.

6. Platt, "Racism in Academia," 35; Ruth Edmonds Hill, ed., *Women of Courage: An Exhibition of Photographs* by Judith Sedwick, based on the Black Women Oral History Project sponsored by the Schlesinger Library, Radcliffe College, 1984, 26.

7. GTH interview with JBB and LNS, October 16, 1985; Frances Williams and Wenonah Bond Logan, *Pudge Grows Up* (New York: Women's Press, 1936), taken from a notation in GTH Papers then housed in Woodruff Library's Archives Department, Atlanta University Center.

8. Jones, *Labor of Love, Labor of Sorrow*, 220–21.

9. John Hope Franklin, *From Slavery to Freedom: A History of Negro Americans*, 5th ed. (New York: Knopf, 1980), 412–13.

10. John Hope Franklin, "A Brief History of the Negro in the United States," in *American Negro Reference Book*, ed. Davis, 65, 72.

11. GTH interviews with LNS, April 24, 1984, July 10 and October 20, 1985, and with LNS and JBB, October 16, 1985, and April 8, 1986; Brochure entitled *A Pilgrimage of Friendship from U.S. to India*, among GTH Papers then housed in Woodruff Library's Archives Department, Atlanta University Center; Franklin, *From Slavery to Freedom*, 390.

12. Richard Bardolph, *The Negro Vanguard* (New York: Vintage Books, 1959), 200–201; GTH interviews with LNS, April 24, 1984, July 10 and October 20, 1985; Paula Giddings, *When and Where I Enter: The Impact of Black Women on Race and Sex in America* (New York: Bantam Books, 1985), 97.

13. Lee, *Beale Street*, 241, 262–66, 282; GTH interview with LNS, April 24, 1984; Annette E. Church and Roberta Church, *The Robert R. Churches of Memphis* (Ann Arbor: Edwards Brothers, 1974), 5, 12–26, 46–57, 67–68, 96, 122.

14. Lee, *Beale Street*, 251, 266; Church and Church, *The Robert R. Churches of Memphis*, 87, 89; Franklin, *From Slavery to Freedom*, 384.

15. GTH interview with LNS, April 24, 1984; Jones, *Labor of Love, Labor of Sorrow*, 8.

16. GTH interviews with LNS and JBB, April 23, 1984, and October 16, 1985, with LNS, July 10, October 20 and 24, 1985; Gladys Gilkey Calkins, "The Negro in the Young Women's Christian Association: A Study in the Development of YWCA Policies and Practices in Their Historical Setting" (M.A. thesis, George Washington University, 1960), 67, 76, 81–88.

17. GTH interviews with LNS, April 24, 1984, July 10, 1985; GTH to Charles Houston, October 31, 1939, in YWCA folder, GTH Papers, AHC.

18. Eleanor Hamilton Payne interview with JBB, May 14, 1984.

19. Ibid.

20. Ibid.

21. Katherine Stoney interview with LNS, San Francisco, June 9, 1992.

22. Bacote, *Story of Atlanta University*, 334–35, 346; GTH interview with LNS, April 24, 1984.

23. GTH interview with LNS, April 24, 1984; Eleanor Hamilton Payne, interview with JBB, May 14, 1984.

24. GTH interview with LNS and JBB, April 23, 1984; Undated letter from Mrs. Edward H. Heller to GTH, shown to LNS from GTH private correspondence.

25. GTH interview with LNS and JBB, April 23, 1984.

26. Eleanor Hamilton Payne interview with JBB, May 14, 1984.

27. Eleanor Hamilton Payne interview with LNS, June 26, 1985; see also *Sweatt* v. *Painter*, 339 U.S. 629 (1950).

Chapter 5: The Emerging Leader

1. Sharon Mitchell Mullis, "The Public Career of Grace Towns Hamilton, a Citizen Too Busy to Hate" (Ph.D. dissertation, Emory University, 1976), 101, 163–65; Genevieve Pou, "Grace Towns Hamilton: The Case for Commitment," *Atlanta Magazine*, June 1, 1967; YWCA manuscript and Neighborhood Union Papers, Trevor Arnett Library, Atlanta University, and YWCA Manuscripts, Sophia Smith Collection, Smith College, Northampton, Mass., cited in Lerner, ed., *Black Women in White America: A Documentary History*, ed. Gerda Lerner (New York: Pantheon Books, 1972), 482, 488.

2. GTH interview with LNS, April 24, 1984, and with JBB and LNS, October 16, 1985; W. E. B. Du Bois, *The Autobiography of W. E. B. Du Bois* (New York: International Publishers Company, 1968), 301; Clarence A. Bacote, *The Story of Atlanta University* (Atlanta: Atlanta University Press, 1969), 289, 374.

3. Robert E. Weaver, "The Negro Ghetto," in *The Making of Black America*, ed. August Meier and Elliott Rudwick (New York: Atheneum, 1964), 2: 173; Nicholas Leman, "Chasing the Dream: Deep South, Dark Ghetto, Middle Class Enclaves," *New Perspectives Quarterly* 8 (Summer 1991): 30; Eli Ginzberg and Dale L. Hiestand, "Employment Patterns of Negro Men and Women," in *The American Negro Reference Book*, ed. John P. Davis (Englewood Cliffs: Prentice-Hall, 1966), 208; *Le Monde Diplomatique* (Paris monthly), January 1992, p. 19.

4. John Hope Franklin, "A Brief History of the Negro in the United States," in *American Negro Reference Book*, ed. Davis, 68, 70; John Hope Franklin, *From Slavery to*

Freedom: A History of Negro Americans, 5th ed. (New York: Knopf, 1980), 383–92; Paula Giddings, *When and Where I Enter: The Impact of Black Women on Race and Sex in America* (New York: Bantam Books, 1985), 217–21; Jacqueline Jones, *Labor of Love, Labor of Sorrow: Black Women, Work and the Family from Slavery to the Present* (New York: Basic Books, 1985), 217.

5. Guichard Parris and Lester Brooks, *Blacks in the City: A History of the National Urban League* (Boston: Little, Brown, 1971), 265; Jones, *Labor of Love, Labor of Sorrow,* 220–21.

6. Giddings, *When and Where I Enter*, 217–18; Ginzberg and Hiestand, "Employment Patterns of Negro Men and Women," 221; Paul D. Bolster, "Civil Rights Movements in 20th Century Georgia" (Ph.D. dissertation, University of Georgia, 1972), 38–40.

7. Franklin, *From Slavery to Freedom*, 393–98.

8. Bolster, "Civil Rights Movements in 20th Century Georgia," 47.

9. Ibid., 46, 58–88; Parris and Brooks, *Blacks in the City*, 250–60; Du Bois, *Autobiography*, 304; Franklin, *From Slavery to Freedom*, 357–59.

10. V. O. Key Jr., *Southern Politics in State and Nation* (New York: Vintage Books, 1949), 623.

11. Jacqueline Anne Rouse, *Lugenia Burns Hope: Black Southern Reformer* (Athens: University of Georgia Press, 1989), 119–20; Clarence A. Bacote, "The Negro in Atlanta Politics," *Phylon* 16 (1955): 342–43; Bolster, "Civil Rights Movements in 20th Century Georgia," 85–88.

12. Giddings, *When and Where I Enter*, 235.

13. Ibid., 236–38; Parris and Brooks, *Blacks in the City*, 290–91, 306.

14. Franklin, *From Slavery to Freedom*, 423–28.

15. GTH interviews with LNS and JBB, April 23, 1984, and October 16, 1985, with LNS, April 24, 1984; GTH interview with Jacquelyn Hall, July 19, 1974, Southern Oral History Program, Wilson Library, University of North Carolina, Chapel Hill; Giddings, *When and Where I Enter*, 257–58; LBG to GTH, August 29, 1957, Lester B. Granger Papers in National Urban League Collection, LC.

16. *Atlanta Daily World*, February 24, 1943, as quoted in Mullis, "Public Career of Grace Towns Hamilton," 107.

17. John H. Calhoun, "Wedding of Town and Gown," *Atlanta Inquirer*, September 19, 1970; Bacote, *Story of Atlanta University*, 422–23; Richard Bardolph, *The Negro Vanguard* (New York: Vintage Books, 1959), 370–71.

18. Hugh Carl Owen, "The Rise of Negro Voting in Georgia, 1944–50" (M.A. thesis, Emory University, 1951), 9–30; Lorraine Nelson Spritzer, *The Belle of Ashby Street: Helen Douglas Mankin and Georgia Politics* (Athens: University of Georgia Press, 1982), 103–5.

19. Nancy J. Weiss, *The National Urban League, 1910–1940* (New York: Oxford University Press, 1974), 4, 8, 10–12, 15–48, 54–60.

20. Ibid., 64–67; Mary White Ovington, *The Walls Came Tumbling Down* (New York: Harcourt, Brace, 1947), 112.

21. Weiss, *National Urban League*, 40–46, 71–76, 79, 80, 84, 89, 129–35, 150, 219, 232–33; Parris and Brooks, *Blacks in the City*, 166.

22. Weiss, *National Urban League*, 92–93, 102, 112, 135–36, 150, 164, 167, 181, 216, 246,

250−64, 284−85, 303−6; Parris and Brooks, *Blacks in the City*, 166−68, 248−60, 274−75, 280−305.

23. Parris and Brooks, *Blacks in the City*, 161−66, 301; Weiss, *National Urban League*, 151, 159−61, 164−75, 246, 292−93; Bolster, "Civil Rights Movements in 20th Century Georgia," 58−60; Mullis, "Public Career of Grace Towns Hamilton," 102−3; Information on founding members of AUL's Board of Directors supplied by John Griffin, Ella Mae Gaines Yates, Dottie Johnson, and Dorothy Pleasant, all of Atlanta.

Chapter 6: The Atlanta Urban League: A Housing Success

1. GTH interview with LNS, July 10, 1985; GTH interview with Jacquelyn Hall, July 19, 1974, Southern Oral History Program, University of North Carolina, Chapel Hill; "The Atlanta Urban League," Atlanta Community Chest paper prepared from facts supplied by Atlanta Urban League, 1956, Lester B. Granger Papers, National Urban League Collection, LC.

2. Robert A. Thompson interview with LNS, February 3, 1986; GTH interview with LNS and JBB, October 16, 1985, and with LNS, October 24, 1985.

3. Katherine Stoney interview with LNS, San Francisco, June 16, 1992; GTH interview with LNS, April 18, 1986; Reginald Johnson to Jerome Johnson, May 5, 1960, LBG Papers; Comments of Philip G. Hammer and Lester B. Granger, from minutes of joint meeting of AUL-NUL Boards, New York City, February 29, 1960.

4. Nancy J. Weiss, *The National Urban League, 1910−1940* (New York: Oxford University Press, 1974), 155, 161, 345n; Guichard Parris and Lester Brooks, *Blacks in the City: A History of the National Urban League* (Boston: Little, Brown, 1971), 307, 398; Statement by J. B. Blayton and GTH, October 21, 1959, on Community Chest financing of local Leagues, submitted to NUL January 18, 1960, in response to LBG complaint of January 11, 1960; Jacob Henderson interview with Duane Stewart, June 8, 1989, Georgia Government Documentation Project, Georgia State University; Sharon Mitchell Mullis, "The Public Career of Grace Towns Hamilton, a Citizen Too Busy to Hate" (Ph.D. dissertation, Emory University, 1976), 150−52.

5. Thompson interview with LNS, February 3, 1986.

6. GTH interview with LNS, April 18, 1986; Mullis, "Public Career of Grace Towns Hamilton," 145; Robert A. Thompson, Hylan Lewis, and Davis McEntire, "Atlanta and Birmingham: A Comparative Study in Negro Housing," in *A Study in Housing and Minority Groups*, ed. Nathan Glazer and Davis McEntire (Berkeley: University of California Press, 1960), 20−23, 25−26, 30−34, 37−38.

7. *An Atlanta Housing Story*, film script produced by Highlander Folk School, n.d., GTH Papers, AHC; Thompson interview with LNS, February 3, 1986; Harold Fleming, "Housing for a New Middle Class," *Survey*, September 1951; George Goodwin, "Honest Cooperation Helps Ease Negro Housing Bottleneck," *Atlanta Journal-Constitution*, July 30, 1950; Dennis R. Judd, "Segregation Forever?" *Nation*, December 9, 1991.

8. "The Atlanta Urban League," Atlanta Community Chest paper prepared from facts supplied by AUL, 1956, LBG Papers; "Report on the Housing Activities of the Atlanta Urban League," November 28, 1951, GTH Papers, AHC; Goodwin, "Honest Cooperation Helps Ease City's Negro Housing Bottleneck"; Thompson interview with LNS, February 3, 1986.

9. Thompson interview with LNS, February 3, 1986; Thompson, Lewis, and McEntire, "Atlanta and Birmingham," 22–23; "Report on the Housing Activities of the Atlanta Urban League."

10. Thompson interview with LNS, February 3, 1986.

11. Minutes, Atlanta Urban League Board meeting, November 18, 1952; Thompson interviews with LNS, February 3, 1986, and October 28, 1993.

12. Thompson interview with LNS, February 3, 1986.

13. Al Kuettner, "Negroes in Atlanta Solved Problem of Housing," UPI news story in *Anniston* (Ala.) *Star*, July 17, 1958, clipping in LBG Papers; Reginald Johnson to Jerome Johnson, May 5, 1950, LBG Papers.

14. Thompson, Lewis, and McEntire, "Atlanta and Birmingham," 23–25, 37–38; Goodwin, "Honest Cooperation Helps Ease City's Negro Housing Bottleneck"; Morris B. Abram telephone interview with LNS, August 14, 1993; "Report on Housing Activities of the Atlanta Urban League."

15. Thompson, Lewis, and McEntire, "Atlanta and Birmingham," 14, 24–25; Ivan Allen Jr., with Paul Hemphill, *Mayor: Notes on the Sixties* (New York: Simon and Schuster, 1971), 71.

16. Morris B. Abram telephone interview with LNS, August 14, 1993.

17. Fleming, "Housing for a New Middle Class."

18. "Report on Housing Activities of the Atlanta Urban League."

19. Thompson, Lewis, and McEntire, "Atlanta and Birmingham," 34–38; "The Atlanta Urban League," Atlanta Community Chest paper prepared from facts supplied by Atlanta Urban League, 1956, LBG Papers; Kuettner, "Negroes in Atlanta Solved Problem of Housing."

20. Thompson interview with LNS, February 3, 1986; *Atlanta Daily World*, June 23, 1951, as quoted in Mullis, "Public Career of Grace Towns Hamilton," 148.

21. Adie Suehsdorf, "Good News," *Atlanta Journal-Constitution Magazine*, January 14, 1951.

22. Goodwin, "Honest Cooperation Helps Ease City's Negro Housing Bottleneck."

23. News clipping, "Thompson Receives 27-Club Award," from *Atlanta Daily World*, May 28, 1955, LBG Papers; GTH interview with Jacquelyn Hall, July 19, 1974.

Chapter 7: At the AUL: Equalizing Funds for Negro Schools and the Rebirth of Negro Voting

1. GTH interview with LNS, July 10, 1985; GTH interview with Jacquelyn Hall, July 19, 1974, Southern Oral History Program, University of North Carolina, Chapel Hill; GTH interviews with LNS and JBB, October 16 and with LNS October 24, 1985.

2. GTH interview with LNS, October 16, 1985.

3. Sharon Mitchell Mullis, "The Public Career of Grace Towns Hamilton, a Citizen Too Busy to Hate" (Ph.D. dissertation, Emory University, 1976), 108–10.

4. "Summary of the Work of the Citizens Committee on Public Education Organized by the Atlanta Urban League 1944 to 1946," GTH Papers, Box 4, Folder 4, AHC; Clarence A. Bacote, "The Negro in Atlanta Politics," *Phylon* 16 (1955): 342; Kathryn L. Nasstrom, "Women, the Civil Rights Movement, and the Politics of Historical Memory in Atlanta, 1946–1973" (Ph.D. dissertation, University of North Carolina, 1993), 19.

5. GTH interviews with LNS and JBB, April 23, 1984, and October 16, 1985; Mullis,

"Public Career of Grace Towns Hamilton," 108–11; "Report of Public School Facilities for Negroes in Atlanta, Georgia," 1944, GTH Papers, Box 4, Folder 1.

6. "Report of Public School Facilities"; GTH interview with LNS, April 18, 1986; Melvin W. Ecke, *From Ivy Street to Kennedy Center, Centennial History of Atlanta Public School System* (Atlanta: N.p., 1972), 282, excerpts in GTH Papers; GTH interview with LNS, April 18, 1986.

7. GTH interview with Jacquelyn Hall, July 19, 1974.

8. Ecke, *From Ivy Street to Kennedy Center*, 282; "A Summary of the Work of the Citizens Committee on Public Education Organized by the Atlanta Urban League, 1944 to 1946," GTH Papers, Box 4, Folder 4; Press release from Citizens Committee on Public Education, August 16, 1946, GTH Papers; Walter O'Meara, letter to GTH, December 15, 1946, GTH Papers.

9. "A Summary of the Work of the Citizens Committee on Public Education"; Ecke, *From Ivy Street to Kennedy Center*, 285.

10. *Atlanta Daily World*, December 17, 1944.

11. *Atlanta Journal*, December 2, 14, 1944; *Atlanta Constitution*, December 3, 12, 1944; *Milwaukee Journal*, editorial reprinted in *Atlanta Journal*, December 27, 1944.

12. Ecke, *From Ivy Street to Kennedy Center*, 287.

13. Ecke, *From Ivy Street to Kennedy Center*, 282, 287–88; "A Supplemental Report on Public School Facilities for Negroes," Atlanta Urban League, 1948, A. T. Walden Papers, Folder 3, Box 34, AHC; "An Analysis of Per-Pupil School Expenditures by Race, 1948–1949, 1949–1950," Atlanta Urban League, August 15, 1950, GTH Papers.

14. *Atlanta Journal*, September 19, 1950; *Atlanta Constitution*, September 20, 1950.

15. GTH interview with Jacquelyn Hall; Statement of Atlanta Urban League, September 22, 1950, GTH Papers; Mullis, "Public Career of Grace Towns Hamilton," 115; GTH interview with LNS and JBB, April 23, 1984.

16. Nancy J. Weiss, *The National Urban League, 1910–1940* (New York: Oxford University Press, 1974), 302; Hugh Carl Owen, "The Rise of Negro Voting in Georgia, 1944–1950" (M.A. thesis, Emory University, 1951), 8–19, 25–30; Lorraine Nelson Spritzer, *The Belle of Ashby Street: Helen Douglas Mankin and Georgia Politics* (Athens: University of Georgia Press, 1982), 64–74; Paul D. Bolster, "Civil Rights Movements in 20th Century Georgia" (Ph.D. dissertation, University of Georgia, 1972), 113, 131; Bacote, "The Negro in Atlanta Politics," 343–45; Thomas Camp interview with LNS, November 7, 1977, tape on file with Georgia Government Documentation Project, Georgia State University, Atlanta.

17. Spritzer, *Belle of Ashby Street*, 88–108; GTH interviews with LNS, July 26, 1977 (transcript in LNS files), and with LNS and JBB, October 16, 1985.

18. GTH interview with LNS and JBB, October 16, 1985.

19. Ibid.; Bacote, "The Negro in Atlanta Politics," 346.

20. Bacote, "The Negro in Atlanta Politics," 347–48; Spritzer, *Belle of Ashby Street*, 105.

21. Owen, "The Rise of Negro Voting in Georgia," 26–28; Bolster, "Civil Rights Movements in 20th Century Georgia," 121, 127, 131.

Chapter 8: A Hospital for the Excluded and the "Hidden Agenda"

1. "A Report on Hospital Care of the Negro Population of Atlanta, Georgia, 1947," Atlanta Urban League, GTH Papers, Folder 2, Box 5, AHC.

2. Winifred Wygal, "The Life and Death of Juliette Derricotte," *Crisis* 39 (March 1932), as reprinted in Gerda Lerner, ed., *Black Women in White America: A Documentary History* (New York: Pantheon Books, 1972), 384–96.

3. GTH to Alfred Stanford, December 30, 1947, and to W. Montague Cobb, Professor of Anatomy, Howard University, January 22, 1948, GTH Papers; Edward R. Embree and Julia Waxman, *Investment in People: The Story of the Julius Rosenwald Fund* (New York: Harper and Bros., 1949), 18, 244; GTH letter to "Dear Friends," December 19, 1947, GTH Papers, Box 5.

4. GTH interview with Jacquelyn Hall, July 19, 1974, Southern Oral History Program, University of North Carolina, Chapel Hill; "Report on Hospital Care"; GTH interview with LNS and JBB, October 16, 1985; GTH to W. Montague Cobb, January 22, 1948, GTH Papers, Box 5; W. Montague Cobb to GTH, January 16, 1948, GTH papers; W. Montague Cobb to R. Hugh Wood, Dean of Emory University School of Medicine, January 23, 1948, GTH Papers, Box 5; Alfred A. Weinstein, "Request for a Grant to Develop a Teaching Program for Negro Interns and Residents and a Post-Graduate Program for Physicians at the Spalding Pavilion," 1955, GTH Papers; Charles R. Drew, M.D., to Paul B. Beeson, M.D., Emory University School of Medicine, January 20, 1947, GTH Papers; Hughes Spalding to G. Arthur Howell, January 8, 1948, GTH Papers.

5. "Report on Hospital Care"; GTH to Alfred Stanford, December 30, 1947, GTH Papers; GTH interview with LNS, October 24, 1985.

6. GTH interview with LNS, October 24, 1985; Hughes Spalding to G. Arthur Howell, January 8, 1948, and to Stephens Mitchell, December 23, 1949, GTH Papers.

7. Hughes Spalding to GTH, October 13, 1948, and February 27, 1950, and to Trustees of the Advisory Board of Fulton-DeKalb Negro Hospital, May 30, 1950, GTH Papers; Sharon Mitchell Mullis, "The Public Career of Grace Towns Hamilton, a Citizen Too Busy to Hate" (Ph.D. dissertation, Emory University, 1976), 132–33.

8. GTH to Louis T. Wright, February 8, 1952, and to L. D. Milton, August 25, 1955, GTH Papers; Lester B. Granger to Jesse O. Thomas, June 1, 1950, Granger Papers, National Urban League Collection, LC; W. Montague Cobb to R. Hugh Wood, January 23, 1948, GTH Papers.

9. G. Lombard Kelly to GTH, January 24, 1948, GTH Papers; Charles R. Drew to Paul B. Beeson, January 20, 1947, GTH Papers; GTH to Louis T. Wright, February 8, 1952, GTH Papers; GTH to W. Montague Cobb, January 22, 1948, GTH papers.

10. Alfred A. Weinstein, "Request for Grant to Develop a Teaching Program," 1955, GTH Papers; Hughes Spalding to R. C. Mizell, July 20, 1948, GTH Papers; GTH to Channing Tobias, September 2, 1951, as cited in Mullis, "Public Career of Grace Towns Hamilton," 136.

11. Alfred A. Weinstein to Hughes Spalding, July 6, 1955, GTH Papers; *Atlanta Journal*, June 27, 1948; GTH to Hughes Spalding, November 21, 1951, GTH to L. D. Milton, August 25, 1955, Hughes Spalding to Emory W. Norris, President of the Kellogg Foundation, August 7, 1953, Hughes Spalding to R. C. Williams, January 7, 1958, Asa G. Yancey, M.D., to Dr. Ira A. Ferguson, Chief of Surgery, Grady Memorial Hospital, August 9, 1955, R. Hugh Wood to Hughes Spalding, April 6, 1954, Alfred A. Weinstein, "Request for a Grant to Develop a Teaching Program," 1955, all in GTH Papers.

12. GTH to Samuel Rothberg, August 12, 1960, GTH to Hughes Spalding, July 9, 1953, Draft of a Proposed Letter from the Board of Directors of the Atlanta Urban League to the Fulton-DeKalb Hospital Authority, March 24, 1960, all in GTH Papers; GTH interview with LNS, October 24, 1985.

13. Hughes Spalding to GTH, February 27, 1950, GTH to Hughes Spalding, February 3, 1950, November 21, 1951, January 28, 1959, Hughes Spalding to GTH, January 29, 1959, all in GTH Papers.

14. GTH interview with LNS, October 24, 1985.

15. GTH to Louis T. Wright, February 8, 1952, GTH Papers; GTH interview with LNS, October 24, 1985.

16. Hughes Spalding to Advisory Board of Trustees, Negro Hospital, Fulton-DeKalb Hospital Authority, April 15, 1950, Hughes Spalding to R. C. Mizell, July 20, 1948, GTH to W. B. Stubbs, November 16, 1949, GTH to Hughes Spalding, June 21, 1949, Hughes Spalding to Advisory Board of Trustees, New Negro Hospital, July 18, 1952, all in GTH Papers; Mullis, "Public Career of Grace Towns Hamilton," 134–35; Hughes Spalding to GTH, June 22, 1949, Hughes Spalding to Advisory Board of Trustees, New Negro Hospital, Fulton-DeKalb Hospital Authority, April 15, 1950, both in GTH Papers.

17. Hughes Spalding to Frank Wilson, Superintendent of Grady Hospital, June 8, 1953, GTH Papers.

18. GTH to Hughes Spalding, July 9, 1953, GTH Papers.

19. GTH to Fred J. Turner, Fulton-DeKalb Hospital Authority chairman, December 9, 1960, GTH Papers.

20. Juan Williams, *Eyes on the Prize* (New York: Penguin Books, 1988), 34, 66–89; GTH to Joseph L. Johnson, Dean of Howard University School of Medicine, May 24, 1954, GTH Papers.

21. Alfred A. Weinstein, M.D., to Hughes Spalding, April 4, 1955, Weinstein to Dean Johnson, April 8, 1955, Helen Harper to GTH, August 18, 1955, GTH to Morris B. Abram, September 22, 1955, Hughes Spalding to Asa G. Yancey, August 14, December 10, 1957, Hughes Spalding to Alfred A. Weinstein, July 28, 1955, GTH to Frank Loescher, Fund for the Republic, March 5, 1956, GTH to L. D. Milton, August 25, 1955, all in GTH Papers.

22. GTH to Hilda Reitzes, Executive Secretary, National Medical Fellowships, June 28, 1958, Draft of a proposed letter from Atlanta Urban League Board of Directors to Fulton-DeKalb Hospital Authority, March 24, 1960, GTH Papers.

23. Stephen Birmingham, *Certain People: America's Black Elite* (Boston: Little, Brown, 1977), 250; Charles R. Drew to Paul B. Beeson, January 20, 1947, Charles R. Drew to GTH, March 27, 1950, GTH Papers.

24. Hughes Spalding to Benjamin E. Mays, April 17, 1950, GTH Papers.

25. Benjamin E. Mays to GTH, March 31 and April 11, 1950, and to Hughes Spalding, April 5, 1950, Hughes Spalding to Stephens Mitchell, December 23, 1949, Hughes Spalding to Benjamin E. Mays, April 17, 1950, all in GTH Papers; GTH interview with LNS, October 24, 1985.

26. Asa G. Yancey to Ira A. Ferguson, August 9, 1955, Hughes Spalding to Alfred A. Weinstein, July 28, 1955, GTH to Hughes Spalding, February 27, 1957, GTH Papers; Asa G. Yancey interview with LNS, April 18, 1985.

27. Asa G. Yancey interview with LNS, April 18, 1985.

28. *Atlanta Constitution*, October 4, December 30, 1961; *Atlanta Journal*, February 21, 1962.

29. Asa G. Yancey interview with LNS, April 18, 1985.

30. Ibid.

31. Eleanor Hamilton Payne interview with JBB, May 14, 1984, and with LNS, June 25, 1985; GTH interview with LNS, July 10, 1985.

Chapter 9: A Leave and a Resignation

1. GTH interview with Jacquelyn Hall, July 19, 1974, Southern Oral History Program, University of North Carolina, Chapel Hill; Katherine Stoney interview with LNS, San Francisco, June 16, 1992.

2. Morton Sosna, *In Search of the Silent South* (New York: Columbia University Press, 1977), 66, 116–20, 160–61; William Clifton Allred Jr., "The Southern Regional Council, 1943–1961" (M.A. thesis, Emory University, 1966), 68–69, 85–86, 298; Katherine Stoney interview with LNS, June 16, 1992.

3. GTH interview with Jacquelyn Hall, July 19, 1974.

4. Sharon Mitchell Mullis, "The Public Career of Grace Towns Hamilton, a Citizen Too Busy to Hate" (Ph.D. dissertation, Emory University, 1976), 191–95; GTH interview with Jacquelyn Hall, July 19, 1974.

5. Nancy J. Weiss, *The National Urban League, 1910–1940* (New York: Oxford University Press, 1974), 151; Philip G. Hammer, letter to JBB, November 8, 1992, in LNS files; Lester B. Granger to Jesse O. Thomas, June 1, 1950, LBG to GTH, August 27, 1957, LBG Papers, National Urban League Collection, LC; LBG remarks before joint AUL-NUL meeting, February 29, 1960, Austin T. Walden Papers, AHC.

6. GTH interview with LNS and JBB, April 8, 1986; LBG to Robert A. Thompson, March 18, 1960, GTH to J. B. Blayton, June 27, 1960, LBG Papers.

7. GTH interview with LNS and JBB, April 8, 1986, and with LNS, April 18, 1986.

8. GTH interviews with LNS, April 24, 1984, and April 18, 1985.

9. Memorandum with various enclosures from Atlanta Urban League Board of Directors to National Urban League Board, January 18, 1960, and Lisle C. Carter, as quoted in minutes of Joint AUL-NUL Board meeting, February 29, 1960, both in Walden Papers; Memorandum from Nelson C. Jackson to LBG, April 12, 1956, LBG Papers;

10. Memorandum of March 4, 1959, from Mahlon T. Puryear, Southern Field Director, to Jackson, J. B. Blayton, summary (dated February 18, 1959) of meeting February 16, 1959, between Theodore W. Kheel, NUL Board President, and committee from AUL Board of Directors, Jackson to LBG, December 22, 1952, GTH to LBG, October 4, 1957, Puryear to LBG, March 18, 1959, LBG to Blayton, January 11, 1960, all in LBG Papers.

11. Weiss, *National Urban League*, 155, 161, 345n; Guichard Parris and Lester Brooks, *Blacks in the City: A History of the National Urban League* (Boston: Little, Brown, 1971), 398; Statement submitted to National Urban League by Blayton and GTH, October 21, 1959, Walden Papers; "The Atlanta Urban League," Atlanta Community Chest document prepared from facts supplied by AUL 1956, Puryear-Jackson memorandum, March 4, 1959, Puryear to LBG, October 7, 1959, all in LBG Papers; Memorandum of

January 18, 1960, from AUL Board to NUL Board, Walden Papers; Hammer interview with JBB, October 11, 1992.

12. Minutes of joint AUL-NUL meeting February 29, 1960, Walden Papers; GTH to LBG, October 4, 1957, LBG Papers; Lisle C. Carter's remarks as quoted in minutes of joint AUL-NUL meeting, February 29, 1960, Walden Papers; Theodore W. Kheel, NUL President, to Blayton, February 6, 1958, LBG to Puryear, December 8, 1959, LBG Papers; Hammer and LBG remarks in minutes of joint AUL-NUL board meeting, February 29, 1960, Walden Papers.

13. LBG to Blayton, January 11, 1960, LBG to Jackson, January 15, 1960, both in LBG Papers.

14. Blayton to LBG, January 18, 1960, LBG Papers; Memorandum from AUL Board of Directors to NUL Board of Directors, January 18, 1960, and Lisle Carter's remarks in minutes of joint AUL-NUL board meeting, February 29, 1960, both in Walden Papers; Kheel to Blayton, March 23, 1960, LBG Papers.

15. Comments of Mrs. Harry M. Gershon at special meeting of AUL Board of Directors, January 18, 1960, and report of the Atlanta Urban League subcommittee on the crisis with the NUL, March 24, 1960, both in Walden Papers.

16. Theodore W. Kheel to J. B. Blayton, March 23, 1960, Walden Papers.

17. Minutes of AUL Board of Directors meeting, March 24, 1960, Walden Papers; Ann Wead Kimbrough, "Jesse Hill Jr.: The Long Road to Success," *Atlanta Weekly*, January 26, 1986; Statement of special subcommittee of Atlanta Urban League's Board of Directors, March 31, 1960, Minutes of special meeting of Atlanta Urban League's Board of Directors, April 5, 1960, both in Walden Papers.

18. LBG to Mrs. J. W. E. Bowen, copy in minutes of AUL board meeting, April 21, 1960, Walden Papers; LBG to Blayton, January 11, 1960, LBG Papers; Statement of Jesse Hill Jr., April 5, 1960, presented to AUL board meeting, April 21, 1960, Walden Papers.

19. GTH to Blayton, June 27, 1960, LBG Papers.

20. LBG to Thompson and to Blayton, Blayton to NUL and to LBG, Henry Steeger to Blayton, all in LBG Papers.

21. Parris and Brooks, *Blacks in the City*, 398–400.

22. Thompson to LBG, April 18, 1961, LBG Papers.

Chapter 10: Hamilton and the Civil Rights Movement

1. Sharon Mitchell Mullis, "The Public Career of Grace Towns Hamilton, a Citizen Too Busy to Hate" (Ph.D. dissertation, Emory University, 1976), 163; *Atlanta Journal*, December 2, 3, 1944; Correspondence with Legislative Black Caucus leaders in Alabama, Florida, and South Carolina, copies in authors' files; *St. Louis Post-Dispatch*, January 24, 1968; *Atlanta Journal*, January 7, 1972; LNS interview with GTH, April 24, 1984.

2. Alton Hornsby Jr., remarks delivered in GTH lecture, Emory University, April 19, 1990.

3. Jack L. Walker, "The Functions of Disunity: Negro Leadership in a Southern City," in *The Making of Black America*, ed. August Meier and Elliott Rudwick (New York: Atheneum, 1963), 2: 342–52; Ella Baker, quoted in Juan Williams, *Eyes on the Prize* (New York: Penguin Books, 1988), 137; Taylor Branch, *Parting the Waters: America in the King*

Years, 1954–1963 (New York: Simon and Schuster, 1988), 193, 198; Ivan Allen Jr., with Paul Hemphill, *Mayor: Notes on the Sixties* (New York: Simon and Schuster, 1971), 81–83.

4. Branch, *Parting the Waters*, 272–76, 278, 284, 345, 351; Walker, "Functions of Disunity," 344, 346; Williams, *Eyes on the Prize*, 126–29, 140.

5. Branch, *Parting the Waters*, 352–78.

6. Ibid., 395–98; Allen and Hemphill, *Mayor*, 39, 92; Alton Hornsby Jr., "The Negro in Atlanta Politics, 1961–1973," *Atlanta Historical Bulletin* 21, no. 1 (1977): 9, 12.

7. Williams, *Eyes on the Prize*, 143–44, 173; Branch, *Parting the Waters*, 414–15, 508, 699–700.

8. Branch, *Parting the Waters*, 434–36, 476–82, 635, 640, 647–72, 680–81, 699, 756–68, 800, 808–9, 823–24, 839–40, 864–70; Williams, *Eyes on the Prize*, 147–61, 164–79, 183, 184–95, 226.

9. Branch, *Parting the Waters*, 876–87, 918, 922; Williams, *Eyes on the Prize*, 197–202, 232.

10. Williams, *Eyes on the Prize*, 252–85; Amelia Platt Boynton, "The Bridge Across Jordan," excerpt quoted in *The Eyes on the Prize Civil Rights Reader*, ed. Clayborne Carson, David J. Garrow, Gerald Gill, Vincent Harding, and Darlene Clark Hine (New York: Penguin Books, 1991), 208–9; Vincent Harding, "We the People, the Struggle Continues," quoted ibid., 228–34; *Baker* v. *Carr*, 396 U.S. 186 (1962); *Gray* v. *Sanders*, 372 U.S. 368 (1962); *Reynolds* v. *Sims*, 377 U.S. 577 (1964); *Wesberry* v. *Sanders*, 376 U.S. 1 (1964).

11. GTH interview with Jacquelyn Hall, July 19, 1974, Southern Historical Collection, University of North Carolina, Chapel Hill; GTH interview with LNS, April 18, 1986; Katherine Stoney interview with LNS, June 9, 1992.

12. Walker, "Functions of Disunity," 346; Allen and Hemphill, *Mayor*, 44; Margaret Rose Gladney, *How Am I to Be Heard?: Letters of Lillian Smith* (Chapel Hill: University of North Carolina Press, 1994), 209–11.

13. Mullis, "Public Career of Grace Towns Hamilton," 208; Grace Holmes DeLorme interview with LNS, January 24, 1986.

14. Eli Ginzberg with Vincent Bryan and Grace T. Hamilton, *The Middle Class Negro in the White Man's World* (New York: Columbia University Press, 1967), jacket description.

15. Allen and Hemphill, *Mayor*, 28; Hornsby, "The Negro in Atlanta Politics," 8–11; Paul Douglas Bolster, "Civil Rights Movements in Twentieth Century Georgia" (Ph.D. dissertation, University of Georgia, 1972), 123; Lorraine Nelson Spritzer, *The Belle of Ashby Street: Helen Douglas Mankin and Georgia Politics* (Athens: University of Georgia Press, 1982), chaps. 5 and 7; Richard Bardolph, *The Negro Vanguard* (New York: Vintage Books, 1959), 370–71; Clarence A. Bacote, "The Negro in Atlanta Politics," *Phylon* 16 (1955): 349.

16. Hornsby, "The Negro in Atlanta Politics," 9–11.

17. Allen and Hemphill, *Mayor*, 43; GTH interview with LNS and JBB, October 16, 1985; Yoriko Nakajima interview with JBB, March 15, 1992, transcript in LNS files.

18. Mullis, "Public Career of Grace Towns Hamilton," 204–20; *Atlanta Journal*, April 20, 1966.

19. *Atlanta Journal*, April 20, 1966; *Atlanta Daily World*, April 25, 1966; *Atlanta Journal-Constitution*, May 15, 1966.

20. Allen and Hemphill, *Mayor*, 11–16.

21. Robert A. Thompson, Hylan Lewis, and David McEntire, "Atlanta and Birmingham: A Comparative Study in Negro Housing," in *A Study in Housing and Minority Groups*, ed. Nathan Glazer and David McEntire (Berkeley: University of California Press, 1960), 26, 31–34; Allen and Hemphill, *Mayor*, 70–72; Hornsby, "The Negro in Atlanta Politics," 13–16.

22. Allen and Hemphill, *Mayor*, 100–116; Hornsby, "The Negro in Atlanta Politics," 15.

23. GTH interview with LNS and JBB, April 23, 1984.

24. Mullis, "Public Career of Grace Towns Hamilton," 201–2.

25. Ibid., 208–10; Genevieve Pou, "Grace Hamilton: The Case for Commitment," *Atlanta Magazine*, June 1967; *Atlanta Constitution*, May 5, 1966; *Atlanta Journal*, May 8, 1966; Rebecca Gershon interview with LNS and JBB, April 23, 1984.

26. GTH to Mayor Ivan Allen Jr., July 13, 1964, copy in LNS files; George T. Smith interview with LNS, April 10, 1986; Horace T. Ward interview with LNS, April 9, 1986.

27. GTH to Allen, July 13, 1964.

Chapter 11: The Lady from Fulton

1. Paul Hemphill, *Atlanta Constitution* column, May 7, 1965; "States Boast Record Number of Negro Lawmakers," *Ebony*, April 1965; "Nine Negroes to Sit in Georgia Assembly," *New York Times*, May 23, 1965; *Atlanta Daily World*, May 6, 1965; *Newsweek*, June 28, 1965.

2. Stephan Lesher, "Leroy Johnson Outslicks Mister Charlie," *New York Times Magazine*, November 8, 1970; Clarence A. Bacote, "The Negro in Georgia Politics, 1880–1908" (Ph.D. dissertation, University of Chicago, 1955), 468, 472; John Dittmer, *Black Georgia in the Progressive Era, 1900–1920* (Urbana: University of Illinois Press, 1977), 101; *Toombs v. Fortson*, 205 F. Supp. 248 (1962); *Baker v. Carr*, 396 U.S. 186 (1962); *Gray v. Sanders*, 372 U.S. 368 (1962); Judge Horace T. Ward interview with LNS, April 9, 1986.

3. Doyle Mathis, "Georgia's Reapportionment History and Process," in *Reapportionment in Georgia* (Athens: Institute of Government of the University of Georgia, 1970), 5–15; GTH interview with LNS and JBB, October 16, 1985.

4. Ward interview with LNS, April 9, 1986.

5. David Levering Lewis, *W. E. B. Du Bois: Biography of a Race* (New York: Henry Holt, 1993), 393; GTH interview with LNS, April 24, 1984.

6. Genevieve Pou, "Grace Hamilton: The Case for Commitment," *Atlanta Magazine*, June 1967; GTH interview with LNS, April 24, 1984.

7. GTH interview with *Atlanta Constitution*, January 7, 1972; Pou, "Grace Hamilton."

8. *Atlanta Constitution*, May 19, 1965, January 20, 1985, September 14, 1986; GTH interview with LNS and JBB, October 16, 1985; Edmund L. Drago, *Black Politicians and Reconstruction in Georgia* (Baton Rouge: Louisiana State University Press, 1982), 45.

9. *Atlanta Journal-Constitution*, September 14, 1986; Pou, "Grace Hamilton"; George Stoney to LNS, May 15, 1992, in authors' files.

10. Barbara B. Reitt, ed., *Georgia Women: A Celebration, 1976* (Atlanta: Atlanta Branch, American Association of University Women, 1976); Mary Givens Bryan, director, Georgia Department of Archives and History, unpublished notes on Georgia's legislative women, 1958, in LNS files; Sharon Mitchell Mullis, "The Public Career of Grace Towns Hamilton, a Citizen Too Busy to Hate" (Ph.D. dissertation, Emory University, 1976), 225, 283, 292;

Calvin Kytle and James A. Mackay, "Who Runs Georgia?" chap. 1, p. 5, unpublished manuscript, 1947, Georgia Government Documentation Project, Special Collections, Georgia State University, Atlanta.

11. GTH interview with *Atlanta Constitution*, May 19, 1965.

12. *St. Louis Post-Dispatch*, January 24, 1968.

13. George T. Smith interview with LNS, April 10, 1986.

14. Ibid.

15. GTH interview with LNS and JBB, October 16, 1985.

16. On Hamilton's legislative power and reputation, see *Atlanta Constitution*, February 16, 1971, January 21, February 25, 1975, *Buckhead-Atlanta* edition of January 11, 1980, all in GTH papers, AHC; on her first bill, see *Atlanta Constitution*, January 21, March 18, 1966, *Atlanta Journal*, May 26, 1966, and Pou, "Grace Hamilton"; Mullis, "Public Career of Grace Towns Hamilton," 236–39.

17. George T. Smith, interview with LNS, April 10, 1986.

18. Pou, "Grace Hamilton."

19. *New York Times*, January 10, 1966; Mullis, "Public Career of Grace Towns Hamilton," 233–35, 242; *Atlanta Daily World*, January 16, 1966; *Atlanta Constitution*, January 11, 1966.

20. Mullis, "Public Career of Grace Towns Hamilton," 244.

21. GTH interview with Jacquelyn Hall, July 19, 1974, Southern Historical Collection, University of North Carolina, Chapel Hill; Helen Howard, "Am I My Brother's Keeper?" and Helen Howard, interview, in Gerda Lerner, ed., *Black Women in White America* (New York: Pantheon Books, 1972), 311, 516–17; Celestine Sibley, *Atlanta Constitution* column, September 14, 1966; William Clifton Allred Jr., "Southern Regional Council, 1943–1961" (M.A. thesis, Emory University, 1966), 300–301; Betty J. Clark interview with LNS, Georgia State Representative Fifty-fifth District, January 30, 1986.

22. Pou, "Grace Hamilton"; Mullis, "Public Career of Grace Towns Hamilton," 250.

23. *Atlanta Constitution*, February 28, November 23, 1967; Lorraine Nelson Spritzer, *The Belle of Ashby Street: Helen Douglas Mankin and Georgia Politics* (Athens: University of Georgia Press, 1982), 57, 127–28, 174; Mullis, "Public Career of Grace Towns Hamilton," 265, 294; Georgia House Calendar, 1970, House Bill 1689, signed into law March 24, 1970.

24. *Atlanta Daily World*, May 4, 13, 1967; GTH interview with LNS, October 24, 1985.

Chapter 12: The Years of Racial Solidarity

1. *Atlanta Constitution*, December 23, 1967, February 15, 20, 21, 1968, January 23, 1969, January 14, 1971; *Atlanta Journal*, January 15, 1969, January 7, 1972; Alex Coffin, "The System May Be Weak but the Mayors Are Not," *Atlanta Magazine*, July 1970, p. 44, GTH Papers, Box 49, Folder 6.

2. *Atlanta Journal*, January 15, 1969; *Atlanta Constitution*, January 23, 1969; GTH to Roger Bruce, Morehouse College, March 13, 1974, GTH Papers; Alton Hornsby Jr., "The Negro in Atlanta Politics, 1961–1973," *Atlanta Historical Bulletin* 21, no. 1 (1977): 11, 20, 21; Clarence A. Bacote, "The Negro in Atlanta Politics," *Phylon* 16 (1955): 333; on third ward revision, see *Atlanta Journal*, February 8, 25, 1969; *Neighbor*, May 12, 1971, in GTH Papers; *Atlanta Journal*, May 16, 1971.

3. GTH interview with LNS, February 2, 1986.

4. Atlanta Charter Commission Fact Sheet, GTH Papers, Box 49, Folder 11; Summary of Charter Commission's first draft, August 20, 1972, GTH Papers; GTH interviews with LNS, February 2 and April 18, 1986.

5. *Northside Neighbor*, September 27, 1972; Letter from Atlanta Branch, NAACP-Political Action Committee, to Atlanta Charter Commission, November 13, 1972, GTH Papers; Hornsby, "The Negro in Atlanta Politics," 30–31.

6. GTH interview with LNS, February 2, 1986; *Atlanta Constitution*, March 14, 1973; Sam A. Williams to GTH, March 19, 1973, GTH Papers.

7. *Atlanta Constitution*, September 10, 1971.

8. *Atlanta Constitution*, March 8, 20, 1969; *Atlanta Journal*, March 7, 11, 1969; Sharon Mitchell Mullis, "The Public Career of Grace Towns Hamilton, a Citizen Too Busy to Hate" (Ph.D dissertation, Emory University, 1976), 263–64.

9. GTH interview with LNS and JBB, October 16, 1985.

10. *Atlanta Journal*, February 16, 1972; Rome (Ga.) *News-Tribune*, February 16, 1972; Deanna Colbert, "A Legislative Summary of the Honorable Grace Towns Hamilton through 1966–1984," unpublished monograph in LNS files; George T. Smith interview with LNS, April 10, 1986.

11. Delmer D. Dunn telephone interview with LNS, March 15, 1986, notes in LNS files.

12. Grace Towns Hamilton, "History of Georgia Reapportionment," 1971–74, Box 79, Folder 2, GTH Papers; Statistical Register of Georgia, information on legislators by color; Betty J. Clark interview with LNS, January 30, 1986; "Taking the Fifth," *Southern Changes* (Southern Regional Council) 8, no. 3 (September 1986): 7–9.

13. *Atlanta Journal*, February 16, 1972; Andrew Young, *A Way Out of No Way* (Nashville: Thomas Nelson, 1994), 109–10; Georgia Election Returns for 1970, Georgia Department of Archives and History.

14. Hamilton Congressional Redistricting Plan as presented to Congressional and Legislative Reapportionment Committees of Georgia House and Senate, June 24, 1971, GTH Papers, Box 79, Folder 17; Reg Murphy column in *Atlanta Constitution*, September 10, 1971; *Atlanta Journal*, June 21, 1971; *Atlanta Constitution*, July 26, December 22, 1971; *Atlanta Inquirer*, September 16, 23, October 14, 23, 1971; *Augusta Chronicle*, December 22, 1971; Letters to U.S. Department of Justice from GTH, November 5, 1971, and from Board of Governors of Fulton County Democratic Party, December 13, 1971, GTH Papers.

15. *Atlanta Journal*, February 16, March 1, 1972; *Macon News*, March 2, 1972; *Bacote* v. *Carter*, cited as 343 F. Supp. 330, opinion of U.S. District Court for Northern District of Georgia, May 17, 1972, Box 81, GTH Papers; Georgia Election Returns for 1972, Georgia Department of Archives and History; Andrew Young, deposition, June 25, 1982, in *Busbee* v. *Smith*, cited as 549 F. Supp. 494 (1982), made available by Georgia Attorney General's office; Andrew Young interview with LNS and JBB, April 8, 1986.

16. *Atlanta Constitution*, February 10, 1972.

17. Celestine Sibley, "The Hamilton Case," *Atlanta Constitution*, February 21, 1975; Linda Meggers, Director of Georgia's Reapportionment Unit, which worked under both House and Senate Reapportionment Committees, interview with LNS, January 28, 1986; GTH interviews with LNS, February 2 and April 18, 1986.

18. GTH interview with LNS, April 18, 1986; *Atlanta Constitution*, January 26, 1970.

19. *Atlanta Journal,* June 3, 1969, March 2, 1971; *Roe v. Wade,* 410 U.S. 113 (1973), and *Doe v. Bolton* 410 U.S. 179 (1973).

20. *Atlanta Constitution,* January 7, May 15, 1972; GTH speech to Woman of the Year banquet in LNS files.

21. *Atlanta Journal,* January 18, 1971.

22. Georgia Election Returns for 1972, Democratic Executive Committee posts, Georgia Department of Archives and History; Remarks by president of Emory chapter of Delta Sigma Rho, presenting Speaker of the Year award to GTH, May 27, 1972, copy in LNS files; *Atlanta Journal,* July 1, 1969.

23. Linda Meggers interview with LNS, January 28, 1986; *Atlanta Constitution,* February 21, 1975, August 7, September 2, 1976, August 3, 1978; *Atlanta Journal-Constitution,* July 16, 1978; Judge Newell Edenfield's discussion of Fulton County Commission's racism found in *Pitts v. Busbee,* 395 F. Supp. 35 (1975); GTH interview with LNS, October 24, 1985.

24. History of the commission controversy and details of legal cases, 1974–76, are contained in the following federal decisions: *Pitts v. Carter* 380 F. Supp. 4 (1974), *Pitts v. Carter* 380 F. Supp. 8 (1974), *Pitts v. Busbee* 511 F. 2d 126 (1975), *Pitts v. Busbee* 395 F. Supp. 35 (1975), *Pitts v. Cates* 536 F. 2d 56 (1976); *Atlanta Journal,* January 24, March 5, 1974; GTH and J. C. Daugherty to Gerald W. Jones, Chief, Voting Rights Section, U.S. Department of Justice, June 4, 1974, Box 78, Folder 5, GTH Papers; *Atlanta Journal,* February 5, 1975; *Atlanta Constitution,* January 24, February 12, 1976; Steven V. Roberts, "Voting Rights and Past Wrongs," *New York Times,* June 13, 1982.

25. *Atlanta Constitution,* February 20, 21, 25, March 1, 21, 1975, January 24, March 5, 1976; *Pitts v. Busbee* 535 F. 2d 56 (1976); *Atlanta Journal,* February 5, March 1, 1975, January 24, February 12, 1976; *Pitts v. Busbee* 395 F. Supp. 35 (1975), *Pitts v. Busbee* 511 F. 2d 126 (1975); LNS interview with GTH, October 24, 1985; *Atlanta Constitution,* June 15, August 10, November 11, 1978.

26. *Atlanta Constitution,* February 21, 1975.

27. Ibid., February 20, 21, March 21, 1975.

28. Ibid., July 23, 27, August 12, September 2, 1976; J. E. Billy McKinney interview with LNS, January 30, 1986.

29. Georgia Democratic Party returns, 1976, Georgia State Archives; Tom Malone, Fulton County Board of Registration and Elections, interview with LNS, April 11, 1986; *Washington Post,* January 20, 1986.

Chapter 13: Waning Solidarity, Growing Power

1. *Atlanta Constitution,* March 20, 1969, January 21, 1975; GTH interview with LNS, April 18, 1986; GTH reply to *Atlanta Journal-Constitution* query concerning her views on county-city merger, Box 78, Folder 6, GTH Papers, AHC; *Atlanta Constitution,* January 28, February 12, 24, March 1, 1972; *Atlanta Journal,* February 24, 1972; Alton Hornsby Jr., "The Negro in Atlanta Politics, 1961–1973," *Atlanta Historical Bulletin* 21, no. 1 (1977): 29–30.

2. GTH interview with LNS, July 10, 1985.

3. *Atlanta Journal,* February 20, November 7, 1974, November 5, 1975; GTH memo to members of Atlanta–Fulton County Study Committee, December 11, 1975, copy in

LNS files; Final Report of Atlanta–Fulton County Commission, December 1977, copy in LNS files; *Atlanta Constitution*, February 7, March 5, November 11, 1978.

4. *Atlanta Journal*, January 28, February 22, 1980; GTH interviews with LNS, April 12 and 18, 1986; copy of confidential memo in LNS files.

5. *Atlanta Constitution*, January 17, 18, 21, February 17, 19, 1980; *Atlanta Journal*, January 7, 28, February 8, 22, 25, 26, 1980; *Atlanta Constitution*, February 3, 1981.

6. J. E. Billy McKinney interview with LNS, January 30, 1986.

7. *Atlanta Journal-Constitution*, October 18, 1981; John Griffin's remarks in Georgia House of Representatives March 12, 1982, copy in LNS files; *Atlanta Journal*, October 21, 1983; GTH interview with LNS, April 18, 1986; *Emory Magazine* 60 (August 1984): 28–29.

8. *Busbee v. Smith*, 549 F. Supp. 494 (1982), 501, citing the position of the U.S. Justice Department on necessary population percentages in majority black districts; Steven V. Roberts, "Voting Rights and Past Wrongs," *New York Times*, June 13, 1982; GTH remarks on "House Reapportionment" before Georgia House August 27, 1981, naming blacks recently elected at large in Fulton County, copy in LNS files; Linda Meggers interview with LNS, January 28, 1986; Andrew Young deposition of June 28, 1982, in *Busbee v. Smith*, cited as 549 F. Supp. 494 (1982); Alton Hornsby Jr., *Chronology of African-American History* (Detroit: Gale Research, 1991), chap. 11.

9. House Speaker Tom Murphy, remarks to Georgia Legislative Black Caucus dinner, October 10, 1992, transcript in LNS files; GTH interview with LNS and JBB, April 23, 1984; Meggers interview with LNS, January 28, 1986; William C. Randall, Black Caucus chairman, 1980–82, interview with LNS, January 29, 1986; Jack Bass, "Atlanta's Mayoral Mishmash," *New Republic*, September 23, 1981; GTH interview with LNS, October 20, 1985, and July 10, 1986, and with JBB and LNS, April 8, 1986; *Atlanta Journal*, August 3, 1984; Julian Bond interview with LNS, January 30, 1986.

10. GTH interview with LNS, October 24, 1985; Randall and McKinney, interviews with LNS, January 30, 1986; Meggers interview with LNS, January 28, 1986.

11. Robert A. Holmes, "Reapportionment Politics in Georgia," *Phylon* 45 (1984): 180; *Atlanta Constitution*, July 14, 16, 17, 1981.

12. GTH statement before House Congressional and Legislative Reapportionment Committee, August 10, 1981, in behalf of her "17–2" plan, copy in LNS files; Barbara Couch telephone interview with JBB, August 3, 1993; Meggers interview with LNS, January 28, 1986.

13. GTH statement August 10, 1981, before House Congressional and Legislative Reapportionment Committee, copy in LNS files; Robert A. Holmes, J. E. Billy McKinney, and Julian Bond interviews with LNS, January 30, 1986, and William C. Randall, January 29, 1986; Meggers interview with LNS, January 28, 1986; *Atlanta Journal*, August 31, 1981; GTH letter to U.S. Justice Department, September 28, 1981, copy in LNS files; Holmes, "Reapportionment Politics in Georgia," 181–82; GTH interview with LNS, February 2, 1986.

14. Robert A. Holmes interview with LNS, January 30, 1986.

15. GTH interviews with LNS, April 24, 1984, and October 24, 1985.

16. Holmes, "Reapportionment Politics in Georgia," 180, 182–87; *Atlanta Journal-Constitution*, September 6, 1981; *Atlanta Constitution*, September 17, 1981; *Busbee v. Smith*, 549 F. Supp. 494 (1982), 500; GTH interview with LNS, October 24, 1985.

17. *Atlanta Constitution*, August 14, September 1, 2, 1981; *Atlanta Journal*, September 3, 10, 1981; GTH interview with LNS, April 24, 1984; *Atlanta Journal*, September 14, 1981; John Sweet conversation with LNS, Atlanta, April 19, 1986, notes in LNS files.

18. *Busbee v. Smith*, 549 F. Supp. 494 (1982), 509; *Atlanta Journal*, June 29, 1982; GTH interview with LNS, October 20, 1985; *Atlanta Constitution*, September 16, 1981.

19. Holmes, "Reapportionment Politics in Georgia," 185.

20. *Busbee v. Smith*, 549 F. Supp. 494 (1982), 497; GTH interview with LNS, October 24, 1985; Holmes, "Reapportionment Politics in Georgia," 185.

21. Young deposition, June 25, 1982, quoted in *Busbee v. Smith*, 549 F. Supp. 494; *Atlanta Journal*, June 30, 1982.

22. *Busbee v. Smith*, 549 F. Supp. 494 (1982), 515; *Atlanta Constitution*, August 9, 1982; Holmes, "Reapportionment Politics in Georgia," 185–87.

23. *Busbee v. Smith*, 549 F. Supp. 494, 500–501.

24. *Atlanta Journal*, July 26, 27, 1982; *Atlanta Inquirer*, July 31, 1982.

25. *Busbee v. Smith*, 549 F. Supp. 494, 518–19, 521; *Atlanta Constitution*, August 31, 1982; *Atlanta Journal-Constitution*, September 19, 1982; *Southern Changes* 8 (September 1986): 7–9; *Atlanta Journal-Constitution*, November 11, 1984.

Chapter 14: A Landslide Defeat

1. GTH interview with LNS and JBB, April 8, 1986; *Atlanta Journal*, August 3, 1984; Campaign Financing Disclosure Reports for GTH, 1974–84, Elections Division, Georgia Secretary of State; GTH interview with LNS, February 2, 1986.

2. Andrew Young interview with LNS and JBB, April 8, 1986; Franklin Thomas interview with LNS, October 16, 1985.

3. Georganna T. Sinkfield and Richard H. Sinkfield interview with LNS, February 2, 1986; *Atlanta Journal*, August 3, 1984.

4. William Randall interview with LNS, January 29, 1986.

5. Susan Howard, "Taking the Torch: Atlanta's Emerging Black Leaders," *Atlanta Weekly (Atlanta Journal-Constitution)*, November 3, 1985; Campaign Financing Disclosure Reports for GTH and Mable Thomas, 1984, Elections Division, Georgia Secretary of State.

6. Fulton County Board of Registration and Elections, returns for Democratic Party primary, August 14, 1986; Georganna and Richard Sinkfield interview with LNS, February 2, 1986; Betty J. Clark and Lorenzo Benn interviews with LNS, January 30 and January 29, 1986, respectively; Campaign Financing Disclosure Reports for GTH and Mable Thomas for 1984 Democratic Party Primary, Elections Division, Georgia Secretary of State; Flyer distributed to Thirty-first District voters by Robert A. Holmes, J. E. Billy McKinney, Douglas Dean, and Tyrone Brooks, copy from GTH files in LNS possession; GTH interviews with LNS, July 10 and October 20, 1985; GTH interview with LNS and JBB, April 18, 1986.

7. Franklin Thomas interview with LNS, October 16, 1985; Rev. G. S. Hardeman, President of AME Ministers' Union, telephone conversation with LNS, April 14, 1986, notes in LNS files.

8. Georganna and Richard Sinkfield interview with LNS, February 2, 1986; Julian Bond interview with LNS, January 30, 1986.

9. Fulton County Board of Registration and Elections, returns for Democratic Party run-off, September 4, 1984; *Atlanta Journal,* September 5, 6, 1984; Georganna and Richard Sinkfield interview with LNS, February 2, 1986; *Atlanta Constitution,* September 7, 1984.

10. GTH interviews with LNS, July 10, 1985, and February 2, 1986; Howard, "Taking the Torch".

11. Betty J. Clark interview with LNS, January 30, 1986.

12. *Atlanta Constitution,* March 7, 1985.

13. GTH interview with LNS, April 8, 1986.

Chapter 15: The Last Years

1. Documentation for Hamilton's work on the Georgia SAC was obtained from records, pamphlets, and correspondence dated variously between 1985 and 1987 which Hamilton gave to LNS in October 1988, having withheld the material for the authors' benefit from the collection delivered two years before to the Atlanta Historical Society. These papers will be deposited in the Hamilton collection at the Atlanta History Center. GTH interviews with LNS (already part of the Atlanta History Center collection) and with Morris B. Abram (by telephone August 14, 1993) provided further documentation.

2. The authors relied on the personal files of Jane Maguire Abram, which she graciously made available for documenting the work of the GTHHP. Other documentation was provided by minutes of its meetings, correspondence, and personal recollections of the authors, which will become part of the GTH collection at AHC.

3. A copy of Hugh M. Gloster's tribute to Henry Cooke Hamilton was made available to the authors by Eleanor Hamilton Payne.

4. Eleanor Payne's assessment of her parents' marriage was made in an interview with JBB on May 14, 1984.

5. The first break in Grace Hamilton's health is based in part on private correspondence between Harriet Towns Jenkins and JBB.

6. Hamilton's honors were documented by newspaper clippings and memorabilia in the authors' possession and by the authors' knowledge of and sometimes participation in the relevant events. All these personal records will be open to the public as part of the GTH Collection at AHC.

7. The recounting of Hamilton's final months in the Briarcliff Nursing Home is based on the authors' personal knowledge, memorabilia made available by the family, and newspaper clippings which are to become part of the GTH Collection at AHC.

Epilogue

1. Material in the epilogue is based on interviews with Mable Thomas and Julian Bond, both on January 30, 1986, and with Georganna Sinkfield on February 2, 1986. The quote from Alton Hornsby Jr. is from his GTH lecture at Emory University on April 19, 1990.

Index

. . .